ANTHONY DOWNS

NEIGHBORHOODS
and Urban Development

THE BROOKINGS INSTITUTION
Washington, D.C.

NEIGHBORHOODS
and Urban Development

THE BROOKINGS INSTITUTION is an independent organization devoted to nonpartisan research, education, and publication in economics, government, foreign policy, and the social sciences generally. Its principal purposes are to aid in the development of sound public policies and to promote public understanding of issues of national importance.

The Institution was founded on December 8, 1927, to merge the activities of the Institute for Government Research, founded in 1916, the Institute of Economics, founded in 1922, and the Robert Brookings Graduate School of Economics and Government, founded in 1924.

The Board of Trustees is responsible for the general administration of the Institution, while the immediate direction of the policies, program, and staff is vested in the President, assisted by an advisory committee of the officers and staff. The by-laws of the Institution state: "It is the function of the Trustees to make possible the conduct of scientific research, and publication, under the most favorable conditions, and to safeguard the independence of the research staff in the pursuit of their studies and in the publication of the results of such studies. It is not a part of their function to determine, control, or influence the conduct of particular investigations or the conclusions reached."

The President bears final responsibility for the decision to publish a manuscript as a Brookings book. In reaching his judgment on the competence, accuracy, and objectivity of each study, the President is advised by the director of the appropriate research program and weighs the views of a panel of expert outside readers who report to him in confidence on the quality of the work. Publication of a work signifies that it is deemed a competent treatment worthy of public consideration but does not imply endorsement of conclusions or recommendations.

The Institution maintains its position of neutrality on issues of public policy in order to safeguard the intellectual freedom of the staff. Hence interpretations or conclusions in Brookings publications should be understood to be solely those of the authors and should not be attributed to the Institution, to its trustees, officers, or other staff members, or to the organizations that support its research.

Foreword

RAPID neighborhood change has long been characteristic of American cities. Whether declining in physical condition and social status from an influx of poor people, or improving through the investments of affluent young newcomers, or being leveled and rebuilt by urban renewal, thousands of U.S. urban neighborhoods have been subjected to swift and radical shifts in their basic character during the past few decades. Residents of these areas typically view such change as a threat that could be avoided if only local officials would adopt the "right" public policies. But drastic neighborhood changes almost always accompany urban development, and hence they cannot easily be stopped or even greatly affected by policies aimed at particular neighborhoods alone. The links between neighborhood change and the general process of urban development—and their public policy implications—are the subject Anthony Downs investigates in this book.

According to Downs's analysis, the nature and direction of urban development in the United States are affected mainly by the desire of many householders to segregate themselves from those they regard as socially, economically, or ethnically different. This desire expresses itself in the establishment of many separate suburban communities politically dominated by middle- and upper-income households, the maintenance of exclusionary zoning laws and building codes, and differential enforcement of such laws in various parts of each metropolitan area. The resulting pattern of urban development concentrates the poorest households in deteriorated neighborhoods near the metropolitan center. There, many find little escape from environments dominated by high rates of unemployment, crime, vandalism, arson, physical decay, broken families, and other social maladies.

vii

Moreover, the way urban neighborhoods change is influenced greatly by conditions and trends prevailing within the larger metropolitan area, such as the rate of net migration of households (of all income levels) and the volume of new suburban housing construction. Ironically, neighborhood decline in older areas can result not only from high net influx of the poor, which causes overcrowding, but also from *low* net influx of the poor, which may lead to housing abandonment.

Downs argues that neighborhood change and many of the nation's most serious urban problems result from institutional arrangements that enable residents to exclude poverty from some neighborhoods, thus segregating the poor but benefiting a majority of urban households. He explores various governmental policies—national, state, and local—aimed at changing these arrangements or offsetting their most negative effects.

This book was written as part of a study of urban decline and the future of American cities carried out at Brookings by Katharine L. Bradbury, Anthony Downs, and Kenneth A. Small. The larger study was funded by the Ford Foundation, the U.S. Urban Mass Transportation Administration, the U.S. Federal Highway Administration, and the Brookings Institution.

Anthony Downs is a senior fellow in the Brookings Economic Studies program. He is grateful to his Brookings colleague Katharine L. Bradbury and to Kenneth A. Small of Princeton University for their criticism and suggestions in the preparation of this volume. He is also grateful to Roger S. Ahlbrandt, Jr., James V. Cunningham, Marcia Kaptur, Norman Krumholz, Edward Marciniak, and John McH. Yinger for their comments on the manuscript; to Diane Hammond for editing the manuscript; to Ellen W. Smith for checking its factual content; to Edith Brashares, Mary E. Burnham, and Thea M. Lee for research assistance; to Anita G. Whitlock for secretarial services; and to Florence Robinson for preparing the index.

The views expressed in this book are solely those of the author, and should not be ascribed to the persons or organizations whose assistance is acknowledged above, or to the trustees, officers, or other staff members of the Brookings Institution.

BRUCE K. MAC LAURY
President

July 1981
Washington, D.C.

Contents

1. Introduction and Main Themes   1
   The Nature of Neighborhoods *1*
   Problems Arising from Neighborhood Change *2*
   Exploring Future Policies Concerning Neighborhoods *4*
   The Necessity for Neighborhood Deterioration *5*
   Federal and State Policies *8*
   City Policies *9*
   Neighborhood Policies *10*
   The Boundaries of This Study *11*

2. What Is a Neighborhood?   13
   Conclusions from This View of Neighborhoods *15*
   Nonmarket Linkages and Self-Reinforcing Expectations *16*
   Organizations within Neighborhoods *19*

3. Neighborhood Stability   24
   Factors in Population Mobility *27*
   Variations in Mobility Rates *31*
   Population Mobility and Neighborhood Stability *33*

4. Urban Growth and Neighborhood Change   37
   The Trickle Down Process and Urban Growth *37*
   The Effect of the Trickle Down Process on Neighborhoods *41*
   Spatial Hierarchy of Neighborhoods *44*
   Differential Code Enforcement by Neighborhood *48*
   Continuous Neighborhood Change *49*
   Some Motives for Socioeconomic Segregation *50*
   Differential Benefits to Households *52*
   The Slowing of Urban Growth *58*

5. Stages of Neighborhood Change   61
   Agents of Neighborhood Change 62
   Stages of Change in Decline and Revitalization 63
   Intensified Land Use 67
   Neighborhood Life Cycles 68
   Housing Construction and Neighborhood Change 70

6. Neighborhood Revitalization   72
   The Nature of Revitalization 72
   Causes of Revitalization 75
   Benefits and Costs of Revitalization 81
   Displacement 84

7. Neighborhood Racial Change   86
   The Arbitrage Model 86
   Differential Incomes 90
   Racial Prejudice 91
   Microdynamic Illustrations of Racial Change 93
   The Negative Effects of Racial Change 96
   Stable, Racially Integrated Neighborhoods 98
   Hispanics in the United States 100

8. Future Urban Developments Influencing
   Neighborhoods   103
   Demographic and Economic Trends 103
   High Gasoline Prices 107
   Neighborhood Decline 110
   Neighborhood Redevelopment 113

9. Limitations on Future Neighborhood Policies   116
   Rhetorical versus Real Possibilities 116
   The Proper Institutional Level for Action 118
   Strategies 119
   Personal Values and the Limits of Public Policies 119

10. Coping with Poverty   124
   Redistributing Incomes within Metropolitan Areas 125
   Deconcentrating the Poor 126
   Improving Access to Housing Credit 129
   Improving Public Schools 131
   Additional Recommendations 134

11. Balancing Suburban Growth and
    Central City Revitalization   136
    Effects of Suburban Growth upon Central Cities 136

Stimulating Central City Revitalization by Limiting Suburban
        Growth 139
Achieving Fairer Distribution of the Social Costs of Suburban
        Growth 141
Providing More Accessible Mortgage Financing for City
        Revitalization 144
Balancing Neighborhood Revitalization and Displacement 146
Encouraging Suburban Growth to Reduce Housing Prices 150
Conclusion 151

12. Physically Improving Central City
    Residential Neighborhoods   153
Available Resources 153
Strategies for Spatially Allocating Resources 155
Treatment by Neighborhood 159
Coping with Housing Deterioration 163
Housing Code Enforcement 164
Assessment Practices 168
Traffic and Transportation 169
Conclusion 171

13. Focusing on Activities within Neighborhoods   172
Some Attitudes of Neighborhood Residents and Their
        Implications 172
Personal Values and Participation in Local Organizations 174
Raising Neighborhood Consciousness 176
Transferring Government Authority to Neighborhoods 177
Transferring Delivery of Some Services to the Neighborhood
        Level 179
Overcoming Neighborhood Resistance to the Location of Key
        Public Facilities 182
Conclusion 184

Index   185

Tables

3-1. Variables in Neighborhood Stability   25
3-2. Neighborhood Characteristics and Residents' Mobility   31
3-3. Annual Household Mobility Rates and Five-Year Population
     Changes for Ten American Cities   32
4-1. Value or Rent of Previous and Current Housing Units   43
5-1. Factors Underlying Decline and Revitalization   66
6-1. City and Metropolitan Factors Underlying Revitalization   75
6-2. Neighborhood Factors Underlying Revitalization   76
11-1. Housing Construction and Changes in Population and Households,
     Twenty Metropolitan Areas, 1970–75   138

11-2. Possible Means of Limiting Suburban Residential Growth
in Order to Stimulate Inner-City Housing Demand   140

12-1. Level of Resources Required for Eight Types of
Neighborhood Treatment   162

Figures

4-1. Destination of Households Moving from Central Cities,
Suburbs, and Nonmetropolitan Areas   45

4-2. Origin of Households Moving to Central Cities,
Suburbs, and Nonmetropolitan Areas   46

5-1. The Neighborhood Change Continuum   65

7-1. Neighborhood Racial Transition in the Arbitrage Model   87

7-2. Neighborhood Racial Equilibrium through Income Equilibrium   91

1

Introduction and Main Themes

DURING the 1970s, interest in neighborhoods, the revitalization of large cities, and suburban sprawl greatly intensified in the United States. Urban policies in the next two decades will continue to focus on these three subjects. However, most discussions of them treat each as though it were separate from the other two. In fact, all three phenomena are parts of the U.S. urban development process. Decisionmakers must understand how they relate to each other if future urban policies, especially those concerning neighborhoods, are to be effective. Providing such an understanding is one goal of this book.

The Nature of Neighborhoods

Three aspects of urban development are fundamental to that understanding. One is *the dynamic nature of urban neighborhoods* (*urban* includes both city and suburbs). Each neighborhood experiences constant inflows and outflows of residents, materials, and money. Consequently, neighborhood stability can be achieved only by balancing these opposite flows, rather than by stopping them. This subject is discussed in chapters 2 and 3.

The second aspect is *the dual nature of urban neighborhoods*. They are not only places to live, valued for themselves, but units of urban development inextricably linked to all other city neighborhoods and to the entire metropolitan area.[1] For example, a new expressway connecting

1. In most of this study, the term *metropolitan area* is the same as the Census Bureau's standard metropolitan statistical area, or SMSA. See Bureau of the Census, *Statistical Abstract of the United States, 1979* (Government Printing Office, 1979), p. 2.

1

downtown with the suburbs may cause multiple shifts of activities and people. Industrial and retail employment (including some displaced by the highway) moves to the suburbs; office employment grows mainly in the downtown area; low-income inner-city households displaced by the highway shift to neighborhoods farther out; households initially living in these neighborhoods emigrate to new suburbs. Thus a major transportation improvement affects the population and land use of dozens of neighborhoods, including many nowhere near the new highway itself. Urban development does not affect every urban neighborhood at every moment, but it does affect some urban neighborhoods at every moment, and all of them over the long run. The nature and some implications of the link between urban development and urban neighborhoods are analyzed in chapter 4.

The third aspect of urban development is *the direct connection between two urban frontiers*: the suburban periphery and inner-city neighborhoods.[2] Although these frontiers are usually far apart, and are occupied by households with very different characteristics, what happens on each greatly affects—and is affected by—what happens on the other. Thus, the nature and pace of suburban growth have profound effects on the rate of decay and the prospects for the revival of deteriorated inner-city neighborhoods. Conversely, the amount and pace of migration of poor households into inner-city neighborhoods affect the demand for new housing at the urban periphery. These connections are dealt with in chapters 4 and 5.

Problems Arising from Neighborhood Change

These aspects of urban development generate major social problems. Explaining how such problems arise and how they affect neighborhood conditions and change is the second goal of this book.

Social and economic segregation of population has long been a basic part of U.S. urban development, especially since World War II. Many of the poorest urban households are concentrated in neighborhoods with other poor households, usually in older parts of big cities. Their environments are often dominated by unemployment, crime, vandalism, drug addiction, broken families, and neighborhood decay. The social costs to

2. The concept of the two frontiers and the link between them is taken from Anthony Downs, *Urban Problems and Prospects*, 2d ed. (Rand McNally, 1976), pp. 11–14.

the residents are severe; the fiscal burdens on their local governments are heavy.

Furthermore, because most households that can afford to occupy newly built housing avoid neighborhoods with many poor households, little new housing is built in inner-city neighborhoods even when vacant land is available. Revitalization of these deteriorated neighborhoods is therefore difficult. These issues are discussed in chapters 4, 5, 6, and 7.

Other social problems stem from the fact that nearly all poor households migrating into metropolitan areas are legally prohibited from moving directly into new-growth neighborhoods at the suburban periphery. Zoning regulations and building codes make housing there too costly for the poor, so they must enter inner-city areas instead. When heavy immigration causes severe overcrowding in those areas, the poor spread into surrounding areas, displacing residents who also move outward. This creates a process of musical chairs in which households move through a spatial hierarchy of city and suburban neighborhoods. Some neighborhoods grow unstable, as one social group replaces another. The nature of the whole process is described in chapter 4, and neighborhood changes are analyzed in chapter 5.

A life cycle is evident in many neighborhoods. They evolve from births as new subdivisons occupied by relatively affluent households, through middle age, when they shelter relatively less affluent households but remain in good condition, to their deaths through decay and abandonment by the poor households that finally occupy them. This phenomenon is related to the concentration of poverty mentioned above, which generates severe fiscal problems for city governments. Neighborhood life cycles are discussed in chapter 5.

Paradoxically, neighborhood decline is caused both by large-scale immigration of poor households, which generates overcrowding and rapid neighborhood change, and by the cessation of such immigration, which generates housing decay and abandonment. If the population in the metropolitan area is stable or declining, and if construction of new housing continues at the suburban frontier, the demand for existing housing in the inner city weakens. Again, a process resembling musical chairs arises, but its cause in this case is excess housing. The new suburban units attract relatively affluent households out of older housing, and the units they leave behind are occupied by other households moving from still older units. As households filter up through the housing inventory, vacancies trickle down to the oldest, most deteriorated neighborhoods.

Consequently, the economic level of the city population declines relative to that of the suburban population, and the real fiscal resources available to the central city government decrease. Moreover, since suburban expansion usually reduces population density, the need for urban travel increases, and energy consumption rises. Chapter 4 describes the connections between the two frontiers; chapter 5 relates them to new housing construction; and chapter 8 discusses likely future relationships between higher energy costs and urban development.

Racial discrimination and the resulting racial segregation by neighborhoods are two additional social problems built into the urban development process. How they operate and some reasons they are likely to continue are presented in chapter 7.

Exploring Future Policies Concerning Neighborhoods

Any policies seeking to cope effectively with the problems of neighborhoods must take into account the processes of urban development described above. The third goal of this book is to explore the implications of these for each level of policymaking relevant to neighborhoods.

Urban development is affected by larger factors, which must also be taken into account: population growth, population shifts, energy costs, jobs. Forecasting such conditions and trends is crucial to creating effective neighborhood policies. Certain of these conditions may change greatly in the 1980s and beyond. For example, the availability of extremely low-cost financing for housing in the 1970s—in real, after-tax terms—stimulated massive building of suburban homes. Many apartment renters bought houses. The movement of households from older city neighborhoods to newer suburbs was enormous, and the effects on urban neighborhoods were pervasive. But in the 1980s the real cost of capital for housing will probably be much higher than in the 1970s; so the rate of home building will be slower in relation to the potential rate of household formation. New dwellings will be smaller and less costly. A discussion of these and other specific forecasts is presented in chapter 8.

Chapters 10 through 13 deal with policies relevant to neighborhoods at various levels of action—federal, state, metropolitan area, city, and neighborhood. Their major themes are summarized in the remainder of this chapter.

The Necessity for Neighborhood Deterioration

Public attention usually becomes focused upon a neighborhood because of either deterioration in its physical condition and declines in the social status and incomes of its residents or an upgrading in both of these accompanied by displacement of some initial residents. Few people realize that a certain amount of neighborhood deterioration is an essential part of urban development in almost every metropolitan area. This necessity arises from the interaction of (1) poverty among a sizable minority of urban households, (2) local regulations requiring housing standards too costly for these households to uphold,[3] (3) the unwillingness of the nonpoor majority to pay the substantial costs of subsidizing poor households to meet housing standards, and (4) the desire of different socioeconomic groups to live in neighborhoods populated mainly by people like themselves.

Poor urban households must live somewhere. Many can afford only older units that have deteriorated enough to substantially reduce the cost of occupying them. Rigorous enforcement of building and housing codes in neighborhoods of nonpoor households and lax enforcement in older more obsolete neighborhoods result in a concentration of physical decay—and poor households—in a few older neighborhoods in each metropolitan area, usually in the central city.

The amount of deteriorated housing in any metropolitan area is not determined solely by such measurable local conditions as the number of poor households, the intensity of their poverty, and the nature of the housing stock. For one thing, poor households can greatly vary the percentages of their incomes they spend on housing. Moreover, how well renters and landlords treat their units influences whether those units will deteriorate and the cost of keeping them from deteriorating. In addition, whether owners of older rental units will abandon or maintain them sometimes depends upon local government code enforcement and public investment in neighborhood improvements. Thus, the total amount of deteriorated housing required within each metropolitan area at any moment depends upon so many factors it cannot be determined precisely.

3. Such universal prohibition is not true of most other nations. Nearly all lesser developed countries, in particular, allow poor households to build new, low-quality housing (often shacks) on vacant land at the periphery of large cities.

Nevertheless, it is clear that several factors increase this amount. These include heavy net in-migration of poor households, the raising of legally required housing standards (which changes the definition of "deterioration"), more rigorous enforcement of existing standards (which may force some poor households out of their units), and demolition of existing deteriorated units. Several other factors tend to decrease the amount of such housing needed. These include a decline in the number of poor households because of either rising real incomes among the poor or net out-migration of poor households, increased public subsidies of housing occupied by the poor, a lowering of legal housing standards, less rigorous enforcement of housing standards, and more rapid construction of housing units than net formation of households in the area.

Both increases and decreases in the amount of neighborhood deterioration occur through systematic processes of change related to the above factors. Descriptions of these processes and their ingredients form the first part of this book.

Because neighborhood deterioration is regarded as undesirable by almost everyone, few officials admit that our institutional structure makes a certain amount of such deterioration necessary to cope with poverty. Their lack of realism makes it difficult to formulate effective public policies concerning neighborhood decline. Moreover, uncertainty about just how much deterioration is necessary allows every official to argue that *any* deterioration found within his or her area of jurisdiction "should be eliminated."

Deterioration can be abolished within any area either by eliminating it altogether or by moving it to some other area. In reality, one community's efforts to reduce deterioration often just move it somewhere else, since a certain amount is necessary somewhere. But most citizens and public officials are interested only in what happens in their own neighborhoods. This attitude is further encouraged by ignorance about what causes neighborhood deterioration and how it is related to the overall urban development process.

Consequently, many public and private efforts to reduce neighborhood deterioration, including some policies for revitalizing neighborhoods, have "beggar thy neighboring neighborhood" effects. Yet it is hard to know in advance whether specific upgrading efforts are of that character or whether they might reduce the total amount of deterioration needed within the metropolitan area. That ambiguity allows officials in good conscience to espouse policies that reduce deterioration in their own areas without asking whether those policies might injure other areas. Moreover, in our society, it is considered permissible for each community to improve itself, even if it does so at the expense of other communities.

As a result, every municipality is engaged in a competitive struggle with other municipalities in its metropolitan area, each trying to get rid of its deteriorated housing and to avoid accepting any more. These struggles are hidden by the unwillingness of anyone to admit that a certain amount of deteriorated housing is necessary to house the area's poorest households. Instead, all espouse the myth that deterioration could be completely eliminated if only everyone tried hard enough. That would in fact be true if nonpoor households were willing to pay the public subsidy costs of helping the poorest households occupy housing that met middle-income standards. But up to now officials of local governments, state governments, and Congress have been unwilling to accept such costs—probably because their constituents are not willing to pay them.

Under these conditions, public officials almost never confront or even discuss the important issue of where the deterioration needed to cope with poverty ought to be located for the good of the entire community. If they did, many residents of the areas selected would become outraged. They would feel their neighborhoods were being relegated to a state of permanent deterioration. Consequently, all "comprehensive plans" use platitudes to avoid dealing with the vital issue of where poor people will live. This situation makes it almost impossible for anyone to formulate realistic overall strategies for coping with neighborhood deterioration in a metropolitan area as a whole, or even in a single large city as a whole.

This outcome does not result from ill will, or ignorance among elected and other officials (though few people fully understand the urban development process). The major social function of elected officials is dealing with conflicts in society with a minimum of disruption and dissension. They probably perform that function better by adopting evasive and ambiguous postures about neighborhood deterioration than by confronting the facts squarely.

To be effective, policies aimed at coping with or reducing neighborhood deterioration must accept the limitations imposed by this situation. Therefore, at all levels of government, specific policies concerning neighborhoods should be designed to improve existing conditions even though they cannot remove the fundamental conflicts and ambiguities described above.

Federal and State Policies

One of the major conflicts relevant to neighborhood change is that between further suburban development and revitalization of central city areas. Construction of suburban housing faster than net formation of households weakens the demand for central city housing and the prospects for revitalization of central city neighborhoods. But such construction aids the poor—and all renters—by increasing the total housing supply relative to demand, thereby putting downward pressure on rents and housing prices (compared to what they would be otherwise). It also helps many households upgrade their dwellings and environments by enabling them to move to newer suburban communities from older, relatively obsolete areas.

There is no simple way to resolve this conflict. In fact, the fragmentation of governmental powers *within* each metropolitan area means that no one there has either the incentive to recognize this conflict or the power to resolve it. However, federal and state agencies have jurisdictions encompassing both the suburbs and central city neighborhoods. Hence federal and state officials should begin taking far more account of the relationships between their policies that affect suburban growth and those that affect central city revitalization and decline. Federal policies concerning reduction of poverty and unemployment in general have immense effects upon neighborhood change, even though they are not aimed at it. So do federal policies aimed at reducing racial discrimination in housing and employment. In addition, other federal and state policies have even more direct effects on neighborhood change, often negative. The federal government has a responsibility to help large cities finance their public services, since those cities contain a disproportionate share of the poverty and unemployment resulting from national economic forces. Hence federal and state policies should redistribute resources from wealthier suburban areas to poorer large cities. One method is to target such resources upon those neighborhoods and residents who have the most intensive needs. This is already done in several federal block-grant, revenue-sharing, and categorical-grant programs.

Federal and state anticity policy biases, such as those in favor of new building and against rehabilitation and maintenance of existing structures, should be removed. Examples of such biases are higher federal funding ratios for new highways than mass transit, more favorable tax treatment of new construction than rehabilitation, and easier funding for building new sewer and water systems than for repairing existing ones. In addition, the federal government can influence local officials to take more realistic attitudes toward areawide needs for deteriorated housing and to formulate and follow overall strategies concerning housing, neighborhoods, and new development. The federal government should also directly support some neighborhood organizations to help them perform their function as watchdogs, monitoring the performance of local government service-delivery agencies.

State governments are channels for some federally financed programs; hence their policies should also reflect many of the considerations mentioned above. In addition, state governments have special concern with big-city public schools, which they finance heavily. In many large cities, public schools have become extremely ineffective at educating those young people who need education most. State governments should consider changing education laws so that disruptive students could more easily be suspended or expelled. They should also consider funding some private alternative schools. The competition might stimulate improvements in public school bureaucracies that will never arise through internal change alone.

One goal of public policy should be to get households who move from central cities to suburbs to pay their fair share of the social costs of coping with the poverty they leave behind. The most practical ways of doing this are federal and state programs for the redistribution of income: federal aid programs for large cities, state power-equalizing and revenue-sharing programs for education, and other federal and state personal-income-transfer programs. In metropolitan areas with tight housing markets, some costs of new suburban infrastructures should be spread over the whole area or state. But in metropolitan areas with relatively loose housing markets, the suburbanites occupying new subdivisions should pay all those costs themselves. Hence no single policy can be developed applicable to all areas.

City Policies

There is a better chance in practice to develop rational overall strategies toward neighborhood decline and revitalization at the city level than at any other—even the neighborhood level. That is because it does not make much sense for city officials to reduce deterioration in one neighborhood by moving it to another, particularly in view of the few municipal resources available for physical upgrading.

An overall strategy is most plausible for policies dealing with the physical upgrading of structures. These include the enforcement of housing codes, the improvement of streets and infrastructures, the demolition of deteriorated buildings, the treatment of tax-delinquent properties, and the encouragement of private investment.

Each city's strategy must balance two sometimes conflicting objectives. The first is encouraging renovation, since it upgrades residents' environments and benefits the city government fiscally. The second is minimizing harm to low-income renters. In loose housing markets, city policies can encourage maximum revitalization, since displaced households can find alternative accommodations without suffering much harm. But tight housing markets pose a cruel policy dilemma, because revitalization may then cause severe hardship for poor displaced households. They probably cannot easily find alternative accommodations without paying much more for them—if then.

Under both conditions—and especially in tight markets—public policy should require payment of some private and perhaps some public compensation to those displaced by revitalization who are poor, have lived in the revitalizing area for some minimum period, and would not have moved otherwise. It may also be desirable to use public subsidies to retain a mixture of different income groups in revitalized areas.

Many other city policies also greatly affect neighborhoods. Examples are property assessment procedures, desegregation of schools, spatial allocation of housing subsidy funds, and regulation of vehicular traffic flows. It is unrealistic to expect city officials to coordinate all these policies so as to benefit neighborhoods. Nevertheless, city leaders could raise the neighborhood consciousness of city officials so they take more account of the impacts of their policy decisions and actions upon neighborhood decline and revitalization.

Neighborhood Policies

Public policies at the neighborhood level itself cannot be expected to embody any overall strategic perspective encompassing larger territories. Local residents naturally tend to be partisans of their particular areas.

They are also very conservative about major changes in existing conditions, no matter how bad, and are much more interested in immediate local improvements than in long-run social reform.

These normal traits make it difficult to find locations for facilities that benefit society generally but impose costs upon nearby residents. Examples are airports, power plants, refuse disposal areas, incinerators, highways, police stations, and mental health clinics. However, designing such facilities to minimize their negative local effects (such as depressing expressways to reduce noise) and directly compensating those bearing such costs (such as paying households living near power plants) can help overcome this difficulty.

Neighborhood groups can encourage property maintenance by internalizing the interdependencies among property owners. Developing such arrangements calls for close cooperation among local financial institutions, local governments, and community organizations. Examples of specific actions these groups can take are requiring that buildings pass code inspections before they can be sold or rented, developing pooled loan funds for rehabilitation, and keeping close watch for code violations.

In fact, big-city neighborhood organizations will become much more important in the future as focal points for community life and citizen participation in local government. Many can take upon themselves some governmental and service-delivery powers through negotiations with city agencies. Such dispersal of power requires the strong support of the mayor and city council. No uniform policy will work in this regard because of the immense variety of needs and capabilities among urban neighborhoods. But for many, such powers can strengthen community organizations and improve neighborhood life.

The Boundaries of This Study

Although this book is about urban neighborhoods, it does not deal with every aspect of that complex subject. It does not present complete analyses of neighborhoods as social structures, or of neighborhood organizations. Instead, it focuses upon those aspects of policies that should be influenced by the links between individual neighborhoods and the urban development process, and it tries to give a realistic account of future trends likely to influence those links. Also, the book does not try to explain why some metropolitan areas have stopped growing while others are still expanding.[4] Rather, it focuses upon the ways in which either growth or stagnation affects the internal structure of each area.

Although urban development is a metropolitanwide process, there are few powerful institutions at that level. The strongest legal, political, and social institutions in each metropolitan area are local. Moreover, they have powerful incentives to ignore the links of neighborhoods to overall development—or to use them for parochial purposes. Thus it is unlikely that many of the recommendations for metropolitan-area policies will be carried out. However, the policy recommendations for other levels could be followed without changes in existing institutions.

The perspective of this book is influenced by the fact that I am an economist; so the methods of economics are prominent in the analysis. However, I have tried to synthesize the work of sociologists, planners, political scientists, biologists, race relations specialists, and other observers. The resulting perspective forms a framework for truly understanding neighborhoods and how they change over time.

4. See Katharine L. Bradbury, Anthony Downs, and Kenneth A. Small, *Urban Decline and the Future of American Cities* (Brookings Institution, forthcoming), for an explanation of differing growth rates among metropolitan areas.

2

What Is a Neighborhood?

To CLARIFY the relationship between what happens in individual neighborhoods and what happens in the overall urban development process, it is vital to define *neighborhood* unambiguously at the outset. That is not easy. For one thing, no one definition has come into widespread acceptance among neighborhood residents themselves, neighborhood organizations, or academic analysts. Second, there are many different geographic scales of neighborhood. People frequently cause confusion by shifting their terms of reference from one scale to another without defining either. Third, few cities have established official geographic boundaries for their neighborhoods. Nevertheless, the basic nature of neighborhoods needs to be clarified as a foundation for the remainder of the analysis.

As the National Commission on Neighborhoods states: "In the last analysis, each neighborhood is what the inhabitants think it is."[1] This subjective definition has two vital implications.

One, a neighborhood's definition varies depending on the geographic scales used by the residents.[2] *The immediate neighborhood* is the small cluster of houses right around one's own house. *The homogeneous neighborhood* is the area up to where the market value of housing noticeably changes or where the mix of housing types or values changes.

1. National Commission on Neighborhoods, *People, Building Neighborhoods*, Final Report to the President and the Congress of the United States (Government Printing Office, 1979), p. 7.
2. The following classification is from Richard P. Coleman, "Attitudes Towards Neighborhoods: How Americans Choose to Live," Working Paper 49 (Cambridge: Joint Center for Urban Studies, 1978), pp. 3–4.

13

The institution-oriented neighborhood is the area in which residents share common relationships with a local institution, such as an elementary school, a church, a police precinct, or a political ward. *The regional neighborhood* is an entire suburb or township or a district within a big city, such as the South Side of Milwaukee. Although each of these scales is appropriate under certain circumstances, they frequently make a neighborhood's boundaries vague and ill defined.

Two, shared participation and viewpoints help create and sustain the neighborhood as a reality for its inhabitants and therefore for the larger community too.[3] The following are examples:

Use of the same space as a focal point for personal interactions. Children interact most intensively with the people living closest to them because they cannot go far from home. But adults, too, use the neighborhood for provision of mutual aid, reinforcement of values, transmission of information and influence, and creation of status.[4]

A common relationship with some nearby institution, such as a church or school. This relationship generates social interactions among members, as in a Catholic parish.

Common membership in an ethnic group. Neighborhoods predominantly Italian, Polish, Greek, Jewish, black, Mexican, and so on persist to this day in most large cities.

Common location in a single residential real estate market area. In the real estate industry, a neighborhood is what local real estate brokers, lenders, appraisers, and residents perceive as the smallest discrete housing market unit beyond the individual structure and block.

Membership in a local political group. Neighborhood residents often form organizations to gain control over neighborhood conditions by influencing some broader government agency, such as the city council or the state highway department.

A relationship to a local public service office. Police precincts are an example.

Agreement on exclusionary arrangements. Often the strongest unifying factor is opposition to an external threat, such as the construction of a new highway or public housing project.[5]

The greater the similarity of boundaries related to each function, the

3. The ideas in this section are taken largely from M. Leanne Lachman and Anthony Downs, "The Role of Neighborhoods in the Mature Metropolis," in Charles L. Leven, ed., *The Mature Metropolis* (Lexington Books, 1978).

4. From Suzanne Keller, *The Urban Neighborhood* (Random House, 1968), chap. 1.

5. For a discussion of "communities of limited liability" see National Academy of Sciences, National Research Council, *Toward an Understanding of Metropolitan America,*

stronger the neighborhood. Each personal relationship among residents springing from these functions reinforces the other ties, forming an invisible network that defines the neighborhood. These intangible networks are as vital to a city as its streets and sewer systems. This approach to neighborhoods, involving both geography and social structure, seeks to resolve the ambiguity concerning the meaning of *neighborhood* pointed out by Suzanne Keller:

From the start . . . the neighborhood unit was both a social and a planning concept. It also had several, somewhat incompatible, objectives. . . . On the one hand, it was to provide convenience and comfort and direct, face-to-face contact in order to restore some sense of community that had been disturbed or destroyed by the specialization and segmentalization of urban life. On the other hand, however, it was also to constitute a special subpart of a larger, more complex totality.[6]

This book combines these two aspects by assuming that *neighborhoods are geographic units within which certain social relationships exist,* although the intensity of these relationships and their importance in the lives of the residents vary tremendously.

The idea of neighborhood can also reflect two different perspectives: the *particular* view of someone located in one spot and looking outward and the *comprehensive* view of someone trying to divide an entire city or metropolitan area into subunits for analysis or administration. People adopting the particular perspective—including most people discussing their own neighborhoods—normally use the smaller scales mentioned above; they also consider the neighborhood an essentially informal social grouping. In contrast, people adopting the comprehensive perspective normally use larger geographic scales to reduce the total number of units they must deal with. They also emphasize relationships between each neighborhood and the larger community and consider the neighborhood a formal organizational or administrative unit. In most cases, I use the comprehensive perspective in this study.

Conclusions from This View of Neighborhoods

Three conclusions derive from defining a neighborhood as "what the inhabitants think it is," in ways that incorporate both a geographic unit

Report of the Social Science Panel of the Advisory Committee to the Department of Housing and Urban Development (Canfield Press, 1975), especially chap. 4.

    6. *The Urban Neighborhood,* pp. 126, 133.

and social interaction. First, neighborhoods can differ greatly in almost all measurable characteristics from one city to another and within a single city.[7] This means neighborhood boundaries must be identified by the local residents in each community; they cannot be defined from afar by national experts or federal officials. Neighborhoods thus locally defined will differ from each other enormously. For example, Cincinnati residents in 1970 defined forty-four neighborhoods. Some were almost entirely residential; others mixed commercial, industrial, and residential. Neighborhood population averaged around 10,000 persons, but ranged from 819 to 28,794. Some had been rapidly growing, others rapidly declining. The population in some was almost entirely white; in others, mainly black; in still others, a mixture of both groups.[8]

Second, people in many residential areas perceive their neighborhoods only on the immediate geographic scale unless local institutions undertake actions that unify the residents. These actions may not be deliberately intended to widen and strengthen the neighborhood, but they will do so if they create unifying relationships among people living in the area.

Third, strong neighborhoods do not depend upon the existence of local organizations specifically designed to create a conscious neighborhood identity. In many vital urban neighborhoods, there are no such *neighborhood organizations*—only *organizations within neighborhoods*, such as churches, schools, political wards, realtors, police precincts, and so on. The distinction between these two types of organizations is discussed in the last section of this chapter.

Nonmarket Linkages and Self-Reinforcing Expectations

Each household in a neighborhood—and therefore the entire neighborhood—is affected by the surrounding households and by the expectations it has about these households. For example, the behavior of people in surrounding households determines how safe it is for the members of another to walk the streets or allow its children to play outside. The size and nature of surrounding housing indicate whether

7. As the National Commission on Neighborhoods concludes, "There is no standard set of characteristics that make a neighborhood; there is no simple, single description accurate for all policymaking purposes." *People, Building Neighborhoods*, p. 7.

8. See Real Estate Research Corporation, "Defining Cincinnati's Neighborhoods, Cincinnati Housing Strategy," Position Paper 1, prepared for the Cincinnati Working Review Committee on Housing, November 3, 1972.

these households have incomes and social status different from its own, or whether they are quite similar. How well nearby housing is maintained affects each household's daily aesthetic pleasure and is another indicator of social and economic status.

These linkages do not occur because of economic market relationships—they flow directly from one household to another and hence are external to markets. Yet such *externalities* have a great effect on the market value of all the housing in the neighborhood and thus affect the owners of property there.

These owners are usually unrelated individuals, each of whom controls only a small part of the entire neighborhood. The value of each owner's property is thus greatly affected by the behavior of persons over whom he or she has no control. Moreover, this inescapable interdependency involves future behavior too. The current market value of every property is essentially the discounted present value of all future streams of income or service it can be expected to produce. Those forthcoming benefits will be affected by how owners of surrounding property behave in the future.

There is an inherent tension between the linkage of neighbors by their nearness and their division into separate and largely autonomous households. Each household is uncertain of its neighbors' future behavior. The degree of its uncertainty depends upon how similar the neighbors' cultural backgrounds are to its own and upon the recent rate of change in neighborhood conditions.[9] Mutual agreement and expectations are especially important concerning personal public comportment, property maintenance, patronage of local institutions, control over children, and sales prices of properties. But neighboring households have very few effective means of coordinating either their behavior or their expectations. Expectations are intangible and are scattered in the minds of thousands of people, including future residents. Since most of these people do not even know each other's identity, effective communication among them is rare and their expectations are possibly incompatible, volatile, and even self-defeating.

Mutual expectations about property maintenance are particularly important among neighboring property owners. As time passes, all property needs repairs and maintenance and sometimes extensive mod-

9. An excellent discussion of how dissimilarity of cultural backgrounds affects behavioral expectations and day-to-day behavior among residents of a single large neighborhood is presented in Gerald D. Suttles, *The Social Order of the Slum* (University of Chicago Press, 1968).

ernization. Owners are more likely to make such investments if they believe they can recover their money through rents, stable or rising property values, or their own consumption. This belief is based on an expectation that the owners of other nearby properties will maintain their properties, too. That expectation in turn is influenced by the past behavior of those other owners. A neighborhood in which nearly every owner quickly carries out any needed maintenance creates an expectation that such behavior will continue. Conversely, each owner in an area terribly deteriorated because of lack of maintenance expects that other owners around him will *not* maintain their properties in the future. Expectations about future property maintenance are affected also by expectations about possible changes in the neighborhood. If a few owners in a well-maintained neighborhood believe, for example, that "undesirable people" are going to move in, or that a new expressway will disrupt the area, they may fail to maintain their properties. Others then adopt negative expectations and in turn let their properties deteriorate. Before long, the deterioration initially expected by only a few has happened, thanks to behavior generated by their negative expectations.

Thus, *crucial to every neighborhood are prevailing expectations there about future property maintenance and other conditions*. These expectations are mutually reinforcing and thus self-fulfilling. This dimension is entirely psychological and intangible, although it is related to existing and recent past physical conditions in the area. Moreover, positive expectations, which sustain good property maintenance in a neighborhood, are fragile. Every neighborhood has some susceptibility to future decline. The following factors increase such susceptibility:

Chance failures of maintenance in properties where fire has occurred, or where legal tangles of ownership remove incentives for owners to keep their properties in good condition, or where absentee owners are indifferent[10]

10. If enough instances coincide in one neighborhood, they can start a vicious circle of negative expectations about its future. The following passage illustrates this conclusion: "Recent studies in two marginal, but not poor, neighborhoods in Philadelphia revealed that almost none of the early abandonment in these neighborhoods stemmed from any of the reasons that are usually cited—problem tenants, high vacancy rates, code enforcement, rents that are insufficient to cover operating costs, or inability to obtain financing for repairs.

"Initially, abandonments were almost all the result of untoward events, such as fires, accidents, or deaths, that led directly or indirectly to serious property damage and the need for expensive repairs which owners declined to make." William G. Grigsby and others, *Rethinking Housing and Community Development Policy* (University of Pennsylvania Department of City and Regional Planning, 1977), p. 47.

Withdrawal of a key local institution, such as a hospital that employs many local residents or a Catholic school that teaches their children

Land-use changes, such as the building of an expressway, a shopping center, or a different kind of housing (a shift from single-family to multifamily dwellings, for example)

The possibility of land-use changes posed by, for example, tentative local government decisions to build a community college or to raze a site for urban renewal

Entry of several households different from the average in the area— poorer, or lower in socioeconomic status, or from a different ethnic background

Transition to lower-income occupancy in adjacent or nearby neighborhoods

Large increases in property taxes that force many owners to put their houses on the market all at once and thereby depress property values

Declining or inadequate public service, such as infrequent garbage collection or poor-quality public schools

Obsolete structures, such as huge single-family houses too expensive to maintain or large multifamily buildings too difficult to manage

Organizations within Neighborhoods

As noted earlier, it is important to distinguish between *organizations within neighborhoods* and *neighborhood organizations*.[11] Organizations within neighborhoods, or *neighborhood institutions*, are any groups that happen to operate in a neighborhood, serving certain people who happen to live there. They include informal organizations like extended families, government service agencies like a public elementary school, religious and social organizations like a Catholic parish, political organizations like the local Democratic precinct team. In contrast, *neighborhood organizations* function in relation to the entire neighborhood perceived as a geographic entity and usually serve all its residents. They are not accidentally related to a specific neighborhood—they were formally created with such a relationship in mind. Many neighborhoods in U.S.

11. I am indebted to Edward Marciniak of the Institute of Urban Life, Loyola University, Chicago, for pointing out the importance of organizations within neighborhoods, as opposed to neighborhood organizations, and for many other helpful suggestions. This chapter presents some basic facts about such organizations without attempting to analyze them fully.

urban areas do not contain any neighborhood organizations defined in this way.

Nearly all U.S. urban neighborhoods contain several neighborhood institutions that perform social and political functions. They enable both children and adults to *develop social and other skills* and to increase their sense of self-worth through interaction with their neighbors. They *promote mutual assistance* among neighbors. They *pressure government and private agencies* to improve services to the area. They *provide some services* that would otherwise not be furnished, or would be less suitable to local needs. They *create a local base of political support* for state, national, or other broader-area policies that would benefit the neighborhood, such as greater unemployment assistance. They *increase the participation of local residents* in formal neighborhood organizations so as to make the latter more effective in meeting their needs.

These functions are defined here in abstract rather than concrete terms so they can be applied to many different activities: education, religion, health care, vocational training, police and fire protection, recreation and entertainment, housing, lending money, and referral to nonlocal expertise. Some of these activities involve organizations within neighborhoods as intermediaries between individual residents or households and city or even national agencies. Other activities involve such organizations more directly, as producers of services or as channels of communication among local residents without much reference to organizations or forces outside the neighborhood. Still other activities are performed by organizations within neighborhoods, like police precinct stations, that are branches of larger agencies.

Children need many services, and their activities are concentrated right around where they live. Therefore, a neighborhood containing many school-age children normally generates dozens of neighborhood institutions. In contrast, a neighborhood containing mainly childless upper-income households in high-rise rental apartments may generate very few. Because of such diversity of neighborhoods, there is a diversity of organizational requirements. For example, a high-income suburb with an elaborate network of public schools, churches, social relationships, bridge clubs, country clubs for golf and tennis, garden clubs, political organizations, and informal contacts among business and local government leaders does not need a formal neighborhood organization. True, if some unusual threat to community stability arises—such as a state government proposal to split the community with a new expressway—the residents may form a formal neighborhood organization to respond to that threat. However, even in that case, they may believe that existing neighborhood institutions are capable of handling the situation.

Some observers contend that the strength and vitality of organizations within neighborhoods affect residents' willingness to improve their neighborhoods. In 1978 Roger Ahlbrandt and James Cunningham surveyed households in six Pittsburgh neighborhoods, probing the relationship between a resident's interactions within the neighborhood's social fabric and his or her satisfaction with, and commitment to, that neighborhood.[12] Each area's social fabric is made up of formal organizations within that area, family relationships, informal relations, political organizations, and religious activities. The more ties each resident has, and the more active he or she is in those relationships, the stronger is the resident's resulting satisfaction with, and commitment to, the neighborhood as a place to live. Consequently, Ahlbrandt and Cunningham believe neighborhood organizations and local governments should devote significant resources to strengthening the social fabric of neighborhoods they want to preserve or revitalize. That includes providing financial and other assistance to families, local newspapers, private schools, public schools, local festivals and fairs, neighborhood organizations, block clubs, and even informal networks within such areas.[13]

Organizations within a neighborhood, then, play such a vital role in performing social and political functions that many neighborhoods need no formal neighborhood organizations. Furthermore, those neighborhoods in which these functions are not being adequately performed should in many cases be enabled to create or strengthen organizations within them rather than to found or strengthen formal neighborhood organizations.

It follows that no uniform national neighborhood policy will be appropriate for all urban neighborhoods, and that a policy of shifting any one set of social and political functions to formal neighborhood organizations is seldom appropriate even within a single city.

Nevertheless, in low-income neighborhoods that contain few functioning neighborhood institutions, where conditions are unsatisfactory and

12. Roger S. Ahlbrandt, Jr., and James V. Cunningham, A New Public Policy for Neighborhood Preservation (Praeger, 1979).
13. Ibid., pp. 198–221.

prospects for improvement poor, new or strengthened neighborhood organizations may be highly desirable.[14]

These neighborhoods not only lack the services normally provided by neighborhood institutions but also may receive poor services from local government agencies, which typically provide their best services to neighborhoods where they get the most pressure from influential residents and neighborhood institutions. To meet this pressure with limited budgets, these agencies often skimp on services to the neighborhoods with the least political influence—usually poor neighborhoods. Strong neighborhood organizations can significantly improve services to their neighborhoods both by pressuring government agencies to act more effectively and by delivering some services themselves.

Neighborhood organizations that monitor the services their areas receive and constantly press for improvements perform toward local government agencies the same function that competition performs in a free market. Most local government service-providers have no real competition. Local ordinances, the nature of the services, and their financing through taxes prevent citizens from seeking alternatives. Hence these agencies often exhibit the classic shortcomings of monopolists: inadequate incentive to work fast or to meet high standards, insensitivity to consumer needs, and a tendency to suit their own convenience at the expense of their customers. One way to overcome these shortcomings is by shifting the provision of local services to private firms, which would compete with each other. But residents of poor areas cannot afford to purchase high-quality services on their own. Unless some type of publicly financed voucher system is used, they must rely upon public service. Another way to overcome the shortcomings of public services is to form

14. But even in these neighborhoods there are usually informal networks of relationships, especially if the residents are members of ethnic groups in which large extended families are common. As one study states: "In fact, contrary to the usual description of the poor neighborhood as 'disorganized,' it serves as a much more effective basis for organized social life than the wealthier neighborhood does. Of necessity, underprivileged groups cultivate patterns of behavior that enable them to survive in relatively inhospitable environments. The residential areas of the poor and the ethnically distinctive are often highly organized, but, as a long series of studies have shown, not in the middle-class pattern. Organization is evident in the presence of various peer groups and gangs equipped with explicit rules and procedures, in ethnic churches, in communication networks, in clear understanding of who the neighborhood turf belongs to, and in the behavior considered proper relative to outsiders. Although these elements of organization may not be approved by the community at large, they provide a basis for regulating social life." National Academy of Sciences, National Research Council, *Toward an Understanding of Metropolitan America*, p. 74.

organizations that protest poor quality and that pressure public service-providers in the same way that fear of losing business to competitors pressures private service providers.

Thus, neighborhood organizations and organizations within neighborhoods have a permanent service-monitoring function wherever local services are provided monopolistically by government agencies—which is almost everywhere.

3

Neighborhood Stability

MOST people regard neighborhood stability as desirable, but they do not realize how dynamic such stability really is in urban areas. In the simplest sense, any neighborhood is *stable* as long as its key characteristics do not change much. These characteristics and the various ways they can change are listed in table 3–1. Thus, neighborhood stability can occur in a new and affluent area and in a deteriorated slum.[1]

However, *neighborhood stability never means lack of movement*, especially of population. About one-fifth of all U.S. households move every year.[2] About half of all households have not moved within the past five years. This means the annual turnover is concentrated in the other half. Therefore, a significant fraction of the households in every neighborhood moves out each year. If a neighborhood is to remain stable, these movers must be replaced by newcomers with similar characteristics. The newcomers may be existing households or newly formed households.[3]

1. True, the term *stable neighborhood* usually means a place that is desirable to live in, as well as unchanging. But I use the term only to refer to lack of change.
2. The Census Bureau surveys recent movers each year. These are defined as those households that moved in the twelve months before they were interviewed. See Bureau of the Census, *Current Housing Reports*, series H-150-76, *Annual Housing Survey, 1976: United States and Regions*, pt. D, "Housing Characteristics of Recent Movers" (Government Printing Office, 1978), p. 1. Although the fraction of these recent movers who shifted residences within the same city is known (as discussed later in the text), it is not known what fraction shifted residences within the same neighborhoods rather than moving into those neighborhoods from elsewhere. This lack of knowledge further limits the inferences about mobility that can be drawn about individual neighborhoods from existing data.
3. The fraction of newly formed households is quite significant. Of the 15.8 million households that moved in 1977, 4.11 million (26 percent) had a different household head in their previous housing unit. Thus, about 5.5 percent of all 75.3 million households were newly formed. *Current Housing Reports*, series H-150-77, *Annual Housing Survey, 1977*, pt. D, "Housing Characteristics of Recent Movers" (GPO, 1979), pp. 1, 7.

24

Table 3-1. *Variables in Neighborhood Stability*

Population change involves shifts in
   Number of households
   Number of residents
   Socioeconomic status
   Age distribution
   Ethnic composition
   Crime rates

Physical change involves shifts in
   Number of structures
   Physical condition of structures
   Vacancy rate
   Mixture of building types
   Mixture of land uses
   Amount and nature of open space
   Amount and nature of vehicle traffic

Economic change involves shifts in
   Market values of property
   Sales prices of property
   Rent levels
   Number of active buyers and sellers of property
   Number of housing units occupied by owners
   Amount invested in maintenance, repair, and renovation of property
   Amount of new construction
   Availability and cost of real estate financing and insurance
   Real estate taxes
   Amount of real estate tax delinquency

Public service change involves shifts in the quality of
   Police and fire protection
   Public schools
   Public transportation
   Street and sidewalk maintenance
   Trash and garbage collection

Psychological change involves shifts in opinions and expectations about
   Socioeconomic status
   Ethnic composition
   Physical condition of structures
   Property values
   Personal and property security
   Public school quality
   Desirability of neighborhood as place to live

So population stability results from balancing two flows of people: one moving out, and another moving in.

The stability of a neighborhood's physical characteristics also depends upon balancing inflows with outflows. The outflows are declines in physical structures caused by demolition, accidental damage, and deterioration from age, arson, vandalism, and economic obsolescence. Unless the outflows are offset by physical inflows consisting of repairs, maintenance, renovations, and new construction, the neighborhood gradually deteriorates.

These stabilizing movements of households, materials, and services also involve economic movements. Money flows into the neighborhood as people buy homes and invest in repairs, modernization, and construction of properties; as patrons purchase goods and services in local stores; and as governments provide services and capital improvements. Money flows out as sellers of property depart; taxes are paid; and profits from renting properties and operating local businesses are withdrawn by absentee owners. Economic movement, too, affects stability. Money inflows must be large enough compared to outflows to keep property values either stable or rising along with general inflation.

Thus, *stability requires constant inflows of people with certain characteristics and of investments in money or in-kind services*. If such inflows do not occur but normal outflows continue, any area will gradually lose population and sink into physical decay. In well-maintained neighborhoods that remain stable for years, the balancing of outflows and inflows seems almost automatic. But the real estate market is simply performing successfully. Hence most residents do not even realize that stability is a dynamic condition until these flows are no longer in balance and the neighborhood begins to change.

Household movements out of neighborhoods are of two types. *Normal turnover* arises from everyday life and is unrelated to expectations that the neighborhood will change. Households move out because of job transfers, deaths, additions to the family that make their dwellings too small, reductions that make them too large, or changes in economic or social status. All neighborhoods experience normal turnover outflow every year, the size depending upon certain traits of the residents (discussed further below). *Neighborhood transition turnover* arises because people expect the neighborhood to change. For example, if some low-income households move into a neighborhood formerly composed entirely of middle-income households, the latter may believe the area will change character; so some may leave sooner than they otherwise would have. Total outflow is the sum of normal turnover and neighborhood transition. Hence one sign of ongoing or impending transition in a neighborhood is a noticeable increase in its rate of outflow.

Factors in Population Mobility

Although inflows and outflows of people are equally important to neighborhood life, accurate data are available only concerning people who move *into* neighborhoods each year. These data are obtained from the Census Bureau's *Annual Housing Survey*, which each year asks a large national sample of households how long they have lived in their present residences. These data are not tabulated for the neighborhood level but for the national, regional, metropolitan-area, and central-city levels. Hence inferences about likely rates of outflow from any specific neighborhood must be drawn from data concerning (1) how larger groups of people with certain characteristics behave, and (2) the fraction of those types of people living in that neighborhood. For example, since older people move far less frequently than young ones, a neighborhood with a high fraction of elderly residents usually has a low normal turnover rate.[4]

In 1976, 19.7 percent of all U.S. households had moved into their present residences within the past twelve months. This fraction has been relatively stable for many years: in 1973, it was 19.2 percent; in 1974, 19.6 percent; in 1975, 18.9 percent; and in 1977, 21.0 percent.[5] However, the rate of normal turnover in any specific neighborhood depends upon certain characteristics of its residents, as follows:

1. The higher the percentage of renters, the greater the neighborhood's rate of turnover. In the entire nation in 1976, 38.0 percent of all renters but only 9.7 percent of all owner occupants were recent movers—that is, they had moved into their current dwellings within the last twelve months.

2. Neighborhoods in the West and South typically have turnover rates higher than those in the Midwest and much higher than those in the Northeast. Regional mobility rates in 1976 were:[6]

4. For many large cities these inferences can be verified by the annual door-to-door surveys conducted by R. L. Polk and Company. See their *Profiles of Change: Management Reports by Census Tract*, and *Profiles of Change: Map Series by Census Tract*, for specific city and year (Detroit: R. L. Polk).

5. All figures from *Annual Housing Survey*, 1977, pt. D, p. 1, and previous issues.

6. *Annual Housing Survey*, 1976, pt. D, pp. 1, 24, 41, 58, 75. These regional mobility differences are *not* significantly affected by migration from the Northeast and the Midwest to the South and West. For example, in the West 3.642 million households moved within

	Percentage of recently moving households		
Region	*All households*	*Owner occupants*	*Renter occupants*
West	26.0	13.6	45.7
South	20.8	10.2	41.6
Midwest	18.3	9.3	38.6
Northeast	14.6	6.3	27.0
United States	19.7	9.7	38.0

3. Neighborhoods with many young households experience much higher turnover rates than those with many older households. Variations in annual turnover rates by age are illustrated by the following 1976 data for all U.S. households containing two or more persons and headed by a male with wife present:[7]

	Percentage of recently moving households	
Age of household head	*Owner occupants*	*Renter occupants*
Under 25	43.5	68.0
25–29	27.9	44.0
30–34	17.5	42.4
35–44	10.0	29.1
45–64	5.2	21.5
65 and over	3.6	14.3

a twelve-month period, but net in-migration *to* the West was only about 128,000 households. If those in-migrants are subtracted from both the number of recent movers and the total number residing in the West, the adjusted mobility rate would be 25.3 percent instead of the 26.0 percent shown in the table. Similar calculations eliminating the effects of interregional migrations also produce small adjustments in the other regions, as follows:

	Percentage of recently moving households		
Region	*Before adjusting for interregional migration*	*After adjusting for interregional migration*	*Percent change*
West	26.0	25.3	−2.8
South	20.8	20.4	−2.0
Midwest	18.3	18.6	1.6
Northeast	14.6	14.8	1.4

The adjustments are made by assuming that net migrating households remained in the regions where they originated and that net households migrating from abroad did not enter the United States. It is impossible to make similar adjustments for the percentages of owner occupants and renters who recently moved in each region. However, they would undoubtedly also be very small. Hence nearly all the regional differences noted in the text table stem from true regional variations.

7. Ibid., p. 2.

As can be seen, owner occupant households with heads under twenty-five years old were twelve times as likely to move as those with heads aged sixty-five and over; young renters were 4.8 times as likely to move as the older renters. Mobility among other types of households is also apparently age-related.

4. Neighborhoods containing many black residents have slightly lower turnover rates than those containing few blacks, *if* both neighborhoods have the same type of housing tenure:[8]

Race of household head	Percentage of recently moving households	
	Owner occupants	Renter occupants
Black	7.8	28.7
All nonblack	9.9	39.9

In almost every age group black households had lower mobility rates than nonblack households with each type of tenure, as well as for both types of tenure combined. In 1976, 56.3 percent of all black households and 32.8 percent of all nonblack households were renters. Since renters are far more mobile than owners, the average annual turnover among all black households (19.6 percent) was almost the same as that among all nonblack households (19.7 percent). However, except for owner occupants with incomes of $15,000 or more, black mobility was lower for both types of tenure at all income levels.[9]

5. Neighborhoods of relatively expensive housing have higher turnover rates than those with less expensive housing. Among owners, the difference is only slight, but among renters the difference is considerable. In 1976, 12.4 percent of owner occupants in homes valued at $50,000 or more had moved during the preceding year; the percentage declined steadily to 5.5 percent of those in homes valued under $10,000. Among renters, the highest turnover rate (47 percent) was for households paying $300 or more a month for rent. Slightly lower rates prevailed for renters paying between $300 and $150 per month. Below $150 rent, turnover rates declined steadily to only 22 percent for households paying under $60 a month. This may reflect high proportions of elderly households among low-income renters.[10]

8. Ibid., pp. 1, 14.
9. Ibid., pp. 2, 15.
10. Ibid., p. 3.

Incomes of neighborhood residents do not greatly affect turnover rate. Low-income owners have turnover rates only half those of high-income owners, but the *absolute* difference between them is less than 6 percentage points, as mobility among all owners is at the low end of the spectrum. Turnover-rate variations among income groups of renters are also small in absolute terms, with the highest rates being in the $5,000 to $10,000 bracket:[11]

	Percentage of recently moving households	
Dollars of annual household income	*Owner occupants*	*Renter occupants*
Under 3,000	6.0	35.8
3,000–4,999	5.2	35.0
5,000–6,999	6.9	41.2
7,000–9,999	8.9	42.1
10,000–14,999	11.1	37.8
15,000–24,999	11.0	37.9
25,000 and over	11.0	33.9

6. Central city neighborhoods have slightly higher percentages of residents moving out each year than suburban neighborhoods or nonmetropolitan neighborhoods with the same form of housing tenure. Suburban and nonmetropolitan neighborhoods have slightly higher percentages of residents moving in.[12]

	Percentage of recently moving households			
	Owner occupants		Renter occupants	
Type of neighborhood	*Moving in*	*Moving out*	*Moving in*	*Moving out*
Central city	8.4	12.6	35.8	38.4
Suburban (inside SMSA but outside central city)	10.3	8.8	40.2	38.0
Nonmetropolitan	9.9	9.0	39.2	38.2

11. Ibid., p. 2. How can variations in neighborhood housing prices be associated with different mobility rates when variations in neighborhood incomes are not? This seeming inconsistency arises because people with the same incomes pay widely varying amounts for housing.

12. Ibid., p. 1. These estimates are somewhat exaggerated because accurate data on place of origin are available only for households that had the same heads before and after moving (73.7 percent). The data for this group were arbitrarily expanded to all recent movers. Because central cities contain high proportions of renters, the percentage of all recently moving households was 22.3 percent in central cities, 19.0 percent in suburbs, and 18.1 percent in nonmetropolitan areas. Thus, in *typical* neighborhoods, central cities undoubtedly have higher rates of movement both in and out than either suburbs or nonmetropolitan areas.

Table 3-2. *Neighborhood Characteristics and Residents' Mobility*

Characteristics related to high mobility	Characteristics related to low mobility
High percentage of renter occupants	High percentage of owner occupants
Location in West or South	Location in Northeast
High percentage of young household heads	High percentage of elderly household heads
Low percentage of black households (tenure held constant)	High percentage of black households (tenure held constant)
Expensive rental housing	Lower-cost rental housing
Central city location	Suburban or nonmetropolitan location

Each of the six observations above assumes that all other factors not mentioned remain unchanged. It is clear that accurately estimating a turnover rate for any one neighborhood requires taking many of these factors into account simultaneously, but because few local data are available, only a rough approximation is possible. Table 3-2 summarizes the impacts of the major factors discussed above.

Variations in Mobility Rates

Mobility rates vary tremendously, both among cities and among neighborhoods within a single city. In the early 1970s, R. L. Polk measured mobility in dozens of U.S. cities for the Department of Housing and Urban Development. Polk tried to survey each household included in the data for two consecutive years. Mobility rates were computed by counting all households present in the first year but not the second plus all present in the second year but not the first, and dividing that sum by the total number of housing units occupied in the second year. This method double-counts movers, unlike the method in the *Annual Housing Surveys*. Thus if Polk's mobility rates are divided in half, they are roughly comparable to the rates from the *Surveys*. Since the Polk surveys computed mobility rates for every census tract, they allow comparisons at citywide and neighborhood levels. The two surveys in each city were not always precisely one year apart and did not cover all households, so the comparisons are approximate.[13]

13. If the number of occupied housing units in a particular city surveyed were exactly the same in both surveys and the surveys were conducted exactly one year apart, the Polk mobility rate would be precisely two times the *Annual Housing Survey* rate.

Fast-growing cities generally have higher household mobility rates than slow-growing ones, partly because the former are in more mobile regions and partly because many in-migrating households are entering them. Yet there are large variations within these two groups, as shown in table 3-3. The difference in mobility rates between declining cities and growing cities is much smaller than the difference in their population changes. The five declining cities had an average overall mobility rate only 6.6 percentage points lower than the average of the five fast-growing cities. In fact, Dayton's mobility rate was identical with Tucson's, and Cleveland's was identical with San Jose's. Moreover, mobility rates for specific groups of households between each pair of cities were very similar. Yet one city in each pair was shrinking rapidly and the other was growing rapidly.

The fourth column in table 3-3 shows the percentage of the housing units in each city that changed occupants between the two Polk surveys. South Bend had the lowest turnover rate and Austin the highest. The

Table 3-3. *Annual Household Mobility Rates and Five-Year Population Changes for Ten American Cities*
Percentage

City and time period for household mobility	All households	House- holds with owner occupants	House- holds with renter occupants	Housing units changing occupants	Population change 1970–75
Declining cities					
Dayton, 1974–75	26.5	9.8	46.3	34.8	−15.6
Cleveland, 1972–73	34.0	16.4	51.7	43.7	−14.9
Rochester, 1973–75	30.2	12.0	47.9	39.7	−10.9
South Bend, 1974–75	17.3	9.1	43.0	22.5	−7.7
San Francisco, 1973–74	8.1	10.5	37.9	35.6	−7.1
Average	27.2	11.6	45.4	35.3	−11.2
Growing cities					
Tucson, 1974–75	26.5	11.7	49.4	n.a.	+12.5
San Diego, 1974–75	34.5	13.3	54.7	45.1	+11.0
Austin, 1974–75	38.5	14.3	66.1	54.0	+19.4
San Jose, 1973–75	34.0	17.5	61.9	47.0	+24.7
Colorado Springs, 1974–75	35.5	16.4	45.4	35.3	+33.3
Average	33.8	14.6	59.6	48.5	+20.2

Sources: Mobility rates, R. L. Polk and Company, *Profiles of Change: Management Reports by Census Tract*, and *Profiles of Change: Map Series by Census Tract* for specific cities and year (Detroit: R. L. Polk, 1972–75). Polk data are divided in half for comparability to Census Bureau data. Population change, Bureau of the Census, *Statistical Abstract of the United States, 1977* (Government Printing Office, 1977), table 23.
n.a. Not available.

fast-growing cities had considerably higher turnover rates than the declining ones, although Cleveland's rate was almost as high as the average of the former group. All of these percentages are much larger than comparable mobility figures from the *Annual Housing Surveys*. This divergence arises from differing survey methods and means of projection to offset data gaps. In fact, R. L. Polk and Company cautions users of all the data mentioned above to focus upon comparisons between areas rather than absolute levels.

Neighborhood mobility variations are revealed by Census Bureau data not presented here, which show census tract mobility rates *within* individual cities. In Austin, mobility of owner occupants in the most dynamic neighborhood exceeded that in the least dynamic by a ratio of 3.2 to 1; in Rochester the comparable ratio was 6.7 to 1. The highest renter mobility rates in any census tracts were also in Austin. Three tracts near the University of Texas exhibited renter turnover rates of 87.5 percent, 78.6 percent, and 78.3 percent. (These rates may seem so high it should be mentioned that all rates in this discussion have been translated into *Annual Housing Survey* equivalents; the Polk rates themselves were *double* these figures.) The lowest renter mobility in any Austin census tract was 36.7 percent—less than half that in the highest. The lowest renter mobility rate for any census tract within these ten cities was 18.9 percent in South Bend—just about one-fourth of the highest renter rate in that city (72.5 percent). From these data, it appears that *variations in mobility rates are much larger among neighborhoods within a city than among averages for different cities*. Some of these intracity variations are undoubtedly caused by different combinations of the mobility-related traits discussed earlier in this chapter. Analyzing in detail the reasons for such variation is beyond the scope of this study. Nevertheless, it is clear that the population inflow required to maintain stability in each neighborhood varies greatly within every city.

Population Mobility and Neighborhood Stability

The *turnover rate* of any neighborhood's population can be defined as the number of households that move out during any period, or the number who move in, divided by the average total number of households living there during the period. Since 19.7 percent of all U.S. households move each year (as of 1976), the average neighborhood experiences a 100 percent turnover in about 5.1 years. Neighborhoods consisting entirely of rental households would reach 100 percent turnover more rapidly and those consisting entirely of owner-occupied households more slowly. When a neighborhood experiences 100 percent turnover in some period, that means the *number* of households moving out has equaled the total number originally living there. But not all the original households have moved away. In fact, 1976 data indicate that 43.9 percent of the residents in the average U.S. neighborhood had lived there for nearly seven years, 29.1 percent for twelve or more years, and 8.6 percent for twenty-seven or more years. Thus, nearly every neighborhood has a significant fraction of "stayers," who remain for long periods no matter what the average rate of population turnover. These stayers often include some of the most important leaders in the community. Many have developed long-term attachments to it that reflect strong commitments to maintaining its quality. Owner occupants are much more likely than renters to become long-term stayers:[14]

Time period household moved into present dwelling	Percentage of households		
	Owner occupants	Renter occupants	All occupants
Within the past 12 months	9.7	38.0	19.7
1 to 1.9 years ago	6.6	15.9	9.9
2 to 6.7 years ago	26.6	26.4	26.5
6.8 to 11.9 years ago	17.4	10.1	14.8
12 to 16.9 years ago	12.0	4.4	9.3
17 to 26.9 years ago	15.7	2.9	11.2
27 or more years ago	12.0	2.2	8.6

The fraction of owner occupants who had lived twelve or more years in their current dwelling was 39.7 percent, that of renters, 9.5 percent.

Thus, *in every neighborhood, the occupants of some housing units remain rooted there for long periods, while the occupants of other units change much more rapidly than average turnover statistics indicate*. A neighborhood containing only owner-occupied units would reach 100 percent turnover in 10.3 years, on the average. But at the end of that period, about 46 percent of its original residents would not have moved. So its 100 percent turnover would occur in 54 percent of its housing units. That implies an annual turnover rate of 17.9 percent for those high turnover units, and a zero rate for the units occupied by stayers.

14. *Annual Housing Survey, 1976*, pt. A, p. 6.

In a neighborhood containing only rental units, 100 percent turnover would occur in 2.6 years, on the average. But at the end of that time, about 42 percent of the original residents would not have moved. Hence all of its turnover would occur in 58 percent of its housing units. This implies a huge annual turnover rate of 66 percent in those high turnover units.

In the average U.S. neighborhood, one-half of all present residents will have departed within about 5.6 years. In order to provide enough occupants to fill the high-turnover half of its dwellings at the end of 5.6 years, the neighborhood must attract incoming households equal to 112 percent of its entire initial household population. During this period, over half those newcomers will have come and gone again. Such half-life replacement periods are longer for neighborhoods with more than two-thirds owner occupants, shorter for those with more than one-third renters. Thus, *the future character of every neighborhood is determined almost as much by the people who will move into it during the next few years as by those who live there now.*

Consequently, the opinion that the absentee market—the *potential* residents—have of any neighborhood is critical to its future. If no households elsewhere similar to those now living there will move in, the neighborhood is bound to change character. So the present residents of a neighborhood never fully control its future destiny. They can affect the larger community's expectations of the area's future by how well they maintain it and how highly they praise living there. But if most people in the larger community downgrade their expectations about the area, the existing residents may be unable to counteract those negative expectations through stronger community organization. No matter how well they convince *themselves* the area has a great future, they must also convince all those potential entrants who are not there. Yet no one knows who or where they are.

How does a well-maintained neighborhood attract all the newcomers it needs to remain stable? Every residential neighborhood is part of the overall real estate market in its larger community. Normal turnover there means large numbers of households are seeking places to live at any given moment. Some will consider residing in a particular neighborhood as long as it is widely perceived as desirable and they can afford it. The key characteristics of each neighborhood listed earlier exert the greatest influence upon its relative attractiveness for any specific household.

However, the following other factors also affect its ability to attract inflows:

The willingness of the local real estate profession to direct into the neighborhood households that are similar to those living there now. If most brokers systematically steer such households somewhere else, the neighborhood may have difficulty maintaining its present character.

The availability of real estate financing in the area

The strength of particular ties to the neighborhood arising from those factors which provide its basic identity. For example, people of Italian stock growing up in a largely Italian neighborhood may want to remain in the neighborhood when they establish separate households.

The strength of housing demand in the city or metropolitan area as a whole. People looking for housing do not usually consider entire cities as relevant market units; instead they examine particular neighborhoods. However, citywide factors sometimes influence their decisions. For example, property taxes are notoriously high in Boston, and all taxes are high in many New York suburbs. Also, population loss in a whole city or metropolitan area cuts housing demand in individual neighborhoods. On the other hand, massive in-migration may raise housing demand in nearly all neighborhoods.

4

Urban Growth
and Neighborhood Change

DURING and after World War II, millions of relatively poor households and many nonpoor ones migrated from rural areas into large cities, and fertility rates throughout the population soared. The neighborhood changes common in large U.S. cities are rooted in the urban development process that emerged to cope with this explosive growth in metropolitan-area population.

This process had to furnish moderate- and middle-income households with larger and higher-quality housing as their families grew and their real incomes rose. It had to expand tremendously the total number of housing units available, while improving the quality of the housing inventory. Since it had to operate largely through markets where choices by individual households were voluntary, it had to cater to certain strong desires held by those households—to own free-standing single-family homes, to own automobiles, to live in neighborhoods that were relatively homogeneous socially and economically, and (among whites) to live in predominantly, and often exclusively, white neighborhoods. Not all these desires are commendable, but they were all strong enough to influence metropolitan-area growth patterns.

The Trickle Down Process and Urban Growth

An urban development based on the trickle down, or filter up, process evolved to meet these requirements. No one person or group consciously designed that process or even articulated the above requirements. Rather, it emerged from separate decisions made and actions taken by millions

37

of households, developers, local governments, federal agencies, home builders, lenders, and politicians. It succeeded in providing excellent housing and high-quality residential environments for a majority of households in metropolitan areas, in spite of huge growth. But it also generated dire problems for millions of the poorest urban households. And it has sustained socioeconomic and racial segregation in nearly all U.S. housing markets.

In the trickle down process, as in all types of urban development, most construction occurs on vacant land at the edges of built-up areas.[1] Therefore, rapid urban population growth is accommodated (except in wartime) by large-scale construction of housing on the peripheries of cities. In most of the world, some of this housing consists of high-quality units occupied by the affluent; more consists of good-quality units occupied by middle- and moderate-income households; and still more consists of low-quality units occupied by the poorest households. The last type often amounts to shacks built by the poor themselves on expropriated land; such barrios may be very extensive when the low-income population is growing rapidly. But in nearly all U.S. metropolitan areas, construction of low-quality housing is prevented by zoning laws and building codes that require high-quality units. Therefore, *new* housing is too expensive for most moderate-income and all low-income households to occupy without direct subsidies. Such households are in effect legally excluded from new-growth areas, which are occupied mainly by middle- and upper-income households. So low-income households are virtually compelled to concentrate in older housing close to the historic center of each metropolitan area.

When these older units were built, their neighborhoods were on the urban periphery and they were occupied mostly by middle- or upper-income households. But as the metropolitan area grew out beyond them, these units trickled down to households relatively lower in the income distribution. During most of their history, these housing units provided good-quality shelter for their occupants, but eventually they were occupied by households too poor to maintain them.

The neighborhoods comprising these housing units also went through stages of relative and then absolute decline (as discussed further in

1. Parts of this discussion of the trickle down process are taken from several earlier works. See especially Anthony Downs, *Opening Up the Suburbs: An Urban Strategy for America* (Yale University Press, 1973), chap. 1.

chapter 5). From the viewpoint of each declining neighborhood, such change was undesirable. But from an areawide perspective, these declines were necessary parts of the trickle down process of accommodating the expanding poor population. Any method of accommodating rapid total population growth requires large-scale construction of housing at the urban periphery. But in the trickle down process, newcomers of all incomes cannot move directly into that new housing, since these units are deliberately made too costly for the poor to occupy directly. Poor households must enter the center of the area and gradually spread outward, successively displacing higher-income households. Thus the trickle down process requires, in effect, a constant outward movement of all income groups whenever the poor population increases significantly. It also results in spatial concentration of the lowest-income groups in older neighborhoods near the center of each metropolitan area.

In some southern metropolitan areas, poor households are less concentrated near the center than implied by this analysis. Greater scatteration of the poor occurs there partly because descendants of slaves were located in small clusters on the urban periphery, as well as in inner-city neighborhoods. Also, legal racial segregation of schools before 1954 allowed more affluent white households to send their children to schools not attended by their low-income black neighbors.

A different explanation of why poor households concentrate near the center of each metropolitan area has been suggested by urban economists Edwin S. Mills, Richard F. Muth, and William Alonso.[2] Centrally located land is more accessible to large clusters of jobs than land farther out; so the average time and money costs of commuting between downtown and farther out are higher. To make up for this disadvantage, land prices per acre tend to fall with distance from downtown, other things equal. This relationship has been well established empirically by studies of many large urban areas around the world. Where land is more expensive, it is used more intensively. Hence residential and other densities are normally higher on the costlier land close to each area's center than farther out.

Because housing consumption tends to rise with income, middle- and

2. Mills, *Urban Economics* (Scott, Foresman, 1972), pp. 71–72, 85–88; Muth, *Cities and Housing: The Spatial Patterns of Urban Residential Land Use* (University of Chicago Press, 1969), pp. 29–34, 311–13; and William Alonso, *Location and Land Use* (Harvard University Press, 1964). This discussion draws heavily upon contributions from Kenneth A. Small, to whom I am greatly indebted.

upper-income households seek bigger houses on larger lots than poor households do. Therefore, these economists argue that more affluent households live relatively far out where land costs per acre are lower. That leaves poor households concentrated in higher-density housing closer in, where they occupy much less land per household and hence spend less on land in spite of its higher cost per acre.

But there is a countervailing argument to this reasoning even within the downtown-centered city model itself. Empirical studies suggest that a major element of commuting cost is the self-perceived value of the time required. This value appears to rise with income, thereby creating an incentive for high-income workers to choose central residential locations. Thus, the theoretical location of various income groups in long-run equilibrium depends upon how fast the demand for housing rises with income, compared to how fast transportation costs (including time value) rise with income. (The issue formally rests upon a comparison between the income elasticities of housing demand and transportation cost.) Muth and Mills argue that the former increases faster than the latter; therefore the transportation-cost theory of land use successfully explains the observed tendency of higher-income households to locate farther out.

But more recent evidence on housing demand casts doubt upon their argument.[3] Data from the experimental housing allowance program—the largest empirical study of housing markets ever undertaken—indicate that most households do not increase their spending on housing anywhere near proportionally to increases in their incomes.[4] Furthermore, recent writings have stressed the positive role of other downtown amenities in the trade-off between space and accessibility. Households may *increase* the proportion of their incomes they spend on some amenities as their incomes rise.[5] If the frequency of downtown trips therefore rises with income, households will shift more toward downtown locations as their incomes rise. Still other evidence indicates that the relation between location choice and income is different among small and large households. In the New York area, 1970 census figures show a tendency for high-

3. See A. Mitchell Polinsky, "The Demand for Housing: A Study in Specification and Grouping," *Econometrica*, vol. 15 (March 1977), pp. 447–61.

4. See Eric A. Hanushek and John M. Quigley, "Consumption Aspects," in Katharine L. Bradbury and Anthony Downs, eds., *Do Housing Allowances Work?* (Brookings Institution, 1981).

5. For evidence supporting this conclusion see Douglas Diamond, "Income and Residential Location: Muth Revisited," *Urban Studies*, vol. 17 (February 1980), pp. 1–12.

income families to live farther from downtown Manhattan than low-income families, but the reverse was true for unrelated individuals.[6] Moreover, this theory assumes all households ignore neighborhood effects—that is, the nature of surrounding households and environments—in choosing where to live. But recent studies of household behavior indicate such effects are important influences upon residential choices.[7]

Thus, it does not appear that even simplified transportation-cost theories of land use can explain the spatial pattern of income-group residences observed in U.S. metropolitan areas. Nor is it likely that the trade-off between housing prices and transportation costs to the city center is the primary factor accounting for the concentration of poor households in inner-city locations. This conclusion is strengthened by the fact that in many urban areas around the world where zoning and other land-use controls are not strongly enforced poor people live at all distances from the urban center, not mainly clustered near it. Hence the central concentration of poverty in U.S. urban areas results to a significant extent from the deliberate exclusionary policies embodied in our urban development process, as discussed earlier.

The Effect of the Trickle Down Process on Neighborhoods

The outward movement of households from older, often deteriorated housing into newer, better quality housing is of two types: massive neighborhood transition and individual household upgrading.

Massive neighborhood transition is the displacement of one income group by a poorer one or the displacement of one ethnic group by

6. Clifford R. Kern, "Private Residential Renewal and the Supply of Neighborhoods," in David Segal, ed., *The Economics of Neighborhood* (Academic Press, 1979), pp. 121–46.

7. For example, see David L. Birch and others, *The Behavioral Foundations of Neighborhood Change* (Cambridge: Joint Center for Urban Studies of the Massachusetts Institute of Technology and Harvard University, 1977), p. 15. About 900 households living in three metropolitan areas were interviewed in 1976 concerning their residential location choices. When asked what had been most important in choosing their existing neighborhoods, they cited twelve factors, eight of which involved neighborhood characteristics rather than distance to downtown or characteristics of the housing unit selected. These eight neighborhood factors were cited as most important by 44 percent of the respondents, whereas other factors were cited by 56 percent.

another, the incoming group being almost always a minority group.[8] In ethnic displacement, noneconomic factors more powerfully influence behavior than purely economic ones; in fact, the incoming group often has incomes as high as or higher than the initial occupants. Ethnic transition is used here to illustrate the dynamics of massive neighborhood transition. But these dynamics are essentially the same whether the newcomers are poorer households, or minority-group members, or both. Thus, in most of the following analysis, *poor households* can be substituted for *minority-group households*, and *high- and middle-income households* can be substituted for *white households*, with little distortion.

When minority-group households first enter an all-white neighborhood on the edge of a large minority-group area, most other white households stop moving in because they do not want to live with minority-group households. As vacancies appear due to normal turnover, most households willing to fill them are minority-group households. Hence the population of the area rapidly shifts from mainly white to mainly minority group. Sometimes this transition is accelerated by panic flight by the initial occupants, who sell out en masse to speculators or minority-group households.

But even when no panic occurs, normal turnover without much white inflow ensures rapid ethnic transition. This is especially true in neighborhoods with high fractions of renters—hence high normal turnover rates. Thus, massive ethnic transition along the edges of a minority-group ghetto results from a combination of (1) the need of minority-group households to acquire more housing because their number is rising, (2) the resistance of all-white neighborhoods far from that ghetto to accepting *any* minority-group residents, as would be necessary if minority-group growth were to be scattered through many areas,[9] and (3) the unwillingness of most white households to move into neighborhoods on the edge of the ghetto once any minority-group households have moved there.

Individual household upgrading is a more continuous process. In every neighborhood some households will attain higher real incomes and social status than most others around them. These households can improve their homes and environment by *upgrading through movement* to other neighborhoods with higher average incomes and social status or by

8. The term ethnic is used throughout to include racial groups.

9. If the newcomers were poor whites, resistance would be through building codes and zoning, as noted earlier. This is one way ethnic transition differs from socioeconomic transition, as discussed further in chapter 7.

upgrading in place through renovating their housing and trying to improve their immediate surroundings. Upgrading through movement is by far the predominant mode. For one thing, it is much easier to attain instant improvement in one's environment by moving to an area that already has higher-quality housing units and amenities than by trying to transform the area where one is living. Second, the steady outward expansion of low-income households in recent decades created a presumption in the minds of many higher-income households in older areas that their neighborhoods would eventually be occupied by poorer households. Hence it is often considered safer to invest in housing farther from the center.

The Bureau of the Census' *Annual Housing Surveys* provide data useful in determining whether households really move upward through the hierarchy of neighborhoods. Table 4–1 indicates that majorities of central city owners, suburban owners, and suburban renters had moved to dwellings of higher value or higher rent. Moreover, the ratios of these groups to those moving to dwellings lower in value or rent were 4.8, 13.8, and 2.2 to 1, respectively. Only 44.1 percent of central city renters moved to higher-rent dwellings, but that is still 1.4 times the number that moved to lower-rent dwellings.[10]

Table 4-1. *Value or Rent of Previous and Current Housing Units*[a]

Household by present location and tenure	Number of households (thousands)	Percentage moving to unit with lower value or rent	Percentage moving to unit with same value or rent	Percentage moving to unit with higher value or rent
Central city owners	170	14.7	15.3	70.0
Suburban owners	445	5.6	17.3	77.1
Central city renters	1,915	30.7	25.2	44.1
Suburban renters	1,430	23.8	23.4	52.8

Source: Bureau of the Census, *Current Housing Reports*, series H-150-76, *Annual Housing Survey, 1976: United States and Regions*, pt. D, "Housing Characteristics of Recent Movers" (Government Printing Office, 1978), pp. 11–13.

a. The data cover the 3.96 million metropolitan-area households that had moved within twelve months of the Census Bureau interview and that had the same heads and occupied housing units with the same type of tenure (renting or owning) before and after moving; households in the highest and lowest value brackets are excluded. These households are 53 percent of metropolitan-area households with the same heads before and after moving, and only 27 percent of *all* households that had moved.

10. The force of these data is limited because (1) inflation was raising most values and rents during this period, (2) households in the lowest and highest home-value and rental brackets could not be counted, and (3) shifts *within* each home-value and rental bracket could not be broken down into upward and downward moves.

Two other sets of data shed light on where households *leaving* central cities, suburbs, and nonmetropolitan areas moved to and where those *arriving* in each of those areas came from. Figures 4-1 and 4-2 indirectly confirm the patterns of moves posited by the trickle down explanation of urban development. They indicate that (1) most moves occur *within* central cities and *within* suburbs as households climb the hierarchy of neighborhoods one step at a time, and (2) more households move from central cities to suburbs than vice versa, since suburbs have newer and higher-income neighborhoods. Over twice as many households moved from central cities to suburbs as moved from suburbs to central cities. However, the absolute numbers moving *within* each type of area were much larger.

Comparing the number of households that moved *from* locations in each type of area (figure 4-1) to the number who *arrived* in each type of area (figure 4-2), the net movement from central cities to suburbs and nonmetropolitan areas is clear:

Area	Households leaving (thousands)	Households arriving (thousands)	Net change (thousands)
Central city	4,309	3,562	− 747
Suburb	3,400	3,945	+ 545
Nonmetropolitan	3,040	3,242	+ 202
Total	10,749	10,749	...

Moreover, those moving out of central cities have higher average incomes than those moving in. From 1975 to 1978, the median income among males sixteen years old and over who moved from central cities to suburbs of the same cities was $12,411, while the median income of those who moved from the suburbs into the central cities of those suburbs was $10,240. The median income of similar persons who moved from central cities to suburbs of other central cities was also higher ($11,651) than that of those who moved in the other direction, from suburbs to other central cities ($8,907).[11]

Spatial Hierarchy of Neighborhoods

In nearly every large urban area throughout the world a spatial hierarchy has arisen containing residential neighborhoods of distinctly

11. Bureau of the Census, *Current Population Reports*, series P-20, no. 331, "Geographic Mobility: March 1975 to March 1978" (Government Printing Office, 1978), p. 73.

Figure 4-1. *Destination of Households Moving from Central Cities, Suburbs, and Nonmetropolitan Areas*[a]

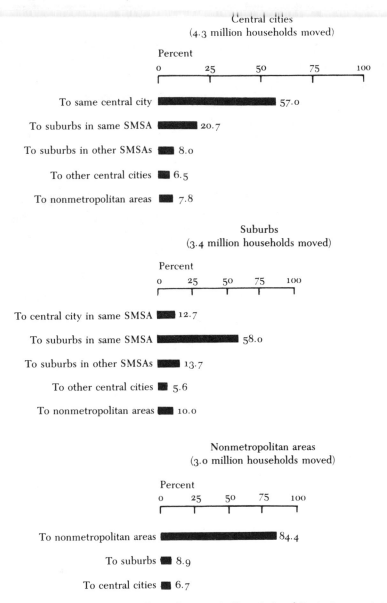

Central cities
(4.3 million households moved)

Percent

| 0 | 25 | 50 | 75 | 100 |

To same central city ▇▇▇▇▇▇ 57.0

To suburbs in same SMSA ▇▇▇ 20.7

To suburbs in other SMSAs ▇ 8.0

To other central cities ▇ 6.5

To nonmetropolitan areas ▇ 7.8

Suburbs
(3.4 million households moved)

Percent

| 0 | 25 | 50 | 75 | 100 |

To central city in same SMSA ▇ 12.7

To suburbs in same SMSA ▇▇▇▇▇ 58.0

To suburbs in other SMSAs ▇ 13.7

To other central cities ▇ 5.6

To nonmetropolitan areas ▇ 10.0

Nonmetropolitan areas
(3.0 million households moved)

Percent

| 0 | 25 | 50 | 75 | 100 |

To nonmetropolitan areas ▇▇▇▇▇▇ 84.4

To suburbs ▇ 8.9

To central cities ▇ 6.7

Source: Bureau of the Census, *Current Housing Reports*, series H-150-76, *Annual Housing Survey, 1976: United States and Regions*, pt. D, "Housing Characteristics of Recent Movers" (Government Printing Office, 1978), p. 5.

a. The data cover the 10.75 million households that had moved within twelve months of the Census Bureau interview and that had the same heads before and after moving, or 74 percent of all households that had moved.

Figure 4-2. *Origin of Households Moving to Central Cities, Suburbs, and Nonmetropolitan Areas*[a]

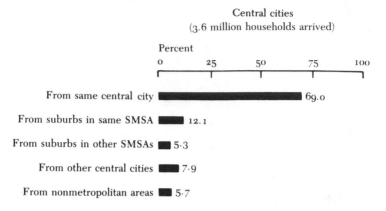

Central cities
(3.6 million households arrived)

Percent

From same central city	69.0
From suburbs in same SMSA	12.1
From suburbs in other SMSAs	5.3
From other central cities	7.9
From nonmetropolitan areas	5.7

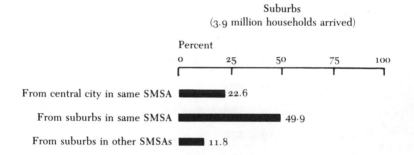

Suburbs
(3.9 million households arrived)

Percent

From central city in same SMSA	22.6
From suburbs in same SMSA	49.9
From suburbs in other SMSAs	11.8
From other central cities	8.8
From nonmetropolitan areas	6.9

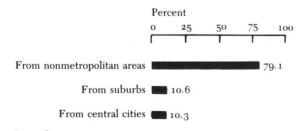

Nonmetropolitan areas
(3.2 million households arrived)

Percent

From nonmetropolitan areas	79.1
From suburbs	10.6
From central cities	10.3

Source: Same as figure 4-1.
a. See note a, figure 4-1.

different average levels of household income and social status. This hierarchy results from the preference of all types of households to live in neighborhoods where most other households have incomes and social status (and sometimes ethnic character) similar to their own. This preference probably springs in part from the desire of many parents to live in an environment that reinforces the values they want to pass on to their children, rather than one that introduces conflicting values.

Such hierarchies are usually not very systematically ordered. The neighborhoods in them may be only vaguely defined, with no precise boundaries, and gradations of income or social status of each neighborhood often overlap. Nevertheless, knowledgeable citizens of most metropolitan areas of the world can readily identify those neighborhoods widely perceived as having the highest income levels and social status and those widely perceived as having the lowest levels. Moreover, they can usually divide the remaining neighborhoods into two or more additional categories of average income and social status. Thus, at least rough spatial hierarchies exist almost everywhere.

In each U.S. metropolitan area, most of the lowest-ranking neighborhoods in this hierarchy are close to the older core of the area, most of the highest-ranking are close to the outer periphery, and most of the middle-ranked neighborhoods are between. This concentration of the poorest households in the center of the urban area results mainly from the prohibition of new, low-quality housing for the poor at the urban periphery, as explained earlier. In big metropolitan areas containing large black populations, there are often two spatial neighborhood hierarchies, one mainly white, and one mainly black.[12] Except in a few cities like Los Angeles, other ethnic submarkets are not usually large enough to form a third hierarchy.

Every metropolitan area necessarily contains one or more neighborhoods regarded as the lowest ranking in its neighborhood hierarchy. But that does not mean they are *absolutely* in bad condition. Some metropolitan areas are so new, so prosperous, so well maintained, or so fast growing, that even their worst neighborhoods are in good condition compared to slums elsewhere. This seems to be true of the "worst" neighborhoods in Seattle, for example. It would be socially destructive to convince the residents there, or the rest of the community, that these

12. The concept of racially separated hierarchies is analyzed in Chicago Urban League, Research and Planning Department, *The Black Housing Market in Chicago: A Reassessment of the Filtering Model* (Chicago Urban League, 1977).

areas are positively undesirable places in which to live. Yet because they are the *least* desirable, they are also the most susceptible to future decline if overall housing demand in the metropolitan area weakens in relation to overall supply for any long period.

Differential Code Enforcement by Neighborhood

Wherever many poor households live, high-quality housing standards for all are impossible to maintain unless society provides costly subsidies for the poor. Hence significant amounts of substandard housing—either deteriorated, overcrowded, poorly built, or lacking complete plumbing— are present in every large metropolitan area in the world except those few, like Stockholm, with extensive subsidized housing programs. Metropolitan areas in the United States nearly all contain significant amounts of such substandard housing, although many poor households live in "decent" units.

This situation poses a dilemma for local governments. They want regulations requiring quality high enough to prevent any substandard housing from "contaminating" neighborhoods occupied by middle- and upper-income households. But these same regulations make it impossible for many low-income and moderate-income households to afford housing without massive public subsidies; and U.S. taxpayers will not pay for those subsidies.

Resolving this dilemma requires maintaining high housing-quality standards in middle- and upper-income neighborhoods (which thereby exclude the poor), moderate standards in moderate-income neighborhoods, and quite low standards in very poor neighborhoods. This can be done by either (1) adopting different legally required standards in different parts of the community; (2) adopting a single high-quality standard but enforcing it in varying degrees in different neighborhoods; or (3) dividing the metropolitan area into separate legal jurisdictions which determine their own standards.

In the United States, the democratic ideal of equal treatment before the law makes it politically unacceptable for a single community to *openly* adopt different housing standards for the affluent and the poor. Furthermore, recent court decisions mandate local governments to provide equal-quality services everywhere within their jurisdictions. However, many small communities and all large cities do engage in differential housing code enforcement in order to reconcile one legal standard with the multiple levels of incomes and housing quality within their boundaries.

The necessity for differential housing standards generates strong pressure for creating separate governments, each controlling the housing standards and land uses within its boundaries. High- and middle-income households can be much more certain of effectively excluding the poor from their neighborhoods if they live in legally separate jurisdictions in which they form heavy majorities and in which they therefore can clearly dominate local government decisionmaking. Hence the spatial hierarchy of neighborhoods tends to culminate in the legal separation of high- and middle-income areas from the central city. Then socioeconomic segregation can be achieved through legal means, rather than just market forces.

Self-determination at such a small spatial scale has both good and bad effects. It encourages healthy personal participation of citizens in local government and great responsiveness of local officials to citizens' desires. But it also solidifies the socioeconomic segregation built into the hierarchy of urban neighborhoods, with its ultimate social injustice to the poorest citizens. This is one of the fundamental dilemmas of our democratic system.

Continuous Neighborhood Change

As long as the population of a metropolitan area is expanding rapidly because of in-migration or natural increase of poor households, a continuous process of neighborhood change must occur. It is like a giant game of musical chairs, in which the object is to give every member of a constantly increasing group a place to sit down by adding more and more chairs to a long line.[13] However, newcomers to the game must start at one end of the line, while new chairs can only be added at the other end. Hence the more newcomers appear, and the more new chairs are added, the more people must move from one end of the line toward the other. From the perspective of each specific chair, there is a constant succession of occupants as the game's total population increases.

13. The "musical chairs" analogy has been used earlier by M. Leanne Lachman and Maxine V. Mitchell in "New Construction and Abandonment: Musical Chairs in the Housing Stock," *Nation's Cities*, vol. 15 (September 1977), pp. 14–15, 40. It was also used by Rolf Goetze in *Building Neighborhood Confidence: A Humanistic Strategy for Urban Housing* (Ballinger, 1976).

Under these conditions, it is difficult to create neighborhood stability in most central parts of the metropolitan area. They experience constant changes in the identity of their residents. When the newcomers entering one year are different in character from those who entered in earlier years, the changes are even greater.

Rapid population growth within a metropolitan area does not always generate widespread neighborhood change. If in-migration is heavy but the newcomers are not poor, they can afford to move directly into newly built subdivisions at the urban periphery. Older, more central neighborhoods will experience normal turnover but not necessarily constant changes of income or status levels. Many metropolitan areas in the South and West have experienced such nontraumatic growth during the past two decades. However, whenever an area's poor population increases greatly, the process of neighborhood change described above inevitably occurs.

Some Motives for Socioeconomic Segregation

Continuous neighborhood change to accommodate growth of the low-income population could be greatly reduced if poor newcomers moved directly into new neighborhoods on the urban periphery, as they do in most of the rest of the world. Then each group of new arrivals could form its own new neighborhood, rather than having to take over existing neighborhoods from other people. However, new low-income neighborhoods would have to contain either quite low-quality housing or heavily subsidized high-quality housing, since that is all many poor households can afford. Moreover, these neighborhoods would be very near new neighborhoods being built for high- and middle-income households.

Up to now the wealthier households in the United States have not accepted the proximity of poor neighborhoods, though it is widely practiced elsewhere. One reason is the role of home ownership in these households' capital accumulation. Many households, especially during the 1970s, came to regard purchasing a home as an investment designed to produce large tax-free capital gains, rather than just as a means of procuring shelter. A household could usually borrow 80 percent or more of the cost of buying a home. Since the median-priced existing single-family home increased in market value by 9.8 percent a year compounded from 1969 through 1979, an average household's initial equity gained close to 50 percent a year in gross terms.[14] Even after deducting interest and other costs, the average annual net profit rate on the household's initial equity investment was enormous—much greater than the average annual increase in the consumer price index of 7.1 percent in the same decade.

Thus, purchasing a home largely with borrowed funds was both an excellent way for households to hedge against inflation and by far the most available means to accumulate capital. Moreover, capital gains from the sale of owner-occupied residences are not taxed if they are reinvested in similar residences within eighteen months. And a law adopted late in the 1970s allows persons fifty-five years old or older to shift $100,000 of such gains out of housing without paying any capital gains tax at all.

These circumstances cause most home owners to regard the market values of their residences, usually the single most important source of their wealth, as crucial to their economic welfare. They therefore consider any neighborhood changes that might reduce the market values of their homes—or just slow appreciation of those values—as economically threatening. Given the widespread desire among American high- and middle-income households to segregate themselves from poorer and minority-group households, these upper-income home owners believe that the entry into their neighborhoods of poorer households might jeopardize the market values of their homes. This belief often functions as a self-fulfilling prophecy, as explained earlier, thereby reinforcing its apparent validity in the minds of the majority. Hence most high- and middle-income households have strong economic motives for legally perpetuating neighborhood socioeconomic and racial segregation, regardless of their personal or social attitudes toward sharing their neighborhoods with poorer or minority-group households.

A second factor supporting exclusionary attitudes among high- and middle-income households is the nature of U.S. public schools. In many other nations, children from such households attend private schools, or most very poor children do not attend school at all, or there is no strong link between where a household lives and which public school its children attend. Therefore, households with very different income levels can live near each other without their children attending the same schools.

Until recently, except where racial segregation of schools was legally established, nearly all U.S. children, regardless of their socioeconomic or ethnic backgrounds, attended the nearest public school. Therefore,

14. National Association of Realtors, *Existing Home Sales* (April 1980), p. 10.

placing neighborhoods differing in average income or ethnic groups near each other at any given distance from the area's center would cause the children from all these groups to attend the same schools. True, if a neighborhood is large enough, it might have an elementary school patronized almost exclusively by its own neighborhood children, but high-school attendance areas are so large they almost invariably encompass many different neighborhoods.

Most high- and middle-income parents want their children to attend schools where other children from similar households predominate, partly because such schools usually provide the most effective academic training. Yet they also want to use public schools, which are far less costly to parents. The only way they can guarantee both these conditions is to live where there are very few low-income neighborhoods nearby. Thus, the nature of U.S. public schools transforms the desire of high- and middle-income households for *neighborhood* socioeconomic segregation—which is found nearly everywhere in the world—into a desire for *regional* socioeconomic segregation—which is much rarer. Recent court decisions mandating the busing of children to schools other than the ones nearest their homes reinforce this desire for regional separation by income group and race. Now the only way for a high- or middle-income household to ensure that its children will attend public schools dominated by children of similar background is to live out of practical or legal busing range of low- and moderate-income neighborhoods.

Differential Benefits to Households

The process of urban development described above has produced high-quality neighborhood and community environments for nearly all high-income households and most middle-income households in U.S. metropolitan areas. It has also provided reasonably good-quality environments for many moderate-income households and some low-income households. The exclusion of the lowest-income households from their neighborhoods benefits all these groups. It prevents them from encountering the physical deterioration and social maladies often associated with extreme poverty.

Moreover, the movement of people from older central cities to surrounding suburbs and newer cities has been essentially an upgrading process. Most of those who moved improved their housing units, their neighborhood environments, and the quality of their lives in general. In the 1977 housing survey, 86.1 percent of all suburban residents and 72.2 percent of all central city residents rated their neighborhoods as either excellent or good.[15] Thanks to massive production of new units, the quality of the nation's housing has risen remarkably since 1950. In 1977, 69 percent of all housing units in the suburbs and 45 percent of all those in central cities had been built after 1949. The suburbs doubled in absolute population between 1950 and 1977, lessening overcrowding in central cities and expanding the choice of housing units available to minority groups there.[16] Thus, contrary to widespread belief, urban development since 1950 has improved the quality of life for a majority of American metropolitan-area households. That is why there is such strong political support for the institutional and legal structures on which this urban development process is based.

But this same process is disastrous for the lowest-income households, many of whom it compels to concentrate in the oldest, most deteriorated neighborhoods. Conditions associated with poverty—unemployment, public dependency, crime, vandalism, delinquency, arson, housing abandonment, drug addiction, and broken homes—are magnified and come to dominate the entire environment. Most households with enough resources to choose other locations either refuse to move into such neighborhoods or soon leave them. Hence these neighborhoods become occupied mainly by households who cannot move elsewhere—the least capable, least self-confident, least resourceful, least hopeful households in the entire urban area. Such desolate conditions do not prevail in all relatively low-income neighborhoods, but they are likely to exist wherever there are very high concentrations of the poorest households.

Some observers believe that concentration of poverty alone cannot account for these conditions.[17] They cite large poverty concentrations in other nations relatively free from such maladies, such as those in Singapore, Japan, Korea, and Hong Kong. They also contend that past

15. Bureau of the Census, *Current Housing Reports*, series H-150-77, *Annual Housing Survey, 1977: United States and Regions*, pt. B, "Indicators of Housing and Neighborhood Quality" (GPO, 1979), pp. 17–18. Similar modest but significant differentials favoring the suburbs over the central city exist for all income levels and all types of households each year of the survey.

16. By 1977, 58 percent of metropolitan-area residents lived in the suburbs. Bureau of the Census, *Statistical Abstract of the United States, 1978* (GPO, 1978), p. 17.

17. Both Norman Krumholz and Edwin Mills have made this observation in response to early drafts of this book.

concentrations of the poor in U.S. cities during the late nineteenth and early twentieth centuries were less subject to such social problems. Based upon the evidence of somewhat different, but equally deleterious, conditions cited by contemporary observers, it does not appear that conditions were any better in earlier concentrated-poverty areas of U.S. cities.[18] Violent crime rates may have been lower, though no accurate data concerning them exist. But exploitation of child labor, sanitation, housing, nutrition, working conditions, and absolute standards of living were all probably worse than those in present U.S. urban poverty concentrations.

On the other hand, there can be little doubt that concentrations of poverty in some—though not all—other nations have not generated the same conditions as in large U.S. cities. Anyone who has visited urban slums in many parts of the world soon learns that behavior there is more influenced by locally prevailing culture than by the similarities of objective conditions among places—such as overcrowding, poverty, or high density. Moreover, certain negative conditions in U.S. urban poverty concentrations are statistically associated with particular ethnic groups. For example, controlling for income level, the incidence of single-parent households with children is more than twice as high among blacks as among whites, and crime rates are higher among nonwhites than among whites.[19] This suggests that the long history of slavery, racial discrimination, and unequal treatment of American blacks adversely influences

18. The Report to the National Commission on the Causes and Prevention of Violence indicates that levels of urban crime and violence were probably higher in earlier periods of American history than they are now. See Richard Maxwell Brown, "Historical Patterns of Violence in America," and Roger Lane, "Urbanization and Criminal Violence in the 19th Century: Massachusetts as a Test Case," in Hugh Davis Graham and Ted Robert Gurr, eds., *Violence in America: Historical and Comparative Perspectives*, Report submitted to the National Commission on the Causes and Prevention of Violence (Bantam Books, 1969).

19. Data on race and single-parent households are from unpublished data from the Bureau of Labor Statistics. Data on race and crime rates are from Marvin E. Wolfgang, Robert M. Figlio, and Thorsten Sellin, *Delinquency in a Birth Cohort*, Studies in Crime and Justice (University of Chicago Press, 1972), p. 54. In a careful analysis of a birth cohort in Philadelphia, Wolfgang, Figlio, and Sellin found that race is strongly related to delinquency status regardless of socioeconomic level. Overall, 29 percent of the white boys in their study, but 50 percent of the nonwhite boys, were delinquent at least once. Within the lower socioeconomic status group, the delinquency rate was 36 percent for white boys and 53 percent for nonwhite boys. For more on this subject see the President's Commission on Law Enforcement and Administration of Justice, *The Challenge of Crime in a Free Society* (GPO, 1967), pp. 44–45; Edwin M. Schur, *Our Criminal Society: The Social and Legal Sources of Crime in America* (Prentice-Hall, 1969), pp. 125–31; and James Q. Wilson, *Thinking About Crime* (Basic Books, 1975), pp. 13–20, 73.

behavior in urban poverty concentrations in which they predominate. Therefore, it may be the concentration of both poverty and race and the larger community's reactions to it that produce the "critical mass" of undesirable neighborhood characteristics found in many large U.S. cities.

That in turn implies that long-term remedies for these conditions are more complex than deconcentrating the poor—which is tremendously complex in itself. Rather, such remedies may have to include ending most remaining racial discrimination throughout society and somehow counteracting the adverse impacts that past racial discrimination has produced in low-income black communities. It is not easy to imagine ways to accomplish these goals, let alone carry them out. However, the difficulties of separating ethnic from economic influences in analyzing the effects of segregation that concentrates the poor and minority groups together are enormous. Therefore, the remainder of this analysis focuses upon the impacts of concentrated poverty.

Some data from Cuyahoga County, Ohio, illustrate how concentrated poverty can become. In 1970 the county comprised ninety-nine residential neighborhoods—thirty-nine in its central city, Cleveland, and sixty in the suburbs.[20] The total population of the county was 1.728 million, of whom 12.2 percent had low incomes (less than $5,000 per household in 1969) and 27.7 percent had high incomes ($25,000 or more per household in 1969). The median neighborhood incomes ranged from $4,454 to $37,500. The ninety-nine neighborhoods were ranked by median income and divided into groups of ten. The ten with the lowest median incomes contained 12.4 percent of the county's total population but 37.7 percent of its low-income population and only 3.5 percent of its high-income population. About 37.1 percent of the 215,000 people living in these ten neighborhoods had low incomes. The six poorest neighborhoods included 115,000 persons, of whom 43.5 percent had low incomes. These six neighborhoods housed 6.6 percent of the county's total population but 23.6 percent of its low-income population and only 1.2 percent of its high-income population.

Thus, poverty in Cuyahoga County was concentrated in a few neighborhoods, all in Cleveland. In fact, the twenty-six poorest neighborhoods in the county were all in Cleveland, as were thirty-four of the poorest thirty-eight. Only two of the forty-nine richest neighborhoods were in

20. The data are from special tabulations carried out by Edith N. Brashares, based on Bureau of the Census, *Census Population and Housing, 1970: Census Tracts*, Final Report PHC(1)-45, "Cleveland, Ohio, SMSA" (GPO, 1972).

Cleveland. The concentration of poverty in this county is greater than in many other large urban areas in America, but only in degree.

As a further test of the hypothesis that urban poverty concentrates in inner-city neighborhoods, similar analyses of 1970 census data were performed for two other areas for which neighborhood data are available for both the central cities and most of their suburbs. These are the Cincinnati and San Diego areas. They differ greatly concerning such characteristics as age, region, growth rates, climate, economic base, and settlement density. From 1970 to 1975, the city of Cincinnati lost 9 percent of its 1970 population and the city of Cleveland lost 15 percent, whereas the city of San Diego gained 11 percent. Yet households with incomes below the poverty level in 1969 were heavily concentrated in only a few neighborhoods in all three of these urban areas:[21]

	Households in the poorest 10 percent of neighborhoods		Households in the poorest 30 percent of neighborhoods	
Area	*Percentage of all households*	*Percentage of all poor households*	*Percentage of all households*	*Percentage of all poor households*
Cleveland	13	37	36	66
Cincinnati	11	33	26	56
San Diego	7	16	35	51

In Cleveland and Cincinnati, the poorest 10 percent of all neighborhoods contained about three times as high a percentage of the whole area's poor households as of its total households. San Diego's poorest neighborhoods housed more than twice the percentage of its poor than of its total population. Moreover, these neighborhoods are all near the centers of the three metropolitan areas, mainly within the central cities. The poorest 30 percent of these urban-area neighborhoods also contained much higher fractions of all poor households. The following table illustrates the concentration of poor households in poor neighborhoods in another way. It shows, for each neighborhood group, the portion of households therein that is poor:

21. Wealth was measured by median income. Data encompassed only suburbs relatively close to the central city. Nevertheless, coverage extended far enough outward so that median incomes of the farthest-out suburbs included were *lower* than those somewhat closer in, indicating the beginning of rural influences. Data for the Cincinnati and San Diego areas are from tabulations made by Beth Burnham, based on *Census of Population and Housing, 1970: Census Tracts*, Final Report PHC(1)-44, "Cincinnati, Ohio-Ky.-Ind., SMSA," and Final Report PHC(1)-188, "San Diego, Calif., SMSA" (GPO, 1972).

Percentage of households that is poor

Area	In poorest 10 percent of neighborhoods	In second poorest 10 percent of neighborhoods	In wealthiest 10 percent of neighborhoods	In all neighborhoods
Cleveland	31	15	4	11
Cincinnati	38	22	4	12
San Diego	24	15	6	11

The proportions of poor households were four to nine times higher in these areas' poorest neighborhoods than in their wealthiest neighborhoods, and two to four times higher than in the urban area as a whole.

A second major group of people besides the poor has also been unfairly injured by the disruptive neighborhood change generated by the U.S. urban development process. It consists of people who preferred to remain in older city neighborhoods but were pressured to move out, partly because of policies biased against the preservation of such neighborhoods. One biased policy made mortgage credit more easily available in new-growth areas than in older neighborhoods. Another resulted in huge federal investments in highways that decentralized settlement, without comparable investments in city public transit. Federal tax laws favored new construction over renovation of commercial, industrial, and rental-housing properties. Massive, federally supported programs in the 1950s and 1960s that razed inner-city housing accelerated the outward spread of low-income groups from these neighborhoods. Yet these programs did not adequately compensate either those displaced or the residents of surrounding areas that became overcrowded.

Many, though not all, of these biases have by now been removed. But they adversely affected millions of persons from 1950 to 1970. Yet it is difficult to separate the negative effects of biased policies from the negative effects of two other factors. First, the low-income urban population was growing rapidly and had to be accommodated somewhere. (However, different policies could have allowed low-cost housing to be built in the suburbs.) Second, most white households—including those living both adjacent to and far removed from minority-group areas—were reluctant to share their neighborhoods and schools with black newcomers. Nevertheless, there is no doubt that the psychological, social, and economic losses millions of households suffered from moving out of neighborhoods they had enjoyed were caused in large part by the way the U.S. urban development process works.

Thus, the arrangements that most U.S. households have created to separate themselves from the very poor and from minority groups impose severe social and economic costs upon the poorest households and upon certain nonpoor households. These costs are closely intertwined with the nation's most serious urban problems, such as unemployment, crime, physical deterioration, and even much personal disorder and despair. But the majority, while rhetorically deploring these problems, resist changes in policy that would reduce them. This fundamental relationship between economic classes explains why it is so difficult to "solve" many of the nation's basic urban problems.

For those problems are not simply accidental results, which can somehow be remedied without altering the arrangements underlying them. Rather, fundamental policies that would alleviate the worst of these problems (even though not eliminating them) would change the entire structure of urban areas and reduce the benefits that structure now provides to the majority of households. In particular, these remedial policies would decrease the spatial concentration of the poorest households by providing them with the opportunities and the means of scattering themselves more widely among nonpoor households. Such policies are discussed further in chapter 10.

The Slowing of Urban Growth

From the viewpoint of most urban households, the U.S. urban development process successfully coped with rapid metropolitan-area population growth, even though it unfairly imposed large social costs upon certain groups. However, when this growth slowed drastically or stopped altogether, this same process produced socially undesirable results, especially when the growth slowdown occurred among the poor.

True, a fall in low-income in-migration usually improves the welfare of any metropolitan-area's poor population considered as a whole. There are fewer poor households competing for the existing stock of lower-cost housing and for available jobs than there would be with continued rapid in-migration. Yet certain very poor neighborhoods shift maladies from those of overcrowding to those of depopulation, which are often equally harmful to the remaining residents.

In the late 1960s and early 1970s, net in-migration of poor rural households into many big cities virtually halted, and fertility rates among the urban poor fell rapidly. Yet the real incomes of many high- and middle-income households were still rising; so home builders continued to create new housing at the urban periphery, perpetuating outward expansion. Upwardly mobile households kept on moving out of the poorest areas into better housing elsewhere, even though few new in-migrants replaced them. The whole process improved the quality of housing and neighborhood environments for those moving upward. But for those left stranded in deteriorated neighborhoods amid abandoned houses, conditions often became worse. Also, central city governments were caught in a fiscal squeeze, with disproportionately large shares of the very poor, who pay few taxes and are expensive to provide for. Moreover, much of the population remaining in neighborhoods being abandoned were households either unwilling or unable to upgrade themselves. Improving their welfare or their neighborhoods became more difficult than ever.

Two questions arise: why do builders continue creating new housing if there is an overall surplus within the metropolitan area, and why don't they locate the new housing on the inner-city land vacated by housing abandonment? They keep on building new units partly because some relatively affluent households with rising real incomes prefer more modern, more spacious homes. Hence there is a market for some new peripheral units, though satisfying it undermines the demand for older, more centrally located housing. Since the developers of new housing are different persons from the owners of older housing, the former are willing to profit by actions that economically injure the latter. When affluent households move to new units, other households upgrade their accommodations by moving into those vacated. Such filtering up of households eventually causes vacancies created by the surplus of housing to trickle down to the oldest, most deteriorated neighborhoods, where many housing units are abandoned or demolished.

Builders do not create many new units on these vacant inner-city sites partly because those sites are not large enough to contain all the new low-density housing involved. Far more important, most households affluent enough to afford newly built housing are not willing to live in neighborhoods still occupied or surrounded by many very poor house-holds. Thus, the basic desire for socioeconomic (and sometimes racial) segregation underlying our entire urban-area neighborhood structure has up to now restricted most new housing to the urban periphery, rather than generating a rebuilding of urban areas from their cores outward.

However, more such rebuilding can be expected in the future after these core areas have more completely emptied out, though it will occur at lower densities than past settlement there.

Slowed population growth in metropolitan areas has some positive results. Pressure no longer is put on inner-city neighborhoods to accommodate incoming poor households. Therefore, some of these neighborhoods not plagued by housing abandonment can probably be stabilized in the near future. With no newcomers poised to "invade" such neighborhoods, local leaders have a better chance to persuade existing and potential residents that these areas can be preserved from further deterioration in physical condition and social status. This tactic is being effectively employed in the South Shore area of Chicago by a locally owned bank focusing upon neighborhood development. The success of such neighborhood organizations in stabilizing neighborhoods has contributed to the recent nationwide rise in political significance of the "neighborhood movement." Moreover, as the absolute number of households in the poorest neighborhoods declines, society can concentrate more resources per household upon improving living standards and future prospects there.

5

Stages of Neighborhood Change

THE FORCES of urban development and growth described in the previous chapter generate three types of neighborhood change; public policy responses to those forces create a fourth. These types are neighborhood decline, neighborhood revitalization, intensified land use, and neighborhood redevelopment. Aspects of the first three are analyzed in this chapter.[1]

Neighborhood decline involves increasing physical deterioration, reduced social status, greater incidence of social pathologies such as crime, and a loss of confidence among investors and property owners in the area's future economic viability. The two kinds found in the United States are *emptying-out decline* and *overcrowding decline*. Though they embody opposite changes in population, they both exhibit all the above symptoms. This book concentrates mainly upon emptying-out decline because it is both more widespread and harder to remedy.

Neighborhood revitalization involves improved physical condition, rising property values, declining incidence of social pathologies such as crime, and increased confidence by investors and property owners in the area's future economic viability.

Intensified land use involves rising density, changes in types of uses, and extensive redevelopment.

1. Neighborhood redevelopment is discussed in chapter 8. Briefly, it is the construction of an almost wholly new environment in neighborhoods from which the former population has completely departed and almost all original structures have been demolished. Government-aided programs such as urban renewal, public housing, and highway construction have been the main force behind redevelopment.

Agents of Neighborhood Change

As shown in chapter 3, a neighborhood changes because some of its characteristics change—its population, its physical state, its economic traits, its public services, or the community's expectations about it. What happens to each of these characteristics is affected by, and in turn affects, what happens to all of the others. Thus, changes in the physical condition of structures affect property values; changes in socioeconomic status affect the reputation of the area as a desirable place to live. These characteristics shift because of decisions made by a variety of people:

1. Households living in the neighborhood.
2. Households interested in moving to the neighborhood.
3. Absentee owners of property in the neighborhood.
4. Neighborhood organizations.
5. Real estate brokers and sales persons.[2]
6. Real estate appraisers and property managers.
7. Financial intermediaries operating in the area, such as officials of savings and loan associations, banks, insurance companies, and mortgage companies.
8. Financial intermediaries not operating in the area but affecting it through their actions, such as officials in secondary mortgage market agencies like the Federal National Mortgage Association and the Federal Home Loan Mortgage Corporation.
9. Local government officials, especially those responsible for providing services to the neighborhood, preparing urban plans covering it, and developing federal financing proposals for actions to be undertaken there.
10. Federal officials supervising programs that affect the area, such as those in the Department of Housing and Urban Development and its many parts important to neighborhoods (for example, the Federal Housing Administration).
11. Operators of local businesses and of national businesses located in or near the neighborhood, who decide how much to invest and how many people to employ.

2. Brokers often specialize. Sometimes a shift from brokers who handle mainly conventionally financed sales to those who handle mainly FHA- or VA-financed sales signals the beginning of racial change in a neighborhood. See Hammer, Siler, George Associates, *The Role of the Real Estate Sector in Neighborhood Change*, prepared for the Department of Housing and Urban Development, Office of Policy Development and Research, HUD-PDR-380 (Government Printing Office, 1979), p. 21.

The decisions of each of these actors create conditions affecting the decisions of the others, often reinforcing tendencies toward neighborhood change once they have begun. Their expectations about an area's future can also create self-reinforcing behavior patterns, as explained in chapter 2.[3] Furthermore, each neighborhood is affected to some extent by what is happening in other areas around it. Therefore, the actors who influence conditions in those other areas may also be important to it.

Stages of Change in Decline and Revitalization

Within any large city it is possible to identify different stages of neighborhood condition or life cycle.[4] One useful scheme classifies residential areas along a continuum of five stages:

Stage 1: stable and viable. These are healthy neighborhoods that are either relatively new and thriving or relatively old and stable. No symptoms of decline have yet appeared, and property values are rising. Some neighborhoods remain in this stage for decades if they have desirable locations near major amenities or if they continue to attract residents who maintain them.

Stage 2: minor decline. These are generally older areas where some functional obsolescence exists. Many younger families with relatively few resources live there. Minor physical deficiencies in housing units are visible and density is higher than when the neighborhood was first developed. Property values are stable or increasing slightly. Often many mortgages are federally insured because some buyers do not have

3. For detailed discussions of these decision processes, see ibid., and James Mitchell, *The Dynamics of Neighborhood Change*, prepared for the Department of Housing and Urban Development, Office of Policy Development and Research, HUD-PDR-108 (HUD, 1975).

4. Much of this section is from M. Leanne Lachman and Anthony Downs, "The Role of Neighborhoods in the Mature Metropolis," in Charles L. Leven, ed., *The Mature Metropolis* (Lexington Books, 1978), pp. 207–24; Mitchell, *The Dynamics of Neighborhood Change*; James W. Hughes, "The Dynamics of Neighborhood Decline," in Hughes, ed., *Suburbanization Dynamics and the Future of the City* (Rutgers University, Center for Urban Policy Research, 1974), pp. 69–77; and George Sternlieb and James W. Hughes, "Analysis of Neighborhood Decline in Urban Areas," prepared for the Department of Housing and Urban Development, PB-230-189 (Rutgers University, Center for Urban Policy Research, 1973), available from National Technical Information Service, Springfield, Va. The definitions are adapted from Donald S. Cannon, M. Leanne Lachman, and Arlyne S. Bernhard, "Identifying Neighborhoods for Preservation and Renewal," *Growth and Change*, vol. 8 (January 1977), p. 36.

substantial equity. The level of public services and the social status of the neighborhood are below those typical of stage 1 areas.

Stage 3: clear decline. Renters are nearly or fully dominant in the housing market. Tenant-landlord relations are poor because of high absentee ownership. Social status is lower than in either stage 1 or stage 2 areas because lower socioeconomic groups predominate in the residential population. Minor physical deficiencies are visible everywhere. Many structures have been converted to higher-density uses than those for which they were designed. Overall confidence in the area's future is weak. There may be some abandoned housing.

Stage 4: heavily deteriorated. Housing is very deteriorated and even dilapidated, and most structures require major repairs. Properties are marketable only to the lowest socioeconomic groups through contract sales. Profitability of rental units is poor, and cash flows are low or even negative. Subsistence-level households are numerous and may even dominate. Pessimism about the area's future is widespread; so is abandonment.

Stage 5: unhealthy and nonviable. Neighborhoods of this type are at a terminal point, marked by massive abandonment. Expectations about the area's future are nil. Residents are those with the lowest social status and the lowest incomes in the region. The neighborhood is considered an area to move out of, not into.

It is important to stress that *neighborhoods can change in either direction along the continuum*. See figure 5-1. For example, a neighborhood in the process of revitalization can move from a stage of clear decline (stage 3) to a stage of only minor decline (stage 2). Thus, the South End in Boston and Capitol Hill in Washington, D.C., moved from stage 3 to stage 1 through spontaneous rehabilitation. Federally assisted code enforcement programs resulted in many neighborhoods moving up from stage 2 to stage 1, or from stage 3 to stage 2. The Hough area in Cleveland improved from stage 5 to stage 4 through extensive demolition. Urban renewal programs caused many neighborhoods to shift from stage 5 to stage 1 through complete redevelopment.

This classification has proved to be a widely descriptive device in measuring neighborhood change. The Real Estate Research Corporation field-tested it in sixty cities where preservation programs were under way.[5] Their results reveal the following conclusions:

5. Real Estate Research Corporation, *Analysis of Data on Neighborhood Preservation Areas*, prepared for the Department of Housing and Urban Development, Office of Policy Development and Research (HUD, 1976).

Figure 5-1. *The Neighborhood Change Continuum*

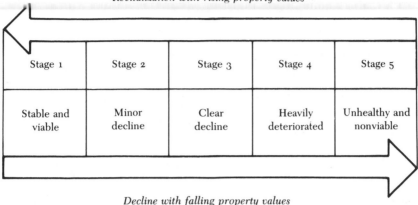

Revitalization with rising property values

Stage 1	Stage 2	Stage 3	Stage 4	Stage 5
Stable and viable	Minor decline	Clear decline	Heavily deteriorated	Unhealthy and nonviable

Decline with falling property values

Source: James Mitchell, *The Dynamics of Neighborhood Change*, prepared for the Department of Housing and Urban Development, Office of Policy Development and Research, HUD-PDR-108 (HUD, 1975), p. 9.

Most cities do not contain any stage 4 or stage 5 neighborhoods. This may seem surprising, since such neighborhoods are notorious in many older cities like Newark, New York City, Cleveland, Baltimore, and Detroit. Yet most of the sixty cities surveyed did not contain extremely deteriorated areas. In Milwaukee, for example, well over half of all residential neighborhoods were in stage 1, and the most deteriorated neighborhoods were between stages 3 and 4. No neighborhoods in Anaheim, California, were below stage 2, and stage 3 was the lowest category found in Rochester, New York.

Neighborhoods at any stage can be stable, or improving, or declining. Thus, three neighborhoods at stage 3 can be similar in condition but different in direction of movement—one declining toward stage 4, another improving toward stage 2, and a third remaining stable in stage 3. Therefore, a complete description of any neighborhood's condition should include both its position on the continuum and its direction of change or the absence of change if it is stable.

Specific factors increase a neighborhood's susceptibility to decline or revitalization. These factors are listed in table 5-1. Any factors that reduce a neighborhood's relative desirability as a place to live or invest reduce the strength of market demand for property there and increase the probability that owners will neglect their properties, thus increasing the neighborhood's susceptibility to decline. The more such factors that are

Table 5-1. *Factors Underlying Decline and Revitalization*

Revitalization factors	Decline factors
High-income households	Low-income households
New buildings with good design or old buildings with good design or historic interest	Old buildings with poor design and no historic interest
Distant from very low-income neighborhoods	Close to very low-income neighborhoods or to those shifting to low-income occupancy
In a city gaining (or not losing) population	In a city rapidly losing population
High owner occupancy	Low owner occupancy
Small rental units with owners living on premises	Large rental apartments with absentee owners
Close to strong institutions or desirable amenities, such as a university, a lakefront, or downtown	Far from strong institutions and desirable amenities
Strong, active community organizations	No strong community organizations
Low vacancy rates in homes and rental apartments	High vacancy rates in homes and rental apartments
Low turnover and transiency among residents	High turnover and transiency among residents
Little vehicle traffic, especially trucks, on residential streets	Heavy vehicle traffic, especially trucks, on residential streets
Low crime and vandalism	High crime and vandalism

present simultaneously, the greater the likelihood that self-reinforcing decline will begin if some triggering event occurs. In fact, a sudden change in one or more of these susceptibility factors can itself act as a trigger starting either neighborhood revitalization or decline.

Reversing neighborhood decline through gradual improvement is much more difficult when an area is in the later stages than when it is in the earlier stages. Attracting enough new resources into an area to reverse decline is far easier when the area is still in relatively good condition, say stage 2, than when it is in a state of advanced decay, as in stage 4. A few stage 5 neighborhoods have been gradually improved to stage 4, and stage 4 neighborhoods to stage 3. But there are far more stage 3 neighborhoods that have been revitalized to stage 2, and stage 2 neighborhoods to stage 1. For an area in stage 4 or stage 5, only complete clearance followed by total redevelopment is likely to restore it to stage 1 or stage 2. Such death and resurrection usually require public assistance, such as urban renewal or a federal urban development action grant.

The effectiveness of specific policies is tremendously influenced by what stage a neighborhood is in when they are applied. Vigorous housing code enforcement, for example, can have precisely opposite effects in stage 2 and stage 4 neighborhoods. Property owners in a stage 2 area still have confidence that values will rise in the future; strict code enforcement encourages them to repair their properties, thereby improving the neighborhood. But property owners in a stage 4 area are normally convinced that values will fall in the future (unless the area has moved up from stage 5, which is unusual). So strict code enforcement will cause many of them to abandon their properties rather than make investments they believe they cannot recover. Consequently, *to improve any neighborhood, policies must be tailored to fit conditions prevailing there.*

Some multistage scheme can be devised for each city to accurately describe its neighborhood conditions. Because of the great diversity of conditions among cities, the definitions of neighborhood stages used here may be less appropriate than others. Local officials should therefore adapt this or some similar approach to their own communities. Without some such classification of neighborhoods by current condition and direction of change, it is impossible to design effective neighborhood preservation or improvement programs.[6]

Intensified Land Use

The most common cause of intensified land use is the growth or expansion of a commercial district. The district attracts large traffic flows that create markets for other activities. Nearby land occupied by single-family homes, for example, becomes desirable for higher-density uses, such as multifamily residences, office space, retail outlets, or commercial parking. All of these uses would greatly increase the value of the land. Developers purchase this land at values based upon its original use, obtain zoning changes permitting more intensive uses, develop it, and reap the profits from its higher values. This process differs from neighborhood revitalization because it does not restore earlier uses but replaces them with higher-density uses.

A second cause of intensified land use is the creation of medium-rise or high-rise residential structures in an area of mainly single-family residences, often near an amenity such as a waterfront. This has occurred

6. Another useful way to look at neighborhood change has been designed by Rolf Goetze, *Building Neighborhood Confidence: A Humanistic Strategy for Urban Housing* (Ballinger, 1976), chap. 3.

along Lake Shore Drive and Lincoln Park on Chicago's North Side, in parts of La Jolla, California, and along much of South Florida's coastline.

Almost always, such intensified land use changes the character of a neighborhood so drastically that the original use does not continue, especially if it was single-family homes. Vehicle traffic rises; parking space dwindles; on-street parking expands (unless prohibited—and often even then); the area's aesthetic appearance is transformed by large buildings, less open space, and commercial signs; and the number of persons entering and leaving the area each day increases enormously. Unless the street system is greatly expanded, the combined result is often a great rise in congestion, noise, and air pollution. A classic case of such transformation is Honolulu's Waikiki Beach. It was once an open area with a beautiful beach lined with parks and a few spacious, rambling hotels. Today the whole neighborhood for many blocks back from the beach is jammed with high-rise hotels and condominium apartments, and thousands of vehicles and pedestrians pass through its streets every day.

In all areas where pressure for intensified land use arises, a strong economic motive exists for property owners to sell to developers. But fear of such an outcome as Waikiki Beach may cause some property owners to oppose that pressure. Such resistance is especially likely in neighborhoods with long-established single-family homes occupied by elderly or high-income households. The former usually do not want to move or change their environment. The latter are less in need of the profits from selling and more able to pay for maintaining the initial environment and amenities, either directly or by giving up such profits.

However, local governments in fiscally squeezed cities tend to encourage intensified land use. It increases taxes and economic activity. Therefore pressures for intensified land use often start conflicts between the owners who want to preserve the area and the groups who want to change it: developers, owners who want to profit from higher land values, and local government officials.

Neighborhood Life Cycles

Most neighborhoods change over time in patterns roughly analogous to a life cycle in living beings. Each is born when vacant land is initially developed for urban use, often as a subdivision built within a short time by a single developer. Hence each neighborhood at first usually contains structures of about the same quality and age. As time passes, the neighborhood can remain perpetually young through continuous maintenance and modernization, or it can begin to "age" through the processes described earlier. If it begins aging, it may continue until it becomes deteriorated and abandoned. When almost wholly abandoned, it has in effect died, thus completing a whole life cycle.

However, this analogy can be misleading. Unlike biological species, neighborhoods have no pattern of development that all must experience in roughly the same way. At any stage in a neighborhood's decline, it may reverse direction and begin revitalizing. This may postpone its old age and death for long periods, even indefinitely. Moreover, many neighborhoods that have died through destruction or almost total abandonment become resurrected through redevelopment either shortly thereafter or much later. Thus, some parts of really old cities like Rome, Athens, Alexandria, Cairo, Peking, and Istanbul have died and been reborn dozens of times. Such total destruction and rebuilding were especially prevalent before the twentieth century, because fires often devastated large portions of big cities. As a result, even in European cities that have existed for centuries, little housing built before 1800 remains in use today.

This diversity of life cycles means that, within a single city, neighborhoods in a variety of stages can exist simultaneously. True, what happens in each neighborhood is strongly influenced by events elsewhere within its metropolitan area. Nevertheless, the revitalization of one or even many neighborhoods in a city does not necessarily mean the others will also be revitalized soon.

However, in cities remaining in active use over long periods, most neighborhoods that have been destroyed or that have become terribly deteriorated eventually are revitalized or redeveloped. True, many once-flourishing cities have been completely abandoned. But if the basic settlement remains, its neighborhoods seem to enjoy a long-term lease on life that includes resurrection from death. Hence in U.S. cities, even those neighborhoods most devastated by abandonment and decay will probably be completely revitalized or redeveloped sometime in the future, as long as the cities do not disappear altogether (highly unlikely unless there is a nuclear war). However, exactly when each neighborhood will be reborn is impossible to forecast.

Housing Construction and Neighborhood Change

Neighborhood change within large cities is closely related to the amount of new housing construction in surrounding suburbs. Hence each can affect the other under different circumstances, even though they are quite far apart spatially. When many poor households migrate into inner-city neighborhoods, the resulting crowding there can stimulate construction of new suburban units, although only relatively affluent households can afford those units. Poor newcomers pour into the inner city, surrounding neighborhoods become more crowded, and nonpoor residents move farther and farther out. The rising total demand for housing increases housing prices throughout the metropolitan area. If prices of existing units rise above the cost of building new ones, home builders start constructing housing on the suburban frontier. If no units were built, relatively affluent households might respond to this demand pressure by simply paying higher prices for existing housing. That is what occurred in large U.S. cities during and shortly after World War II, when many poor households crowded into inner-city neighborhoods, but very little new housing was built.

Conversely, large-scale new housing construction on the suburban periphery can cause changes in inner-city neighborhoods, even though few residents of the latter can afford the new units. When large, modern units are built on the suburban frontier in greater numbers than the net increase in households throughout the metropolitan area, those units attract households out of older neighborhoods, creating vacancies there. Gradually, these vacancies trickle down through the inventory, ultimately settling in the oldest, least desirable units in neighborhoods where the poorest households live. Hence new housing occupied entirely by affluent households eventually reduces crowding throughout the metropolitan area, assuming the number of households is not growing apace. If new housing greatly exceeds net household formation, housing demand may drop so sharply in the most deteriorated neighborhoods that they begin to be abandoned.

Rising real incomes can also generate neighborhood change, as households move to "better" neighborhoods. This drives up the prices of housing in these neighborhoods, which may lead to construction of housing at the suburban frontier—with all the results described above.

Falling transportation costs can also generate outward movement by making suburban housing more accessible and less costly to live in. As more affluent households respond by moving outward, the relative prices of closer-in housing decline. This encourages poor households to improve their housing too.

6

Neighborhood Revitalization

THE REVITALIZATION of older urban neighborhoods, including many that were highly deteriorated, increased markedly in the 1970s. Revitalization upgrades housing, changes population composition, and improves city property-tax bases. However, it may also displace low-income residents, often causing resentment among those affected and adverse political reactions among their elected representatives. This chapter describes neighborhood revitalization and analyzes its causes, benefits, and costs.

The Nature of Revitalization

Two types of revitalization are widely recognized: gentrification and incumbent upgrading. A neighborhood may be affected by either or both.

In gentrification, relatively affluent newcomers buy and renovate homes in run-down neighborhoods. The poorer initial residents are forced out. The newcomers are usually childless households—such as young professional couples. They make major investments of money and their own labor in upgrading their homes. Because of their relatively high incomes, they are able to finance the improvements privately, usually with conventional mortgages.

In incumbent upgrading, residents of a run-down neighborhood rehabilitate their housing themselves. Since they have relatively low incomes, they usually need assistance from publicly financed programs or subsidies.[1]

1. One effective form of assistance is the neighborhood housing services program. This

72

Spontaneous revitalization, which means that which occurs with little or no direct aid from governments, thus usually means gentrification. However, the revitalization of areas really devastated by abandonment usually requires the use of public funds to demolish deteriorated properties, assemble sites, and help private investors achieve complete redevelopment. Public authorities assume most of the risk.

Revitalization always raises the average cost of occupying housing in neighborhoods concerned. The improvement of housing units deteriorated below the legal housing code requires substantial investments of money and labor. Owners of these units—and financial institutions lending them the money—would not make such investments unless they thought they could get a reasonable return on them. Therefore, these properties must produce much greater revenues, including implicit returns to owner occupants, after revitalization than before.

Revitalization also raises property taxes of housing in the neighborhoods concerned. Assessed values increase along with market prices, assuming the local assessor responds quickly to changed market conditions. Increased property taxes may be accompanied by improvements in public services. However, from the residents' perspective, increased property taxes are real costs. Moreover, when enough properties have been rehabilitated to enhance the attractiveness of the entire neighborhood, the values of unchanged properties are raised, along with their property taxes.

These increases in real occupancy costs and property taxes are a barrier to low-income people, both initial residents and others wishing to live in revitalized areas. Without public subsidies, they often cannot reside in rehabilitated dwellings or even in nonrehabilitated dwellings in a revitalized neighborhood. If they are renters, the increased costs are passed on to them through higher rents. If they are owner occupants, their property taxes go up. Possible subsidies include limiting property taxes in relation to household income (circuit breakers), postponing increased property taxes until the initial occupants sell or move, and subsidizing rents for low-income renters. However, the link between revitalization and higher occupancy costs is inherent in the nature of revitalization. It affects the displacement problem and possible resolutions of it, as discussed later.

---

program is analyzed in detail in Roger S. Ahlbrandt, Jr., and Paul C. Brophy, *Neighborhood Revitalization: Theory and Practice* (Lexington Books, 1975).

Revitalization of both types has been cited by some observers as an early sign of a full-scale "city renaissance" in the future. The credibility of this view partly depends upon how widespread revitalization is. A 1975 Urban Land Institute survey found that private renovation was occurring in about half of all U.S. central cities, and in three-fourths of those with populations over 500,000. However, the number of units renovated from 1968 through 1975 was estimated at only 50,000.[2] In those same eight years, 13.4 million new housing units were privately built.[3] Thus private rehabilitation contributed far fewer units than private construction to the overall supply of standard-quality housing. Furthermore, in the 1970s expenditures on housing renovation and repair were much lower than those on new housing.[4] In 1970, renovation expenditures were 61 percent of construction expenditures. This ratio rose to 74 percent in 1975 when housing starts dropped during the recession. But in 1978 they were 49 percent of new housing construction costs. Hence renovation and repairs in 1978 were actually *smaller* in relation to new housing construction than in earlier years. Moreover, only a tiny part of renovation and repair spending occurs in revitalizing neighborhoods, which are themselves a small fraction of all urban neighborhoods.

A crucial question about revitalization is whether it should be conceived of in terms of an *area* or the *initial residents* of an area. One way to revitalize any area occupied by poor households is to replace them with more affluent households that can better afford high-quality housing. This occurs in gentrification. It can certainly upgrade an area's physical condition, social status, contributions to local taxes, and general reputation. However, it may be vehemently resisted by initial residents who do not want to leave for the benefit of wealthier newcomers. Whether the initial residents gain from gentrification depends upon whether they are renters or owners, whether compensation is paid to those displaced, and whether the ultimate rise in property values occurs before initial owners sell to the newcomers. The rest of this chapter focuses on revitalization itself. The fate of the initial residents is considered in the analysis of displacement problems in chapter 11.

2. J. Thomas Black, "Private-Market Housing Renovation in Central Cities: A ULI Survey," *Urban Land*, vol. 34 (November 1975), p. 6.

3. Bureau of the Census, *Statistical Abstract of the United States, 1979* (Government Printing Office, 1979), p. 779.

4. Ibid., pp. 773, 789.

Table 6-1. *City and Metropolitan Factors Underlying Revitalization*

Factor	Operation
Demand side	
Strong downtown business district with growing employment	Creates demand for housing close to downtown jobs
Rising real incomes	Increase households' ability to rehabilitate housing
Formation of many small, childless households	Increases households that need less space, are oriented to urban amenities, and do not need public schools
Rapid in-migration of nonpoor households	Increases demand for good-quality housing
No in-migration of poor households	Permits older neighborhoods to stabilize
Supply side	
Long commuting times to downtown business district	Make living near downtown more desirable
Strong restrictions on suburban development	Limit suburban housing and jobs, enhancing city housing and jobs
Rapid increases in prices of suburban housing	Make city housing more attractive
Loose housing market	Enables poor households displaced by revitalization to find adequate housing, possibly reducing resistance to revitalization
Rents not controlled	Encourages property maintenance and investment in new rental units
Easy condominium conversion	Increases owner occupancy

Causes of Revitalization

Factors on both the demand and supply sides of the housing market can cause the revitalization of a neighborhood. Moreover, these factors can be at the metropolitan and city levels (see table 6-1) and at the neighborhood level (see table 6-2).

Neighborhood revitalization is always associated with rising demand for the housing in that neighborhood—both as a cause for the renovation and as an effect of it. Local increases in demand sometimes are part of a citywide rise in demand, as in Seattle in the late 1970s, but they can

Table 6-2. *Neighborhood Factors Underlying Revitalization*

Factor	Operation
Demand side	
Proximity to amenity such as lakefront, oceanfront, park, or downtown	Enhances long-term value
Good public transportation	Enhances convenience, especially for households with more than one worker
Access to high-quality public or private schools	Enhances attractiveness to households with school-aged children
No nearby public housing with school-aged children who would dominate the public schools	Enhances attractiveness to households with school-aged children and incomes high enough to support renovation
Perceived in community as safe	Enhances attractiveness as place to live
Proximity to revitalized neighborhoods	Creates expectation that revitalization will work here as well
Supply side	
Single-family housing	Simpler to rehabilitate than multifamily housing; fewer management problems
Housing with interesting architectural features such as high ceilings, fireplaces, carved woodwork	Attractive to young households, which are most likely to rehabilitate
Brick housing	Easier to rehabilitate than frame housing, easier to care for, lasts longer
Multifamily housing suitable for condominium ownership	Owner-occupied property better maintained and residency more stable than rented property
Financial institution willing to provide mortgages and home-ownership loans	Makes ownership and rehabilitation easier
Commitment by local government to upgrade infrastructure and public services	Reassures private investors of long-term value of homes
Strong neighborhood organization dominated by home owners	Creates pressure on local government to enforce housing codes and improve public services
Housing and other structures in relatively good condition	Encourages private investment by owners and lenders

also occur in cities experiencing declining total housing demand, as in many large Northeastern and Midwestern cities in the 1970s. The factors underlying both types of rising demand stimulate revitalization.

One demand factor is the tendency for some households to move closer to downtown when their real incomes rise. Most households seek more floor space and more land as their real incomes increase; so many move farther from the center of urban settlement where land is less expensive.[5] (The desire for socioeconomic and racial segregation stimulates similar responses to rising incomes.) Yet about 10 percent believe the "best place to live" is a large city, because of its activities and amenities.[6] This fraction equals about eight million households as of 1980, or about one-third of all the households living in central cities. Small as it is, this group forms a large potential market for housing in revitalizing neighborhoods, larger than the residential capacity of such neighborhoods up to now.

Among the households with a strong desire for urban living are small households formed by young people living apart from their parents; married couples who both work outside the home, having postponed having children or decided never to have any; divorced persons with or without children; elderly couples; and single persons of all ages. Moreover, the real incomes of many of these households (those with two earners) are rising rapidly.

The number of these small, urbane households important to central city housing markets is on the rise.[7] About 77 percent of the 1970–77 increase in U.S. households was in one- and two-person households. In 1970 they were 47 percent of all households; by 1977 they had risen to 52 percent. More important, from 1970 to 1977, small households in central cities rose by 2.107 million, although *total* central city households rose by only 1.756 million. Thus, *in the cities, small households increased by 19 percent while all other households decreased by 4 percent*.

Other studies of households that moved into large cities also indicate the importance of small households to neighborhood revitalization. Over half (55 percent) of households that moved in late 1977 into certain St.

5. Most urban economists believe this tendency is overriding, as discussed in chapter 4. See Edwin S. Mills, *Urban Economics* (Scott, Foresman, 1972), chap. 4, and Richard F. Muth, *Cities and Housing: The Spatial Pattern of Urban Residential Land Use* (University of Chicago Press, 1969), pp. 7–14 and chap. 2.

6. Paul K. Mancini and Martin D. Abravanel, "Signs of Urban Vitality and of Distress: Citizen Views on the Quality of Urban Life," in Department of Housing and Urban Development, Office of Policy Development and Research, *Occasional Papers in Housing and Community Affairs*, vol. 4 (GPO, 1979), p. 23. The survey of over 7,000 households was made in 1977. Thirty percent of respondents thought living in the suburbs was best, 24 percent preferred rural areas, 20 percent preferred small cities, towns, or villages, and 10 percent liked a medium city. Among those actually living in large cities, only 26 percent thought them the "best place to live."

7. Data from Bureau of the Census, *Current Housing Reports*, series H-150-77, *Annual Housing Survey, 1977: United States and Regions*, pt. A, "General Housing Characteristics" (GPO, 1979), p. 3.

Louis neighborhoods with revitalization potential consisted of one or two persons.[8] A 1976 survey of the Atlanta metropolitan area revealed that households moving *into* the city from 1970 to 1976 were smaller (averaging 3.11 persons) than households that moved *out of* the city in the same period (3.30 persons).[9]

Another reason the demand for older central city housing rose among relatively affluent households is that it fell among very poor households. The reduced in-migration of low-income households to many Northeastern and Midwestern cities markedly slowed the transition of city neighborhoods to low-income occupancy. That increased the possibility of relative stability in such areas, thus helping persuade potential newcomers that investments there would retain their value.

The desirability of home ownership as a hedge against inflation, plus rising real incomes among many households, also stimulated the demand for older single-family homes in big cities in the 1970s. The average annual rate of increase in the consumer price index was 7.1 percent in that decade, or almost triple what it had been in the 1950s and 1960s. Yet the median price of existing single-family homes rose even faster, averaging an annual gain of 9.8 percent in the 1970s.[10] Consequently, the number of owner-occupant households within central cities increased by 1.046 million from 1970 to 1977—a gain of 10 percent, whereas renter-occupant households increased only 6 percent. This increase in owner-occupied dwellings was about 60 percent of the increase in all households in central cities, pushing the fraction of owner occupants from 48 percent in 1970 to 49 percent in 1977.[11] Most of these home buyers were renters purchasing their first homes and moving from other dwellings nearby. One researcher estimated that 70 percent of households who bought homes in central cities in 1975 and 1976 were relocating within the same city; two-thirds were renters who had never owned a home before.[12]

8. Joseph C. Hu, "Who's Moving In and Who's Moving Out—and Why," *Federal National Mortgage Association, Seller/Servicer*, vol. 5 (May-June 1978), p. 23; see also Hu, "The Demographics of Urban Upgrading," *Seller/Servicer*, vol. 5 (November-December 1978), pp. 30–37.

9. John D. Hutcheson, Jr., and Elizabeth T. Beer, "In-migration and Atlanta's Neighborhoods," *Atlanta Economic Review*, vol. 28 (March-April 1978), p. 8.

10. Housing price data are from the National Association of Realtors, *Existing Home Sales* (January 1980), p. 10.

11. *Annual Housing Survey*, 1977, pt. A, p. 3.

12. Franklin J. James, "The Revitalization of Older Urban Housing and Neighborhoods," in Arthur P. Solomon, ed., *The Prospective City: Economic, Population, Energy, and Environmental Developments Shaping Our Cities and Suburbs* (Massachusetts Institute of Technology Press, 1980), p. 148.

Their desire for home ownership undoubtedly stimulated revitalization in many central city neighborhoods.

Another related demand factor is the steady increase in the number of office jobs in big-city downtowns. These jobs created a need for city housing, especially in huge metropolises, where commuting from the suburbs at the periphery is extremely time-consuming. Examples are New York City, Chicago, Los Angeles, and San Francisco.

The demand for close-in housing is also affected by other factors. These include attitudes toward personal safety and perceptions of security in the city and suburbs; belief in the quality of city public schools compared to suburban public schools; desire for segregation from households poorer or of different ethnic origin; and the importance attached to entertainment and cultural activities most often found near downtowns. These factors differ among households, depending upon their life-cycle positions and other variables. Crime rates, for example, are of less concern to young adult households than to elderly households, and public schools of less concern to childless households than to households with school-aged children.

Supply factors also influence neighborhood revitalization. Some of these make the alternatives to older city housing less desirable or less available, like sharp increases in suburban housing prices and local government restrictions on new development. Other factors make older city housing more desirable or more available. Since prices of newly built homes rose even faster than those of existing ones, many households with only moderate resources seeking to buy homes had to focus upon older, less costly units in city neighborhoods.

Some observers believe recent revitalization resulted primarily from a relative fall in the price of inner-city land when older neighborhoods declined.[13] Land values temporarily dropped below their true equilibrium levels. Astute entrepreneurs bought such land at very low prices and rehabilitated the structures on it. Some of these entrepreneurs were households creating units for their own occupancy, but many sold or rented the units they had rehabilitated.

Land prices alone, however, do not explain why so many households with money were willing to live in areas formerly considered terribly undesirable. Rather, many demand and supply factors acting in concert during the late 1960s and the 1970s generated the surge in central city

13. Neil Smith, "Toward a Theory of Gentrification: A Back to the City Movement by Capital, Not People," *Journal of the American Planning Association*, vol. 45 (October 1979), pp. 538–48.

revitalization, especially the slowdown in housing construction in 1974 and 1975. Moreover, many of these factors reinforced each other by creating positive expectations about future property values. Just as negative expectations become self-fulfilling and contribute to neighborhood decline, so positive expectations reinforce each other and contribute to revitalization.

The probability that any particular neighborhood will revitalize is a function of all its demand and supply factors. To identify those neighborhoods most (or least) likely to revitalize and to measure the probability of revitalization in a particular neighborhood, its characteristics and those of its metropolitan area and city can be compared to the conditions listed in tables 6-1 and 6-2. A condition opposite of one shown in the table is likely to inhibit revitalization. For example, a neighborhood with a high proportion of multifamily rental housing is much less likely to revitalize than one with high proportion of single-family, owner-occupied dwellings. These tables suggest why revitalization has been increasing in the past few years. Many of the factors in table 6-1 have been growing. At the neighborhood level, several factors account for recent revitalization: stronger neighborhood organizations, more willingness of local financial institutions to provide mortgage credit and home improvement loans, and greater local government commitments to improve neighborhood infrastructures, often with money from a federal community development block grant. The other factors in table 6-2 vary substantially from one neighborhood to another.

Certain other societywide trends have also encouraged recent neighborhood revitalization. These include rising energy costs (further discussed in chapter 8), increased suburban traffic congestion near job clusters that made commuting downtown more onerous, and greater ownership and use of automotive vehicles that contributed to traffic congestion.

However, there is no evidence that more American households are beginning to prefer living in high-density cities. Most still favor the low-density suburban or small-town living they have traditionally desired.[14] Thus, recent increases in neighborhood revitalization appear to result from changes in the composition of U.S. households and in the conditions and opportunities facing them, rather than from any change in their fundamental desires.

14. See James, "Revitalization of Older Urban Housing and Neighborhoods," pp. 130–59.

Benefits and Costs of Revitalization

Like most significant social changes, neighborhood revitalization has both benefits and costs, usually affecting different people. Designing policies to respond to these benefits and costs requires understanding them and whom they affect.

Benefits

Beneficiaries and the gains they receive are as follows:

The local government gains taxes from higher assessments on properties, plus greater conformity to its housing codes. It also retains many middle-income households that otherwise would move to the suburbs, and attracts some middle-income suburban households into the large cities. For example, the average income ($15,517) of Atlanta households that moved into the city between 1970 and 1976 was higher than the average income ($14,017) of households that lived there since before 1970.[15] Most evidence shows that large cities are still losing high-income households through out-migration.[16] Yet they would be losing even more and would be gaining no higher-income newcomers if revitalizing areas were not attracting some of them. These households pay higher income taxes and are more likely to participate in neighborhood affairs than low-income households.

Initial owners of property gain from higher property values, regardless of whether or not they improve their own properties and whether or not they sell them. If they live in their properties, they benefit from the improved environment. If they rent, they benefit from higher rents. If they sell, how much they gain depends on how much the neighborhood has already improved.[17]

Early-arriving owner occupants have the advantages of initially low property prices and of living in an improved area convenient to downtown and other urban amenities. The earlier in the revitalization process a home purchaser buys, the greater the potential capital gain, but the

15. Hutcheson and Beer, "In-Migration and Atlanta's Neighborhoods," pp. 8, 9.

16. The average income of households moving out of Atlanta to the suburbs during 1970–76 was $21,121. See ibid., p. 8.

17. See Ann B. Schnare, *Household Mobility in Urban Homesteading Neighborhoods: Implications for Displacement*, prepared for the Department of Housing and Urban Development, Office of Policy Development and Research (GPO, 1979), p. 39.

larger the risk that no gain will materialize, and the more effort the purchaser usually must put into improving his or her dwelling. This risk is demonstrated by a study of fifteen areas in St. Louis with revitalization potential, which shows that major revitalization was occurring in only six as of mid-1978.[18]

Late-arriving owner occupants do not gain as much from rising property values as the preceding group, but they assume smaller risks and also benefit from living in an improved, convenient neighborhood.

Developers profit by buying run-down units and rehabilitating them for either rental or resale to incoming households who can afford higher occupancy costs. These entrepreneurs, often working on a small scale, are primarily seeking profits. However, they also perform a positive social service by improving properties, therefore helping upgrade the whole area.

Speculators profit by buying properties, holding them without improving them, and selling them at higher prices. Their motive is also profit, but by drawing attention to the area's prospects and helping to make community attitudes toward its future more positive, they, too, perform a social service. However, speculators harm society if they allow their properties to deteriorate further during their ownership.

All citizens of the city gain from having a higher tax base, lower crime rates in revitalized areas, and more potential citizen leadership. The extent of their fiscal gain depends upon whether residents of the revitalized area demand added services more costly to the local government than the additional taxes they pay. If so, the citizenry in general may actually lose fiscally from revitalization. However, it is usually assumed—without much evidence—that revitalization causes larger tax increments than local government cost increments.

Federal taxpayers benefit slightly from revitalization insofar as it aids local governments fiscally, thereby reducing their need for federal aid.

Costs

Parties injured by revitalization and the costs it imposes upon them are as follows:

Displaced residents of revitalizing areas compelled to move elsewhere must bear the normal inconveniences of moving. In addition some

18. Hu, "Demographics of Urban Upgrading," p. 32.

households, especially the elderly, must abandon long-established social networks.

However, the moving costs of those households who would have moved anyway are not attributable to revitalization. Most young renters, for example, might have moved anyway. Over the several years of the typical revitalization period, a very high fraction of all the initial renting residents—except for the elderly—would probably have moved out of the neighborhood anyway. Though it is difficult to determine their numbers, it is conceptually necessary to estimate them in order to measure the costs of revitalization. Both renters and owner occupants can be displaced. However, a study of the higher occupancy costs in neighborhoods where urban homesteading took place showed those costs were far more likely to displace renters than owners.[19]

Renters who cannot find housing of equal quality and convenience at the same price as their former housing suffer additional losses. In cities with tight housing markets these losses may be quite high, especially if the displaced households have been in the same units for many years.[20] The tenants most likely to have been in one unit for a long time are the elderly, who also have the greatest difficulty replacing their social networks. Thus, elderly renters are likely to suffer doubly from displacement.

Owner occupants compelled to move because of higher property taxes clearly suffer a loss, even though it may be partly offset by the higher market value of their homes. Households with relatively fixed incomes may be unable to cope with higher current property taxes without somehow "cashing in" on the increased equity in their homes. Unless they use reverse-equity mortgages or other such devices, they may have to sell their homes to pay the higher taxes on them—thus forcing a move. This real cost can be disguised as "no net loss" if the increased equity realized at sale exceeds the higher property taxes, but it is nonetheless genuine. Elderly households are the most likely to be in this situation.

Suburban land and property owners suffer slight losses in the values

19. See Schnare, *Household Mobility in Urban Homesteading Neighborhoods*, pp. 38–39.

20. Long-term tenants typically have lower rents than short-term tenants, partly because landlords trade lower rents for lower turnover and stability. In 1977 central city renters who had moved into their units within the past twelve months paid 6.7 percent higher rents than the average for all central city renters, although their incomes were only 2.5 percent higher. *Annual Housing Survey, 1977*, pt. D, "Housing Characteristics of Recent Movers," pp. 3–4.

of their properties insofar as revitalization shifts the demand for housing from suburban neighborhoods to older portions of large cities. These losses are not very noticeable, however, and there is no way to know in which suburban neighborhoods they occur.

Suburban local governments also suffer slight losses insofar as retention of more relatively affluent households within large cities "deprives" such governments of net fiscal surpluses from having those same households as residents. These losses are also likely to be very small and impossible to trace.

Big-city minority-group politicians whose political power is based upon ethnic segregation of neighborhoods could lose political power if revitalization scatters formerly concentrated blacks or other minority-group members, especially to areas outside the city limits. However, as of early 1980 revitalization has been on a small scale and most displaced households have probably remained in the cities concerned, so this cost has not yet been very large.

Displacement

The above discussion shows that *the major costs of revitalization fall upon households who would not otherwise have moved but are displaced by rising occupancy costs they cannot afford to pay*. It is easy to exaggerate the number of households who bear such costs, because many who move out of revitalizing areas would have moved even if upgrading had not occurred. It is also easy to dismiss the legitimate complaints of truly displaced households as unwarranted, because the city government is usually a beneficiary of revitalization.

In reality, displacement is the result of large disparities in purchasing power in a free-enterprise economy, plus occasional shortages of adequate housing in specific markets. Local laws in the United States require all households to consume relatively high-quality housing based upon middle-class perceptions of how people "ought to live." Many households cannot afford such "decent" housing without subsidies. Yet the nation does not provide these subsidies in sufficient quantity. Consequently, many households occupy housing that does not meet legal or widely accepted standards.

As long as there is enough decent housing available to supply the needs of more affluent households, poorer ones can occupy substandard housing undisturbed (unless the local government enforces housing codes). But during housing shortages, affluent households are also attracted to that substandard housing. They are able to outbid its poor occupants in both the rental and purchase markets. If society allowed relatively low-quality—but still "decent"—housing to be built, it might be possible to provide shelter that even poor households could afford. But low-cost housing is forbidden by law in almost all U.S. metropolitan areas; so poor displaced households must scramble for places to live in the existing inventory. When housing markets are very loose, the social advantages of revitalization outweigh the costs of displacement enough so that society—and the more affluent newcomers—can adequately compensate the displaced. When housing markets are very tight, the social costs of displacement may be so large that adequate compensation is not possible. How communities can permit revitalization and justly offset its costs is discussed in chapters 11 and 12.

7

Neighborhood Racial Change

THE MOST important neighborhood change in U.S. cities since 1945—
and perhaps for some time before that—has been in racial occupancy.[1]
This shift has been primarily from white to black occupancy, though shifts
from Anglo-American to Hispanic occupancy have récently grown also.
Racially segregated housing markets are characteristic of U.S. metropolitan areas. Therefore, when a neighborhood changes from white to black
occupants, *it actually shifts from one housing market to another*. This
makes racial change different from the types of change discussed in
chapter 5, which do not involve a switch in markets.

The Arbitrage Model

The many studies of neighborhood racial and ethnic change made by
sociologists, demographers, community organizers, and economists are
too vast to summarize here. Instead, I use a spatial arbitrage model
developed by economists to analyze some aspects of the dual housing

1. Technically, *racial* refers to one of the four or so major racial groups in the human
species; *ethnic* refers to any of hundreds of nationality groups. In the United States,
perception of racial differences is more widespread, more intense, and has more important
effects than perception of nationality differences. Therefore, racial segregation has more
profound effects than ethnic segregation. However, the Hispanic groups currently entering
American cities often are descended from some combination of Spanish, Indian, and black
African ancestors. To simplify the discussion in this chapter, *racial* applies to black-white,
Hispanic-Anglo, and Hispanic-black differences, even if these applications are not technically
in accordance with Census Bureau definitions. Moreover, although the discussion focuses
often on black-white relationships, its implications also apply to Hispanic-Anglo and
Hispanic-black relationships.

Figure 7-1. *Neighborhood Racial Transition in the Arbitrage Model*

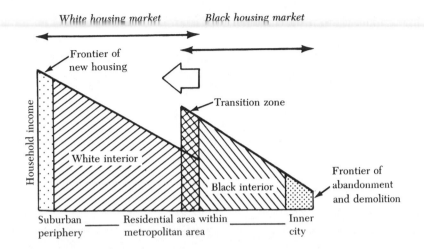

market.[2] It is diagrammed in figure 7-1. According to this deliberately oversimplified model, most white households in a metropolitan area live in one wholly segregated zone, called the white interior. The outer edge of this zone (at the left in figure 7-1) is the frontier of construction. Most minority households reside in another segregated zone, called the black interior (at the right in figure 7-1). These two interiors are separated by a border, spanned by a transition zone. Within this zone live both white and black households. The poorest black households—including newcomers from outside the metropolitan area—live along the frontier of initial entry, shown at the right edge of the figure.

Within each interior zone is a hierarchy of neighborhoods like that described in chapter 4. The neighborhoods in each hierarchy have differing average incomes, with the poorest areas to the right and the most affluent to the left in the figure. Thus, the most affluent black neighborhoods and the poorest white neighborhoods lie adjacent to the transition zone. Hence the residents in the minority neighborhoods

2. The concept of neighborhood arbitrage and much of the analysis in this chapter are taken from Charles L. Leven and others, *Neighborhood Change: Lessons in the Dynamics of Urban Decay* (Praeger, 1976). The application to individual housing units is derived from Paul N. Courant and John Yinger, "On Models of Racial Prejudice and Urban Residential Structure," *Journal of Urban Economics*, vol. 4 (July 1977), pp. 272–91. The basic arbitrage model was developed by Martin J. Bailey, "Note on the Economics of Residential Zoning and Urban Renewal," *Land Economics*, vol. 35 (August 1959), pp. 288–92. It was developed further by Richard F. Muth, *Urban Economic Problems* (Harper and Row, 1975).

adjacent to the zone often have higher incomes than residents in nearby white neighborhoods, even though average white incomes are much higher than average minority incomes over the entire market.

Average housing prices decline from left to right across the diagram. They are highest along the frontier of construction, somewhat lower in the white interior, lower than that in the transition zone, lower still in the black interior, and lowest of all along the frontier of abandonment and demolition on the far right, where the most destitute black households are clustered. Prices are highest on the frontier of construction because new units cost more than existing ones. They are higher in the white interior than in the transition zone because many white households do not wish to live near minority households and will pay a premium for housing in all-white areas. In addition, white incomes are typically higher in the white interior. Prices are higher in the transition zone than the black interior because some black households prefer living in that zone, because either they want to have some white neighbors, or they want newer housing than exists in most of the black interior, or both.

Neighborhood racial change occurs when the transition zone moves (leftward in the diagram) into the white interior. This transfer of housing in the transition zone in response to differences in the prices that white and minority households are willing to pay for the same housing units is called arbitrage.

This entire model market would exhibit spatial stability and economic equilibrium if (1) every household occupied a housing unit, (2) prices in the transition zone of housing units of the same quality were the same for both groups, (3) no net changes occurred in number of households and number of housing units in any zone, and (4) no changes occurred in the incomes of individual households and groups of households in relation to the incomes of other individuals and groups.

However, in dynamic cities many factors can upset equilibrium. For example, a large inflow of poor minority households to the black interior drives up prices for housing there. Households in the black interior then are willing to pay more for housing in the transition zone than white households are willing to pay for the same units. White home owners who move out of the transition zone are more likely to sell to black households than to other white households, since the former will pay higher prices. Speculators may hasten change by buying homes from white households and selling them at higher prices to minority households.

As a result, more and more housing in the transition zone shifts from white to minority occupancy. The area becomes less desirable for those whites who do not like living near minority households, causing its housing prices to fall even lower in the white housing market. Eventually, the transition area becomes predominantly minority in occupancy and is part of the black interior. The border and the transition zone have shifted farther into the white interior. The immediate cause of their movement is the process of arbitraging. However, the ultimate cause is the in-migration of the poor black households into the black interior.

Whenever such a movement of the border line occurs, the total supply of housing available to black households expands. If that supply rises faster than the number of such households, prices of units available to black households will fall. Eventually the prices they are willing to pay for housing in the new transition zone fall. Housing stops shifting from white to minority occupancy, and the racial border stops moving. However, if the original cause—in this case, in-migration of poor black households—continues, the price differential may continue in the new transition zone. The racial border keeps moving—as happened in many cities in the 1950s and 1960s.

Any change in condition that causes minority households to be willing to pay more than white households for housing in the transition zone can generate such a movement of the racial border. Building on the frontier of construction may create a surplus in the white community, lowering housing prices in the white interior, and lowering the prices whites are willing to pay for homes in the transition zone. If these prices are lower than the prices minority households will pay for the same units, the racial border moves to the left.

In some cases, such a movement may help stimulate home building at the frontier of construction. When massive in-migration of minority households raised housing prices in the transition zone, prices rose in the white interior because of the premium whites were willing to pay to avoid minority households. This generated sufficient demand to support construction at the urban periphery. This was certainly not the only factor stimulating such construction; others, such as rising real incomes and greater use of automobiles, were also involved. But the movement of the racial border line clearly contributed to—and was in turn furthered by—suburban home building.

Differential Incomes

When minority households in the transition zone have higher incomes than white households there, the border moves into the white interior. This is a persistent cause when, as shown in figure 7-1, the highest-income neighborhoods in the black hierarchy are those closest to the white community. These neighborhoods usually contain the newest, best-quality housing available to blacks, because blacks obtain additional housing mainly through racial transition of previously white areas. Under such conditions, since profits can be made by shifting housing from white to black occupancy, these shifts will continue to take place *if* purely economic considerations dominate real estate transactions in the transition zone. So the border line will keep marching farther into white territory.

Neighborhood racial equilibrium can then be reached only if black households are distributed at distances from the center appropriate to their incomes. For this to occur within the reality of the dual market, the black community must occupy one or more wedge-shaped pieces of the entire market. See figure 7-2. Blacks and whites of a given income would occupy housing of the same quality, but in segregated neighborhoods. Blacks in the transition zone would no longer have higher incomes than nearby whites; in fact, that is why equilibrium would occur and the border would stop moving.

This type of equilibrium has probably come close to taking place in some large metropolitan areas. In Chicago the black community spread out in large fingerlike extensions from its original position near the central business district. In New York City the black community leapfrogged, establishing segregated enclaves at significant distances from the center, often in the suburbs. In some cities both have happened.

However, in many metropolitan areas, the black community has not spread across enough types of neighborhood to achieve such equilibrium. Because they are discouraged by white hostility from looking for housing in all-white areas, many high- and middle-income black households are still constrained from achieving their true housing and neighborhood preferences. Furthermore, even if black occupancy were spread across many types of neighborhoods, individual black households would still not enjoy the same range of choice in quality of housing and neighborhood environment as whites. These are the social costs blacks continue to pay because of white prejudice and the resulting segregated housing.

Figure 7-2. *Neighborhood Racial Equilibrium through Income Equilibrium*

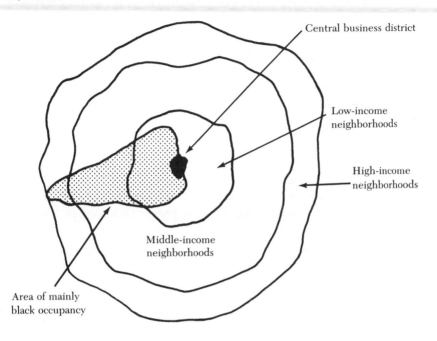

Central business district

Low-income neighborhoods

High-income neighborhoods

Middle-income neighborhoods

Area of mainly black occupancy

Racial Prejudice

White racial prejudice underlies the dual market system itself, but also affects housing prices in both markets. Such prejudice takes three forms. Sellers and landlords (both white and black) *practice racial price discrimination*, often charging black buyers and renters more than white ones for the same housing units, particularly in areas where both groups are looking for housing.

White households that want to *avoid living near blacks* pay more for otherwise similar housing in white neighborhoods than in integrated neighborhoods, pushing housing prices higher in the white interior than in the transition zone.[3] What is more, white expectations about the future of neighborhoods in the transition zone depress prices for housing there. As Leven and his colleagues describe the process,

3. See James R. Follain, Jr., and Stephen Malpezzi, *Dissecting Housing Values and Rent: Estimates of Hedonic Indexes for Thirty-Nine Large SMSAs* (Washington, D.C.: Urban Institute, 1980), pp. 53–65.

Observing the apparent pattern of neighborhood change, [white] householders began to devalue their property in an effort to "get out" even before the boundary had shifted. That is, in neighborhoods that lay along the apparent path of transition, expectation alone brought a drop in values. The effect of this, of course, was to accelerate the entire process.[4]

Various actors *exclude blacks from all-white neighborhoods*. Realtors and lenders are evasive toward blacks about available housing and financing. Some white households are openly hostile toward entering black households. A 1977 study shows that 27 percent of black couples looking for apartments encountered such negative discriminatory treatment.[5] Such discrimination, by restricting black housing demand to the transition zone and the black interior, could cause a net decline in the demand for white-occupied housing and a rise in demand (and prices) for black-occupied housing.[6] Thus exclusion *can* raise the price of housing in the black interior above that in the white interior for otherwise identical units.

However, the largest, most recent, and most complete study of this subject indicates that in the mid-1970s blacks paid significantly *less* than whites for housing of comparable size and quality. James Follain and Stephen Malpezzi analyzed the relationships between rent and housing value and specific characteristics of housing in thirty-nine metropolitan areas, isolating the influence of the race of the occupant on the cost of a housing unit.[7] They found that, for housing of comparable quality, blacks paid an average of 15 percent less to buy and 6 percent less to rent than whites paid. However, these variations differed by metropolitan area and, in fact, blacks paid higher prices in six rental markets and two

4. Leven and others, *Neighborhood Change*, p. 43.

5. Ronald E. Wienk and others, *Measuring Racial Discrimination in American Housing Markets: The Housing Market Practices Survey*, Department of Housing and Urban Development, Office of Policy Development and Research (Government Printing Office, 1979), ES-8.

6. For a somewhat different view, see Chicago Urban League, Research and Planning Department, *The Black Housing Market in Chicago: A Reassessment of the Filtering Model* (Chicago Urban League, 1977). This publication argues that suburban housing construction does not significantly aid the black community, because any additions to the total housing inventory are absorbed by "disinvestment and neighborhood deterioration" in low-income black areas. Hence the trickle down or filtering process is harmful to poor blacks, rather than ultimately beneficial to them, because it "destroys urban neighborhoods . . . without expanding housing choice, improving housing quality, or reducing housing costs" (p. 70). The authors argue for policies that will stabilize black neighborhoods and end deterioration and abandonment, rather than upgrading through movement.

7. Follain and Malpezzi, *Dissecting Housing Values and Rent*, pp. 53–65.

ownership markets of the thirty-nine examined. Nevertheless, the existence of statistically significant discounts for black renters and owners in
the vast majority of these markets has two important implications. First,
the relative housing situation of blacks has improved since the early
1950s. Second, many whites are willing to pay premiums to live in
segregated neighborhoods, even though they could reduce their housing
costs by moving into mainly black neighborhoods. The microdynamics of
such choices are discussed below.

This analysis shows that the purely economic factors in the arbitrage
model cannot fully account for actual behavior in a dual housing market,
for they do not take into account exclusionary behavior that keeps high-
and middle-income blacks from moving directly into white neighborhoods.
Such exclusion causes pressure for neighborhood racial change to build
up along the racial border line. Also, white racial prejudice lowers the
demand for housing in the transition zone, thus pushing housing prices
there below those in the white interior. This creates "bargains" in the
transition zone, very attractive to black households trying to improve
their housing. Thus, illegal exclusionary tactics plus other manifestations
of white racial prejudice create both economic and noneconomic incentives
for blacks themselves to perpetuate the dual housing market by confining
their moves out of mainly black areas to transition zones. This is one
reason it is so difficult to alter racially segregated housing patterns once
they have become established.

Black preferences for living in mainly black neighborhoods could also
account for some racially segregated neighborhoods. But opinion polls
have long shown that many black households prefer living in racially
mixed neighborhoods, though they define "mixed" as containing large
fractions of blacks.[8]

Microdynamic Illustrations of Racial Change

The racial transition of an individual white neighborhood clearly
illustrates this form of neighborhood change. As the racial border line
gets closer to this neighborhood, more and more whites perceive it as
likely to become a black neighborhood in the near future. The number
of white households willing to move into vacancies arising from normal
turnover gradually declines. Their unwillingness is caused partly by their

8. William Brink and Louis Harris, *Black and White* (Simon and Schuster, 1967), pp.
232–33.

prejudice against living with blacks and partly by their fear of future declines in property values, which they associate with black occupancy.

Ironically, the unwillingness of white households to move into the neighborhood is a crucial reason for its changing. No flight or panic among white residents is required to make racial change almost inevitable, once additional white households cease to move in. As property becomes vacant through normal turnover, its owners have no alternative to selling or renting to blacks, and the neighborhood gradually becomes more and more black in occupancy. The critical factor is not how fast whites move out but that *whites do not move in*. Stable, racially integrated residential patterns require the elimination of this unwillingness of whites to move into a neighborhood that blacks are entering.

When black households start moving in, the initially depressed prices of housing tend to rise. Not only are the incomes of most blacks moving in higher than the incomes of most white residents, but white property owners can charge blacks more than they could have charged white buyers and renters.[9] Thus property values fall *before* blacks enter the neighborhood but rise *after* they begin entering in large numbers, especially if they are buying the housing.[10]

What happens after this transition to occupancy by mainly high- or middle-income blacks depends upon two factors. (1) *The rate of growth of the city's low-income black population*. If this population is rapidly increasing, the neighborhood will continue to change as poor black households move out of the inner city. If this population is stable, the neighborhood will probably remain middle-income for a longer period. (2) *The demand for housing among black high- and middle-income households*. Where the demand is strong, housing prices in the neighborhood will remain high long after the racial change. However, where demand is weak, prices will drop and low-income black households will begin to move in. Eventually, the neighborhood will trickle down within the hierarchy of black neighborhoods toward occupancy by lower-income households.

A completely different but very insightful way to look at neighborhood racial segregation has been developed by Thomas Schelling.[11] He analyzed

9. Courant and Yinger, "On Models of Racial Prejudice."

10. See Luigi Laurenti, *Property Values and Race* (University of California Press, 1960), and Anthony Downs, "An Economic Analysis of *Property Values and Race* (Laurenti)," *Land Economics*, vol. 36 (May 1960), pp. 181–88.

11. Thomas C. Schelling, *Micromotives and Macrobehavior* (Norton, 1978), pp. 137–66, and Schelling, "Dynamic Models of Segregation," *Journal of Mathematical Sociology*, vol. 1 (July 1971), pp. 143–86.

how individual white and black households would move, assuming each group has a certain tolerance limit on the racial mixture in its immediate vicinity. For example, assume that neighborhood x has ten blocks containing one hundred white households and no black households. These households are willing to live in an area containing up to 25 percent blacks, and each white household will move when its block exceeds that percentage. These white households are willing—may even prefer—to live in a racially integrated neighborhood, but by their definition of that term.

Further assume that the city's black households are increasing in number and also prefer to live in racially integrated neighborhoods. However, their definition of the term is any area containing up to 75 percent blacks. In a certain year, six black households move into one block of neighborhood x. The whites remaining on that block now have predominantly black neighbors, in violation of their preferences. Those whites will move to some other block in the neighborhood or to some other neighborhood. If the six black households had moved into several blocks, no whites would have had more than 25 percent black neighbors, so none would have moved for reasons related to race.

In either case, blacks will continue moving into the neighborhood since it is now integrated—which blacks in that city prefer. As they enter, the chance that a white household will find itself living with more than 25 percent black households increases; so the likelihood it will move increases. These moves create more opportunities for additional blacks to move in. Once the entire neighborhood contains more than 25 percent black households, the withdrawal of the remaining whites will proceed rapidly. Moreover, no other whites with similar views concerning racial integration will move into the area, since they will recognize that it has more than 25 percent blacks. Within a relatively short period, the area will become entirely black. Notice that this process ends in complete racial segregation even though *all* households, both white and black, are willing to live in what they regard as a racially integrated neighborhood.

Because definitions of integration differ among whites and blacks, stable integration is extremely difficult to achieve. There is a whole range of black-white mixtures that blacks believe constitutes integration, but that whites do not. Blacks keep moving in after the percentage of blacks in the area has surpassed the level that whites regard as acceptable, and the whites then withdraw altogether.

By analyzing combinations of preferences concerning integration and behavior of households under each combination, Schelling demonstrates how unlikely it is for stable neighborhood integration to result from unconstrained household choice. Whenever whites and blacks do not agree almost exactly on what constitutes an acceptable mixture, the behavior of individual households is likely to produce a result that leads to the complete withdrawal of one group or the other. Even if the initial mixture is acceptable to members of both groups, if they do not agree upon the *limits* of an acceptable mixture, more of one group will keep entering the area until its share of the total surpasses what is acceptable to the other group.

Segregation is thus inevitable as long as (1) both groups regard neighborhood racial composition as important in choosing where to live, and (2) they have incompatible beliefs about the acceptable limits of racial integration. Given these factors, achieving stable, racially mixed neighborhoods probably requires the use of racial quotas in some form.

The Negative Effects of Racial Change

Massive neighborhood racial change from white to black occupancy has several serious negative impacts. Since 1945 hundreds of white neighborhoods have changed to mainly black occupancy. Many of the white households initially living in these neighborhoods would have liked to remain and would have remained had it not been for racial transition. The nearly total transition of their neighborhoods from white to black occupancy caused them serious losses, especially the elderly whose remaining wealth was tied up in their homes and whose social contacts were nearby. Furthermore, many of the black households that moved into these neighborhoods would have preferred to continue living in a racially mixed area.

Black home buyers in transition neighborhoods often do not realize as much price appreciation as do white home buyers in the white interior or the suburban periphery. When a neighborhood reaches the lower levels of the white hierarchy of neighborhoods and shifts into the top of the black hierarchy, it is often occupied by black households with incomes higher than those of the departing whites. This prevents prices from falling when whites leave (after an anticipatory decline, as noted earlier). Thus the black households have paid a premium for the housing in the first place. The black middle class provides a very small market; so the neighborhood trickles down through the black hierarchy to lower-income groups fairly fast. A study of neighborhoods in St. Louis and Houston concludes that "neighborhoods undergoing racial transition, and to an even greater extent, nonwhite neighborhoods tended to experience more rapid succession to lower-income occupancy than similar white neighborhoods."[12] This arrangement penalizes black middle-income households. They are the buyers in the majority market, sustaining housing values for the latter, and the sellers in the minority market, which frequently cannot sustain those values.

Furthermore, these black households cannot always separate themselves spatially from lower-income households, as white affluent households can. In 1975, 44 percent of all nonpoor black households—but only 9 percent of nonpoor white households—in central cities lived in poverty areas.[13] The result is social compression, which makes black neighborhoods more economically mixed than most white neighborhoods.[14] The mixture weakens neighborhood cohesion and community organization. Children of these black middle-income households frequently go to schools dominated by children from low-income households, an arrangement in which both groups lose. Lower-class children benefit from going to school with middle-class children only when the latter are a majority—rarely the case in black public schools.

When overall surpluses of housing exist in some metropolitan areas, excess vacancies trickle down through the inventory to the lowest-income, most deteriorated neighborhoods. Serious decay and abandonment often occur in such areas, most of which are occupied by poor blacks at the bottom of the dual hierarchy of neighborhoods. Accompanying physical decay are such maladies as high rates of crime, vandalism, arson, drug addiction, and unemployment. Desire to escape from these conditions generates a strong outward push among black moderate-income households, independent of the outward pull caused by better housing opportunities elsewhere. Hence middle-income blacks who moved earlier to higher-status neighborhoods sometimes find a second wave of black households with lower incomes following them. So the former move again in hopes of finding a neighborhood that will remain stable.[15] This need

12. Kerry D. Vandell, "The Effects of Racial Composition on Neighborhood Succession," paper prepared for the 1979 joint meeting of the American Real Estate and Urban Economics Association and the Regional Science Association, p. 28.

13. Bureau of the Census, *Data Book for the White House Conference on Balanced National Growth and Economic Development* (GPO, 1977), p. 113.

14. Donald I. Warren, *Black Neighborhoods: An Assessment of Community Power* (University of Michigan Press, 1974), pp. 14–15, 31–33.

15. The need for such stability within the black community is cogently argued in Chicago Urban League, *Black Housing Market in Chicago*.

to move frequently in search of stability is naturally upsetting to black middle-income households, just as the need to flee from crisis-ghetto conditions is upsetting to moderate-income blacks.

Racial change has occurred so often in the past that most whites believe it is inevitable, once blacks have begun entering a neighborhood. Whites also believe property values always fall when such transition occurs. Racial change does occur, and property values often do decline, but both are caused mainly by white middle-income households refusing to enter after blacks have begun moving in. Thus, whites attribute to black entry an outcome caused by their own behavior, a form of blaming the victim for an undesirable result.

Racial transition has one positive impact: it has enormously expanded the supply of housing available to black households. As long as white exclusionary tactics and price discrimination keep black households from moving into the white interior, there must be some mechanism to expand the black housing market. Racial transition has been that mechanism. Since 1950, blacks and other minorities have improved the quality of their housing substantially by this means.

But without racial exclusion and price discrimination, the entire metropolitan-area housing supply would be available to blacks. Until whites stop exhibiting racial prejudice in housing markets, massive racial transition of neighborhoods along racial border lines is likely to continue, although at a slower pace than in the past because of slower black population growth.

Stable, Racially Integrated Neighborhoods

Is racial stability impossible in neighborhoods near the racial border? In answering this question, it is necessary to distinguish between stability along the entire border and the stability of one or a few neighborhoods there. Overall stability is impossible as long as any of the conditions discussed above prevail—a growing black population, growing suburbs, income differences between blacks and whites in the transition zone, and especially white discrimination. This discrimination is unlikely to decline greatly, since most of those who discriminate do not bear its costs. These are the white households who refuse to live in the transition zone because of their attitudes toward blacks and their fear of falling property values. Persuading them to take what they believe are serious economic and social risks for an abstract social goal is extremely difficult.

Stabilizing the racial composition of particular neighborhoods along the border probably accelerates racial change elsewhere along the border as long as white discrimination dominates housing markets. However, stability in at least some racially integrated areas is a goal worth trying for. It can be achieved by blocking economic forces with noneconomic forces.[16]

One noneconomic strategy is to enhance the attractiveness of the neighborhood to white households and persuade black households not to concentrate in any one spot in great numbers. The goal is to keep enough white households moving into the neighborhood to maintain its integrated character by keeping the market strong enough so that property values are stable or rising. Oak Park, Illinois, has successfully used this strategy for several years, enforcing its housing code and providing many services to households—aid in housing rehabilitation, counseling, referring black households to housing away from the border, and even providing home-value insurance. Skyrocketing suburban housing prices have contributed to the success of the Oak Park program. The program requires constant effort to influence the market so that purely economic forces do not perpetuate the movement of the border into the white interior.

A second noneconomic strategy is using racial quotas to attain and keep a certain racial balance. A whole neighborhood, say a large rental or cooperative housing project, managed by one organization, is most likely to be able to use a quota system successfully. Several large private rental projects on Chicago's South Side maintained racially integrated (60 percent white) occupancy for many years through such deliberate use of discrimination. Since these projects were very popular and were surrounded by mainly black neighborhoods, they had long waiting lists of black applicants. If the management had accepted applicants on a first-come, first-served basis as vacancies appeared, without taking race into account, the projects would soon have become majority-black in occupancy. According to the experience of similar projects throughout the United States, the remaining white occupants would eventually have left.[17]

Deliberate discrimination, even though clearly aimed at achieving racial integration rather than at excluding all blacks, has recently been

16. The noneconomic forces common in the past were regrettable: violence toward blacks crossing the racial border line and exclusion of blacks from housing by some white real estate professionals and some landlords. Vestiges of the latter remain.

17. Most white Americans do not want to live in neighborhoods where they are not the majority. For a discussion of this attitude see Anthony Downs, "Alternative Futures for the American Ghetto," *Daedalus*, vol. 97 (Fall 1968), pp. 1338–41.

attacked as illegal by several black housing applicants, supported by the Department of Housing and Urban Development. But the Supreme Court has upheld taking race into account to achieve racial integration in education, including the use of racial quotas in assigning students to schools. The same arguments can be applied to housing. Universal application of quotas in housing is both impractical and undesirable, but selective application should be permitted when quotas are clearly used to achieve racial integration. If this method of attaining racial stability along the racial border line is banned, stable, racially integrated neighborhoods will be even more difficult to achieve.

Hispanics in the United States

Although blacks are the largest ethnic minority group in the United States, the Hispanic population is growing at a much faster rate. From April 1970 to October 1977, Hispanic households rose 60 percent, black households, 29 percent, and all others (hereafter referred to as Anglo households), 17 percent.[18] In October 1977 the United States contained nearly 4 million Hispanic households and nearly 8 million black households.[19] If growth continues at the same rates as in the seventies, there will be more Hispanic households than black households in the year 2004. Projections that take into account illegal immigration and the larger size of Hispanic households indicate that Hispanics will surpass blacks numerically in the 1990s or even the late 1980s.

Without counting the many illegally present Hispanics overlooked by the census, over 20 percent of the 1980 population of the following cities were Hispanics:[20]

City and state	Hispanic population (percent)
El Paso, Texas	63
Miami, Florida	56
San Antonio, Texas	54
Corpus Christi, Texas	47

18. Bureau of the Census, *County and City Data Book, 1977*, A Statistical Abstract Supplement (GPO, 1978), table 4.

19. Bureau of the Census, *Current Housing Reports*, series H-150-77, *Annual Housing Survey, 1977: United States and Regions*, pt. A, "General Housing Characteristics" (GPO, 1979), pp. 1, 33, 45.

20. Bureau of the Census, unpublished preliminary data.

City and state	Hispanic population (percent)
Santa Ana, California	44
Albuquerque, New Mexico	34
Los Angeles, California	28
San Bernardino, California	25
Tucson, Arizona	25
San Jose, California	22
Stockton, California	22

Moreover, in some very large cities, although Hispanics were small percentages of the total 1980 population, they were large in number: 1,405,957 (20 percent) in New York City; 422,061 (14 percent) in Chicago.

The large absolute size of this group combined with its rapid growth mean that many urban neighborhoods are becoming Hispanic in occupancy. Experience indicates that Hispanics, like blacks, tend to live together in neighborhoods segregated from other groups. However, there are differences, one being that the Hispanic community is divided into several distinct national groups with different cultural backgrounds. They include Cubans, Mexican-Americans, Puerto Ricans, and small groups from other Latin American nations, such as Colombia and Guatemala. Although there are black national groups, too, from Caribbean and African countries, their members are so few compared to the many descendants of American slaves that they seldom form separate residential communities.

Second, skin color has significant implications among Hispanics. Those with light-colored skin (often of European background) integrate easily into Anglo neighborhoods, unlike light-colored blacks. As a result, Hispanics are less residentially segregated than blacks.

As one study points out,

An overview of residential segregation in 35 Southwest cities yields one clear-cut finding. Mexican Americans are without exception substantially less segregated from the dominant group than are Negroes, but the level of segregation for both groups has remained high. Focusing only on the two largest minorities, the results show the following general rank order: the most severe segregation exists between Negroes and white Anglos, the next highest . . . between Mexican Americans and Negroes, and the lowest . . . between Mexican Americans and Anglos. Within the Mexican-American group there is also some segregation between the native born and foreign born.[21]

21. Leo Grebler, Joan W. Moore, and Ralph C. Guzman, *The Mexican-American People: The Nation's Second Largest Minority* (Free Press, 1970), pp. 286–87.

Residential segregation appeared to be greater (1) the larger the city, (2) the greater the fraction of large households among the minority groups, (3) the greater the income differentials between the minorities and Anglos, and (4) for the larger of the two minority groups.[22]

A third difference between Hispanics and blacks is that as Hispanics improve their economic circumstances they tend to remain in the same locations rather than, as many blacks do, move to "better" neighborhoods. They add rooms or purchase more homes nearby. This tendency springs from their desire to remain near relatives, perhaps to provide them with economic assistance, and also near other Hispanic residents, merchants, and cultural centers. Therefore Hispanic neighborhoods typically contain a broader spectrum of incomes than black and Anglo neighborhoods.

Since the Hispanic population is now the fastest growing group in many large cities—often the *only* group increasing in size—many neighborhoods are changing from Anglo to Hispanic. However, because typically Hispanics are more likely than blacks to move directly into Anglo neighborhoods, growth in the Hispanic population may not cause as much neighborhood transition as the same growth in the black population.

Hispanics will play crucial roles in the future of many large American cities. Careful studies of their behavior and their treatment by the larger society are needed.

22. Ibid., pp. 287–88.

8

Future Urban Developments Influencing Neighborhoods

ANY ANALYSIS of future social conditions is necessarily tentative and speculative. The immense diversity of cities and neighborhoods further complicates forecasting, since no one projection can apply to all or even most places. However, precise assumptions are not crucial to the conclusions in this and succeeding chapters if the direction of the assumptions is true.

Demographic and Economic Trends

A number of trends relevant to urban neighborhoods can be charted with some confidence.[1]

Urban population growth. A Census Bureau projection indicates that total U.S. population will increase by 38 million from 1980 to 2000 (growth was 46.8 million between 1940 and 1960 and 48.0 million between 1960 and 1980).[2] The urban *share* of this growth will be lower than it was in the 1950s and 1960s because net migration out of metropolitan areas to nonmetropolitan areas will continue. But larger *absolute* population growth in the 1980s than in the 1970s will cause an absolute expansion

1. See also Katharine L. Bradbury, Anthony Downs, and Kenneth A. Small, *Urban Decline and the Future of American Cities* (Brookings Institution, forthcoming).

2. Bureau of the Census, *Statistical Abstract of the United States, 1980* (Government Printing Office, 1981), pp. 6, 7; and *Data User News*, vol. 16 (January 1981), p. 2. The actual count in 1980 was 226.5 million—over 4 million higher than shown in the first publication above. Urban (metropolitan) areas gained 21.9 million in population in the 1960s, about 15.7 million in the 1970s, and will probably gain 13 million or 14 million in the 1980s. Ibid., p. 19.

of metropolitan areas similar to that in the 1970s, though smaller than in the 1950s and 1960s.

Hispanic in-migration. The largest groups coming into urban areas will be Hispanics, mostly from Mexico. (This assumes no massive inflows of other immigrant groups, such as those from Southeast Asia.) These newcomers will congregate primarily in cities near the Mexican border, such as San Antonio, El Paso, Albuquerque, San Diego, and Los Angeles. However, significant numbers will enter many other large cities, too. Most will initially have low incomes compared to other residents.

Snowbelt to sunbelt migration. Between 1960 and 1965, 62 percent of the U.S. population growth was in the South and West; that share rose to 90 percent between 1970 and 1980. In the latter period, the Northeast barely maintained its total population. It grew only 0.2 percent compared to 15.1 percent for the rest of the nation. This trend will be more pronounced in the last two decades of the century.[3]

Diversity of population growth. As in the past, there will be a great diversity of population growth rates among metropolitan areas in the 1980s and 1990s. From 1970 to 1975, 26 of the 121 standard metropolitan statistical areas (SMSAs) containing the nation's largest cities lost population. The rest gained varying percentages of population, as follows:[4]

Percentage growth rate category	Number of SMSAs
0.0–11.9	79
12.0–19.9	10
20.0 and over	6

City population loss.[5] The trend evident in the 1970s in cities will continue: from 1970 to 1975, 97 of the 153 largest cities lost population—compared to only 56 that lost population in the 1960s. Forty-one of these cities lost over 6.5 percent of their population, hence they probably lost households, too. (These figures do not include gains from annexation.)

Changes in age distribution.[6] The young population, aged fourteen to

3. Bureau of the Census, *Statistical Abstract of the United States, 1980*, pp. 12, 396.

4. Based on Bureau of the Census, *County and City Data Book, 1977*, A Statistical Abstract Supplement (GPO, 1978), and unpublished data from the Bureau of the Census; data for New England from Bureau of the Census, *Current Population Reports*, series P-25, "Population Estimates and Projections" (GPO, 1977), nos. 649–98.

5. Bureau of the Census, unpublished data.

6. *Statistical Abstract of the United States, 1978*, p. 9.

twenty-four years old, will decline between 1980 and 2000, especially from 1985 on. But record numbers of young people will be entering their late twenties and early thirties. The group aged thirty-five to forty-four will grow faster than any other in both percentage and absolute terms. And the population aged sixty-five and over will grow more rapidly than the population as a whole.

Changes in size and number of households.[7] Small households will continue to increase faster than households in general. From April 1970 to October 1977 households increased by 19 percent, but one-person households rose by 42 percent and two-person households by 24 percent. By 1977 over half of all households were composed of one or two people.

High cost of capital. The annual flow of capital into home mortgages rose from $12.8 billion in 1970 (13 percent of all funds raised by nonfinancial institutions in that year) to $110.2 billion in 1979 (28 percent of all such funds in that year).[8] This immense increase in housing financing was encouraged by rapid increases in home prices, incomes, and the general price level; relatively low rates of mortgage interest in *real* terms; the ability to borrow most of the cost of purchasing a home; and the deductibility of mortgage interest from federally taxable incomes. Even though nominal mortgage interest rates had soared to record levels by early 1980, the inflation rate rose much faster than anticipated; so *real* interest rates in the late 1970s were *lower* than in preceding decades.[9] Mortgage funds will not be available at such low real interest rates in the 1980s and beyond. Consumers, discouraged by the low real rates of interest paid for savings, are saving less of their current incomes than at any period in recent decades. This restricts funds available for mortgage

7. Bureau of the Census, *Current Housing Reports*, series H-150-77, *Annual Housing Survey, 1977: United States and Regions*, pt. A: "General Housing Characteristics" (GPO, 1979), table A-1.

8. *Federal Reserve Bulletin*, vol. 58 (June 1972), p. A73.1; and *Federal Reserve Bulletin*, vol. 66 (June 1980), table 1.59.

9. See Douglas B. Diamond, Jr., "Taxes, Inflation, Speculation and the Cost of Homeownership," paper prepared for the midyear 1979 meeting of the American Real Estate and Urban Economics Association; and Frank de Leeuw and Larry Ozanne, "Housing," in Henry J. Aaron and Joseph A. Pechman, eds., *How Taxes Affect Economic Behavior* (Brookings Institution, 1981). Douglas Diamond calculated that the *real* mortgage interest rate fell from 4.02 percent in 1970 to 1.89 percent in 1977 and 2.01 percent in 1978. He computed an index of the real, after-tax costs of owning a standardized home in each year from 1970 through 1978. His index *fell* from its base of 100.0 in 1970 to 62.5 in 1978—thus dropping 4.7 percent per year. This remarkable decline in the true costs of owning a home tremendously encouraged households to shift from rental to ownership and helped stimulate the record levels of new housing construction in the 1970s.

loans. They will continue such behavior in the future unless borrowers pay higher real interest rates or savers are given new tax benefits.

Slower growth of real incomes. Per capita disposable personal income in 1972 dollars rose at compound annual rates of 1.23 percent from 1950 to 1960, 2.98 percent from 1960 to 1970, and 2.47 percent from 1970 to 1979.[10] However, it rose only 1.76 percent a year from 1973 to 1979, including a decline from 1973 to 1974. Median family income in 1978 dollars rose at compound annual rates of 3.25 percent from 1950 to 1960, 2.96 percent from 1960 to 1970, and 0.79 percent from 1970 to 1978.[11] By either measure, real income growth slowed dramatically in the 1970s. This occurred mainly because of higher energy costs, higher taxes, a drastic fall in productivity growth, and accelerated general inflation—forces likely to continue.

Slower increases in state and local government spending. The rapid growth in state and local government spending and employment from 1950 to about 1975 will cease. More functions will shift from the public sector to the private sector. Cities with falling populations may experience fiscal squeezes that will severely restrict the public services they can deliver.

Residential segregation. Socioeconomic and racial segregation seem very likely to continue. The analysis in the rest of this book is based upon that assumption. This does not imply approval, only recognition of its deeply rooted nature in our society.

Urban neighborhoods and urban development in the last part of the twentieth century are going to be affected by all the demographic and economic trends described above. Cities in the Southwest may experience the same neighborhood change from Hispanic in-migration that Northern cities experienced in the 1950s and early 1960s from in-migration of rural blacks. The reduction of the youthful population should lower unemployment rates, which are highest in this group. The growing elderly population will have more political power and will demand more public services than in the past.

The huge proportion of young adults at ages when they are forming households and buying homes will push the demand for housing very high. Small households, especially childless ones, adapt to city life and city housing more easily than the large households of the 1950s and 1960s. However, suburban housing will also be in demand, especially by the

10. *Economic Report of the President, January 1980*, p. 229.
11. Ibid., p. 232.

largest age group, the thirty-five to forty-four-year-olds. The slowdown in real income growth and the rising real cost of borrowing mortgage money will further the demand for older housing in both cities and suburbs. The ten-year record in housing starts set in the 1970s will probably not be matched in the decades ahead.[12] More mortgage money would be available if borrowers would pay savers and lenders much higher *real* rates of interest, but the trend is toward tight mortgage money.

If 60 percent of growth in population between 1980 and 2000 occurs in metropolitan areas—a reasonable estimate—23 million more persons would need to be absorbed, or 15 percent more than the total 1977 metropolitan population.[13]

Most of these 23 million persons will have to live in the suburbs. Big cities have lost only about six million persons since 1960,[14] many from extremely overcrowded neighborhoods. No one wants those bad old days returned. Furthermore, much of their population loss resulted from a shift to smaller household size, not fewer households, so there are no *excess* housing units in many cities. Moreover, many neighborhoods that lost population have deteriorated and could not be occupied without complete redevelopment, which is unlikely for reasons explained later in this chapter. Therefore, big cities cannot absorb much future SMSA population growth—it must occur in the suburbs.

High Gasoline Prices

Many urban commentators believe rising energy prices and absolute oil shortages will generate a revival of large cities in the 1980s and beyond. They argue that huge increases in gasoline costs will make long-range commuting uneconomical. Workers will live nearer their jobs, businesses will locate in—or remain in—cities, near public transportation.

---

12. From 1970 to 1980, 17.8 million new private housing units were started (21.3 if mobile homes are included). Bureau of the Census, *Construction Reports*, series C20, "Housing Starts," June 1980 (GPO, 1980), tables 1 and 6.

13. In the 1960s, 91 percent of population growth occurred in metropolitan areas; the 1970–77 portion was 51 percent. These percentages are distorted by changes in the number and size of areas considered standard metropolitan statistical areas. The 243 SMSAs of 1970 contained 89.3 percent of total population growth of the 1950s and 82.8 percent of the 1960s; 43.1 percent of 1970–78 growth (of noninstitutional population) was in these 243 SMSAs. The 51 percent figure is total growth in all 279 SMSAs that existed in 1977. See *Statistical Abstract of the United States, 1979*, p. 17.

14. Based on unpublished data from the Bureau of the Census.

These observers further contend that society must restrict urban growth to higher densities than in the recent past, making use of all vacant sites in a city before building on the urban periphery. Cities would be developed to their maximum. Neighborhood decline and abandonment would be reversed, and neighborhood revitalization would take place in all but those cities in areas with falling populations.

This forecast greatly exaggerates the likely effect of high gasoline costs on household behavior. First, housing itself is a much more important component of a household's budget than travel. Since suburban housing costs less than city housing of equivalent quality, households may gain by living in the suburbs even with high gasoline prices.[15] Second, there are many decentralizing forces: preference for low-density living, dependence on automotive vehicles by households and businesses, new building technology that makes many buildings in cities obsolete, new communications technology that reduces the need for concentrating activities together, lower crime rates in the suburbs, the desire of most middle- and upper-income households to segregate themselves from poorer ones, and the desire of many whites to segregate themselves from minority groups.[16] Most of these forces are not reduced by higher energy costs. Third, households are less likely to adjust to higher gasoline prices by changing settlement patterns than by driving slower, making fewer long trips, using car pools, planning local trips more carefully, and shifting to more fuel-efficient cars (a trend clearly under way in 1980).

In reality, settlement densities, once established, are very hard to alter. They are easiest to change in fast growing areas—in the South and West—but average densities in most large metropolitan areas will not change much. Furthermore, over 60 percent of all the housing units that will exist in 2000 are already built. In 1980, close to half of all the metropolitan-area jobs and over 60 percent of all occupied housing units were in the suburbs. Even in 1975, only 19 percent of all metropolitan-area jobs were held by suburban residents commuting into cities; 8 percent were held by city residents commuting to the suburbs.[17] Hence the net commuter inflow involved only 11 percent of all these jobs, a percentage that is undoubtedly smaller now. The number of workers who might move into big cities to cut commuting costs is thus not very large.

15. *Annual Housing Survey, 1977*, pt. A, table A-2.
16. See Bradbury, Downs, and Small, *Urban Decline*.
17. Author's estimates for 1980; and *Current Population Reports*, Special Studies, series P-23, no. 99, "The Journey to Work in the United States: 1975" (GPO, 1979), table F.

If the current price of gasoline doubled, the average suburban resident who works in the central city would save only about $123 a year in commuting costs (in 1977 dollars) by moving to the city.[18] The average worker, including those who commute within cities and suburbs, would save only about $50 a year by making such a move.[19] Adding the cost savings on gasoline for nonwork travel (about $113 a year) brings the cost advantage to households living in the city to about $163 a year. This incentive is not trivial, but it will probably not cause many households to shift residences.

Of course, the more gasoline prices rise, the greater the motivation to change locations. If gasoline cost $5 a gallon, more households would move into cities. However, transportation analysts believe that this price would make it economically feasible to develop and use synthetic fuels to power automobiles and trucks.[20]

Higher gasoline prices also create little net motive for business firms to relocate in cities. In fact, a city firm might compete better for high-quality labor by moving to the suburbs, since more workers commute from there into cities than the reverse. Higher trucking costs from costlier gasoline are also unlikely to cause firms to change location. Much of the cost of relatively short trucking trips consists of loading and unloading, not movement. Moreover, trucks usually skirt metropolitan centers; hence even if firms moved their locations to shorten truck trips, they might not move closer to these centers.[21]

Prolonged and severe petroleum shortages would cause some adjustments, mostly individual voluntary decisions. Governments are unlikely

18. Author's calculation based on ibid., tables F and H; and Bradbury, Downs, and Small, *Urban Decline*. Sixty-four percent of workers who lived and worked in central cities and 81 percent of those who lived in the cities and worked in the suburbs drove to work. Their average one-way trips were 5.6 and 10.1 miles, respectively. Assuming 240 round trips a year, a vehicle with fuel efficiency of 20 miles a gallon, and an increase from $1 to $2 a gallon for gasoline (5 cents more a mile), the average commuter in each group would pay an extra $86 and $195 a year, respectively, to continue commuting. Eighty percent of workers who lived and worked in the suburbs and 76 percent of those who lived in the suburbs and worked in the cities drove to work. Their average trips were 11.5 miles and 7.4 miles, respectively. Their average increases in the cost of commuting would be $209 and $142 a year, respectively. Thus, a worker employed in a central city and living in a suburb could reduce the cost *increase* by $123 ($209 to $86) by moving to the city.

19. Ibid.

20. Anthony J. Wiener and others, *Future Decisions for Public Transportation: A Basis for Decision*, Final Report, prepared for Department of Transportation, Urban Mass Transit Administration, Research and Education Division, Report no. UMTA-NY-11-0017 (UMTA, 1978), pp. iv, 36.

21. Bradbury, Downs, and Small, *Urban Decline*.

to impose higher densities on urban growth or tightly restrict peripheral expansion, because such controls would be politically feasible only if they saved huge amounts of petroleum. And even rigorous controls would save relatively little petroleum. For example, assume the state government compelled a metropolitan area to approximately triple the average density of half of its future development—from, say, five housing units an acre to fifteen units an acre. Persons living in the higher-density portions would reduce total miles driven by about 40 percent.[22] How much gasoline that would save depends upon how fast the area was growing (since the savings could affect only new growth) and how much of its commuting was by suburbanites. Assume that suburban households grew 8 percent a year (a fast rate) and accounted for 85 percent of all vehicle mileage. By the end of ten years, driving mileage would be 20 percent less than it would have been without any restrictions.[23] That is not a large saving compared to what could be saved by other means (such as using more fuel-efficient cars) and in light of the severity of the oil shortage required to win political acceptance of land-use controls.

Many individual households, however, especially those with two or more persons employed outside the home, would want to live where commuting by public transit was possible. Therefore, acute oil shortages would increase demands for housing near public transit and for an expanded transit system. Urban growth would be more compact than if no shortages existed. Even higher gasoline prices without supply interruptions will probably keep urban development somewhat more compact than if gasoline were cheap. Also, the possibility of gasoline shortages will affect where some households locate. These individual decisions will increase demand for city housing and stimulate revitalization of many neighborhoods, but they will not reverse or even stop urban sprawl.

Neighborhood Decline

At any moment most neighborhoods are stable, neither declining nor revitalizing.[24] The two kinds of neighborhood decline described in chapter 5—emptying-out and overcrowding—are caused by large flows of people

22. Boris S. Pushkarev and Jeffrey M. Zupan, *Public Transportation and Land Use Policy* (Indiana University Press, 1977), chap. 2.
23. Bradbury, Downs, and Small, *Urban Decline*.
24. Using Boston as an example, in 1975 about half of its housing stock was in stable neighborhoods, about a third in revitalizing neighborhoods, and about a sixth in declining neighborhoods.

passing *through* on their way to something better. Whether the factors that stimulate these flows are part of urban development between now and the year 2000 depends partly on the strategies of policymakers and on the settlement decisions of households. But it depends most critically on conflicting forces within the social system itself—what Marxists call social contradictions.[25] The clash of these forces generates problems and tensions that cannot be eradicated without altering basic social structures. But those same social structures also successfully meet many profound human needs, often benefiting a majority of the society's members. Hence there is immense resistance to changing them.

Furthermore, most people do not realize the indissoluble connections between specific problems and tensions they believe need solving and the underlying social structures they value so highly. So they press their leaders to solve these problems but oppose any actions that might really do so effectively. Neighborhood decline in U.S. cities is precisely such a profoundly rooted social problem.

One social contradiction underlying such decline is a conflict between the high-quality standards required for all new housing and other construction and the low incomes of a significant fraction of the population. Therefore, *new housing must decline in quality before the poor can occupy it without subsidies*. Yet taxpayers have always considered providing housing subsidies for *all* poor households too costly. And lowering standards for at least some new housing is considered undemocratic. It would require explicitly recognizing the inequality inherent in the nation's distribution of wealth and incomes. Even more important, it would permit poor households to live in new-growth areas close to affluent households—an outcome bitterly opposed by the latter. Thus, neighborhood decline is an inescapable result of (1) poverty in our society, (2) the high quality of housing enjoyed by the majority, and (3) the arrangements we have created to isolate the nonpoor spatially from the poor.

Another social contradiction contributing to neighborhood decline is maintaining the value of existing housing versus building more new housing. City governments and owners of existing property want to maximize the value of the older housing inventory. But home builders,

25. Such contradictions are not confined to capitalist societies but are present in all societies, including Marxist ones. They differ only as each social system differs in its nature and the types of social dominance within it. Social contradictions are inherent in the conflicting impulses of human nature and the conflicts of interest among individuals. For a Marxist view of urban problems and analysis, see Manuel Castells, *The Urban Question: A Marxist Approach* (Massachusetts Institute of Technology Press, 1977).

developers, and suburban landowners profit from the construction of additional housing at the urban periphery. They are motivated to keep building new housing long after it has begun undermining the value of existing units. This tendency is inherent in all free-enterprise markets. New products erode the markets for older ones by stressing the desirability of the new and by raising consumer standards. The free-enterprise system also continuously weakens the acceptability of many existing *social* arrangements. Hence, as their real incomes rise, city households become less and less willing to keep on living in what they perceive as relatively obsolete structures and neighborhoods.

The third and fourth social contradictions underlying neighborhood decline are socioeconomic segregation and racial segregation. There is a conflict between the desire of higher-income households to segregate themselves from poorer ones and the desire of poorer households to share in high-quality housing, neighborhoods, public facilities, and services. A similar tension exists between the desire of many whites to segregate themselves from minority-group members and the desire of the latter to enjoy equal access to good housing and neighborhood amenities. This conflict is currently evident in struggles over public school quality and desegregation.

Fifth, there is a social contradiction between the necessity for true neighbors to share certain human values of cooperation and community responsibility and the unwillingness of society to intervene where children are not taught these values or are learning values that destroy neighborliness. Public schools are prohibited from teaching moral values and prevented from expelling disruptive students; so many in poverty areas end up teaching almost nothing effectively. Yet the same philosophy of nonintervention allows children whose families are themselves broken or wracked with severe problems to be exposed to the commercial values of the media and the often-savage values of the street. Furthermore, the social arrangements that benefit the urban majority cause hundreds or thousands of such distraught families to become concentrated in certain areas. As a result, many residents there never have the conventions of civilized life instilled in their minds and behavior. This creates an environment completely the opposite of a true neighborhood. Most households will leave these environments as soon as they can, and those who must remain live in fear.

Financial aid alone is not enough to remedy this last social contradiction. Higher incomes or improved job opportunities would allow many households to escape from these neighborhoods, but they would not change the behavior of the destructive households who remain. No one has yet resolved, even in theory, how society can cope with these destructive households or help them change their self-damaging behavior. The problem is not trivial. Destitute households that are not destructive are unfairly compelled to bear most of the social costs of those which are.

These social contradictions create self-aggravating trends that perpetuate urban decline in general. For example, the departure of middle-income households from a central city discourages other middle-income households from staying or moving in. Their political power in the city weakens, and public spending shifts more toward activities benefiting low-income households. At the same time, if the local tax system is at all progressive, the departure of these households raises per capita taxes on all that remain, further reducing the city's attractiveness to middle-income households. Similar processes occur at the neighborhood level.[26]

At least some neighborhoods in U.S. cities will continue to decline during the twentieth century as long as the conditions sustaining these social contradictions remain, as long as continued suburban expansion undermines the market for older, central city housing, and as long as there is net in-migration of many low-income households into big cities. Some of the neighborhoods that decline in the future might be outside the central city, or in older suburbs, or in suburbs built right after World War II.

Neighborhood Redevelopment

Over the past few decades, many older, central city neighborhoods in Detroit, Cleveland, New York City, Newark, St. Louis, and other big cities have deteriorated into a devastated condition of serious abandonment. As each such deteriorated zone grows larger, the possibility of redeveloping it becomes more intriguing and important to central city governments.

However, redevelopment of largely vacant land requires new construction. Yet that is so costly under present building codes that only middle- and upper-income households and high-profit-margin businesses can

26. See Katharine L. Bradbury, Anthony Downs, and Kenneth A. Small, "Some Dynamics of Central City–Suburban Interactions," *American Economic Review*, vol. 70 (May 1980, *Papers and Proceedings*, 1979), pp. 410–14.

afford to occupy the resulting structures without subsidies. But most such prosperous households and businesses will not enter any area that contains many low-income households in an environment of decay and abandonment. Hence, for any such "hole in the doughnut" to be redeveloped, large chunks of it must first be completely emptied out. Then they can be rebuilt as unified environments marked by high-level security and middle- or upper-income population dominance.

This dual requirement poses major obstacles in most big cities. It is politically difficult to clear the remaining poor from a deteriorated neighborhood so it can be redeveloped for much wealthier residents. Nearly every large city needs a higher fraction of nonpoor households to strengthen its tax and employment bases. But the higher the percentage of poor in a city's population, the more unpopular it becomes among voters for the government to forcibly relocate poor households. This is true even when doing so improves their housing quality and neighborhood environments. Such relocations were common in the 1950s and 1960s as parts of the urban renewal and highway programs. But institutional changes, partly resulting from antipoverty programs, have greatly increased the ability of poor households to politically resist such treatment unless they receive appropriate compensation, as they should. Consequently, few elected officials today have the political strength to carry out such relocations.

In addition, the need to redevelop these areas on a large scale makes normal real estate procedures unprofitable there. Most private developers cannot afford to assemble and clear the big sites necessary to create whole new environments. Nor can they hold such sites through the long periods required to finally market them, after eventually overcoming the many local political obstacles to development. Therefore, large-scale redevelopment of abandoned neighborhoods will probably require major public subsidies. It must at least involve public eminent domain powers, especially for land assembly, clearance, and holding.

Only such clearance and rebuilding will restore the vitality of these areas. In the 1950s and 1960s, federal programs financed land assembly, clearance, and holding of these neighborhoods in many cities. In Chicago, for example, hundreds of acres south of the central business district were cleared of slums. Highways, public housing, subsidized private housing, universities, hospitals, and industries were built. Thousands of poor households were displaced into surrounding neighborhoods—stimulating major changes there.

Perhaps such redevelopment will occur in the future where no major displacement is required. But who will provide the money? City governments are financially strapped; furthermore, it is politically hazardous to spend any of these limited funds subsidizing developments for the nonpoor. Federal and state officials are also under budgetary pressure to restrict overall spending and political pressure to focus subsidy funds on the poor.[27] Moreover, the urban renewal program of the 1950s and 1960s is regarded by many as a failure; so its precedent is often rejected.[28]

Why not rely upon spontaneous revitalization rather than public funding? After all, it is happening in many formerly poor residential neighborhoods across the nation. And it often takes place without governmental displacement of the poor, large-scale land assembly, or public subsidies. But spontaneous revitalization does not occur in areas containing mostly multifamily structures too large for individuals to rehabilitate, large public housing projects, and massive abandonment. Such areas are seldom near marketable amenities like jobs, recreation areas, hospitals, or universities.

Eventually even the most devastated areas of active cities will be rehabilitated. They might even be rebuilt with single-family homes or low-density industrial buildings competitive with those in the suburbs. A very successful low-density, single-family sudivision has been built in Toledo, Ohio, on urban renewal land less than a mile from downtown. But in the near future, perhaps even for decades, many of these areas will remain abandoned and unused. These "land banks" will remain visible signs of the long-run trend toward low-density settlement in older U.S. cities.

27. However, the federal urban development action grant program shows that programs that do not focus all funds on the poor can be accepted.
28. Although it is extremely difficult to evaluate such a large and complex program, I believe it was not a failure. The benefits to the cities probably exceeded its costs. See Anthony Downs, *Urban Problems and Prospects*, 2d ed. (Rand McNally, 1976), chap. 5.

9

Limitations on Future Neighborhood Policies

DISCUSSIONS of future policies concerning urban neighborhoods must recognize certain practical limitations on what can actually be done. A policy that appears in theory to be a great solution to some pressing problem may be useless in reality. Perhaps no institutions exist to execute it, or no leaders have incentives to support it, or it requires completely unattainable coordination among many agencies, or it is likely to run afoul of some other hidden but very real obstacle. The most important such limitations are briefly described here as a preface to the policy analysis in subsequent chapters.

Rhetorical versus Real Possibilities

Distinguishing rhetorical policy proposals from real action possibilities is vital but not always easy. The boundary is vague between policies that are so marginal they will not threaten the majority who benefit from existing institutions and policies that change those institutions enough to seriously injure that majority. Moreover, the basic environment is constantly changing, often altering the whole system.

Public officials must respond in some way to legitimate complaints of those suffering from the social contradictions described earlier. They are under great pressure to do something, or to *appear* to be doing something. Yet they cannot change the fundamental causes of the problems involved, or even publicly propose to do so, because those causes are rooted in majority-benefiting arrangements.

Whole public agencies have found themselves in this dilemma. In the

1960s, the Economic Development Administration (EDA) was created with the stated purpose of assisting rural areas suffering from sharp declines in employment and population. A major cause of their decline was that most federal policies and many private ones were attracting economic activities to metropolitan areas. An effective federal attack on rural economic decline would have had to alter those other federal policies, which were benefiting millions of Americans and were strongly supported by the administration and Congress. So there was no real possibility of getting either the federal government or the private sector to stop draining population and jobs from rural counties.

In view of these realities, what could EDA really accomplish? Its *actual* mission—as distinct from its *stated* one—consisted of two functions. One was serving as a symbol of federal concern, something for which individual congressmen could take public credit. This symbolic function is both significant and worthwhile. Suffering people need to realize those in authority are sympathetic to them, even if not much can be done to alter their plight. The second function was to provide some help to the depressed areas with loans, grants, and economic planning. However, this aid was very small both from a national viewpoint and in relation to the basic problem. It certainly could not solve that problem. Yet it significantly benefited at least some people in depressed rural areas.

Similarly, one of the central missions of the Department of Housing and Urban Development (HUD) is to "rescue" declining cities. Yet their decline is caused largely by the overall urban development process, which benefits a majority of urban households. There is little political support for changing that process so as to avert big-city decline. Hence, this mission of HUD's is impossible to achieve, but the department cannot admit that fact. Rather, it must be genuinely concerned for those suffering from urban decline and deliver a certain amount of real aid to them—though far less than required to end their problems.

Clearly, this situation limits the federal policies that can actually be carried out in response to urban problems—including those of declining neighborhoods. It usually rules out profound reforms or basic changes in the social institutions or processes causing those problems, regardless of how desirable such reforms and changes may be in the long run.

Nevertheless, it is sensible for federal officials to balance federal aid to further urban growth and development with federal assistance in maintaining the vitality of older existing urban areas. Unfortunately, as discussed further in chapter 11, there is no simple way to strike such a balance. Federal and state governments could evade this issue by using revenue sharing to shift funds and responsibility to local governments. However, Congress will probably not relinquish federal powers to that degree, and federal bureaucrats will try to continue adding regulations both to achieve national goals and to justify their existence.

The Proper Institutional Level for Action

Logically, the best level on which to respond to many forces that change neighborhoods is the metropolitan-area level. But government powers there are fragmented, especially concerning land use, because there are so many small suburban governments. Such division increases the responsiveness of each government to its own citizens, which is clearly desirable. But it thereby allows high- and middle-income households to dominate the local governments where most of them live; so these localities adopt exclusionary ordinances that prevent poor households from residing there. The suburban beneficiaries of the urban development process know that any attempt to cope with the problems it generates would reveal their partial responsibility for those problems. Solutions would—legitimately—impose higher costs upon them; hence they oppose such solutions by resisting any shift of land-use controls to the metropolitan level. Their resistance seems likely to continue blocking such shifts in the foreseeable future.

Active citizen participation within declining neighborhoods further prevents creation of a rational overall policy for managing urban development. People are relatively conservative concerning any alteration in their own neighborhood, for reasons discussed in chapter 13. Hence they vigorously resist highly visible interventions that change the status quo. But decentralized, hidden, or systemwide processes affecting their neighborhood continue without much interference. For example, neighborhood residents may organize to prevent a proposed new apartment project near them. But they do nothing about the refusal of middle-income households to move into their neighborhood after low-income households begin moving in. They do not even understand how this refusal affects them. Yet such implicit boycotting of their neighborhood by potential residents probably has more influence on its future than the project they managed to prevent. However, creating policies to counteract such boycotts is probably impossible as long as governments in each metropolitan area are so fragmented.

On the other hand, there are solid reasons why most urban policies are probably best designed at the local level. Most important is the fact that American cities vary enormously in population, area, density, climate, age, reliance upon public transportation, relationship to outlying suburbs, racial composition, growth rates, economic vitality, age distribution of the population, form of government, amount of housing vacancy and abandonment, crime rates, and stability. Hence the programs and actions in each city should be tailored to suit specific circumstances there. Only local decisionmakers can choose instruments properly fitted to such diverse needs and conditions. Even a program aimed at national goals, if it is to apply different policies and actions to different communities, must rely upon the judgments and measurements of city and neighborhood officials and residents concerning what conditions truly exist in each place.

Strategies

The analyses in the following chapters sometimes use the term *strategies*. Few American governments normally adopt overall policies that could reasonably be considered strategies—that is, long-range, coordinated sets of many different actions aimed at well-defined and consistent goals. Each government or agency consists of many officials acting simultaneously, without much coordination. Moreover, these officials react on a day-to-day basis to often-conflicting pressures from diverse sources. The result is an almost accidental set of acts and policies containing many inconsistencies.

It may therefore seem unrealistic to discuss strategies toward neighborhoods, as I do in chapter 12. Nevertheless, every set of neighborhood-related policies adopted by any level of government is its de facto neighborhood strategy; so that fact should be recognized explicitly, no matter how inconsistent each strategy's elements. Perhaps such recognition will help public officials make their policies toward neighborhoods at least somewhat more consistent.

Personal Values and the Limits of Public Policies

In a free society, public policies cannot determine, or even greatly influence, crucial aspects of the way neighborhoods function. In particular, they cannot impose personal values or basic social structures (such as forms of families, households, churches, informal groups, and neighborhood organizations) upon neighborhood residents. Yet the creation of values and social structures and their transmission from each generation to the next are among the most vital social functions within individual neighborhoods.

Moreover, deficiencies in these elements are among the most important and most intractable aspects of neighborhood life in many areas, especially where poverty is concentrated. Family structures are weak, with many single-parent households in which adolescent children are often influenced more by peer groups than by adults. Values dominating interpersonal relations are often grounded on low self-esteem, feelings of personal powerlessness, hostility toward others, admiration of criminal and other antisocial behavior, lack of respect for hard work or education, and general cynicism.[1]

Some observers argue that these values should not be considered inferior to more traditional working-class and middle-class values. Rather, they are just "different" because those holding them view life from a perspective that varies greatly from that of the dominant working and middle classes. In fact, such values may seem to be a rational response to the difficult, struggle-laden environment facing people in these neighborhoods.

Nevertheless, I believe such values harm those who hold them, harm their immediate neighbors, and harm society in general. In areas where these values are dominant, conditions are inimical to peaceful, fruitful living for most residents. High rates of crime, vandalism, unemployment, illegitimacy, alcoholism, arson, drug addiction, and family instability prevail. Great personal insecurity pervades every aspect of life. Many children are not allowed to play outdoors without adult supervision; extortion and violence undermine public education; the elderly fear to go out on the streets; and interpersonal relationships become laden with suspicion. Young people are discouraged from adopting attitudes toward learning and work that would enable them to escape from such conditions by developing skills marketable in the larger society. Hence their dependence upon public assistance and illegal activities is perpetuated.

Furthermore, this situation creates major social costs that must be

---

1. For a discussion of how ghetto life influences such attitudes and values, see Garth L. Mangum and Stephen F. Seninger, *Coming of Age in the Ghetto: A Dilemma of Youth Unemployment,* Policy Studies in Employment and Welfare Number 33 (Johns Hopkins University Press for the Ford Foundation, 1978), chap. 4.

borne by the remainder of society. They include much higher-than-average government expenditures for providing social services, welfare payments, unemployment compensation, and police and fire protection. Some large public housing projects probably best exemplify the dominance of such values. Those projects are not true "neighborhoods" because not enough of their residents share the kind of values based upon mutual respect that are necessary for a fruitful common life.[2] These "nonneighborhoods" did not arise spontaneously; they were created by public policies that brought large numbers of destitute, broken households together—and isolated them from others.

As this example shows, these adverse situations do not stem only or even mainly from the values of the local residents. They also result from unjust discriminaton—past and present—against those residents by the rest of society, and from exploitation of them through various institutional arrangements, as described earlier. Such adverse treatment has been especially harmful to ethnic minorities, who often live in neighborhoods of concentrated poverty. Blacks in particular have had to endure centuries of slavery, family disruption, discrimination, and segregation surpassing the adversities of any other group of Americans. Many of the values described above have undoubtedly developed in response to such treatment.

Yet regardless of how these values came into being, they have destructive impacts upon the quality of life in many concentrated-poverty neighborhoods, and upon society generally. This conclusion is not based upon "racism" or any other biased perspective but upon simple recognition of reality. In addition, nearly all attempts to improve the quality of life in such areas without changing the residents' values have failed, even when those attempts were supported by significant resources. Many newly rehabilitated homes have been reduced to shambles within a few years. Expensive public school "enrichment" programs have produced no improvements in academic achievement or other measurable outputs. True, antipoverty programs enabled some residents to upgrade themselves into the middle class via the public bureaucracy. But those programs usually failed to improve the areas where those people formerly lived.

These discouraging results are not universal; there are also many instances in which government programs have clearly helped upgrade

2. I am indebted to Edward Marciniak for pointing out both this example and this aspect of it.

significant numbers of people, and sometimes whole neighborhoods. But where the values of a large fraction of the residents have remained dominated by those traits described above, public policies have usually failed to improve the quality of life. Such success is not likely in the future either, because public policies in a democracy only rarely alter people's fundamental perspectives on life. Perhaps that is true in all other forms of society as well.

If public policies cannot change values and basic social structures directly, but changes in those elements are essential to improving the quality of life in many concentrated-poverty areas, how can such changes be brought about? Many ethnic groups that entered the United States in the past, such as the Irish, Chinese, Japanese, and Italians, were treated as harshly when they first arrived as are members of other minority groups today. Some groups exhibited social symptoms very similar to those evident in the black community today, such as high rates of illegitimacy, broken families, unemployment, and crime. The gradual evolution of values that enabled them to change their circumstances eventually emerged from within their own communities—aided by an expansion of economic and political opportunities available in the large society.

True, the circumstances of these other groups were nowhere nearly as difficult as those of blacks. Moreover, the recent shift of many unskilled manufacturing jobs out of large cities into nonmetropolitan areas and foreign nations has reduced upward-mobility opportunities for today's poor city dwellers relative to those in the past. But a similar evolution of values within the "culture of poverty" that dominates many concentrated-poverty neighborhoods today is needed to produce really significant, long-run improvements there, in my opinion.

This emergence must be assisted by provision of expanded opportunities for many residents there—especially for those who succeed in developing the qualifications for advancement in the larger society. Many of the public policies advocated in this book are aimed at such expanded opportunities. One approach is to provide more opportunities for residents of concentrated-poverty areas to gain greater control over their own lives and environments. This includes both job opportunities and chances to exert more influence over local affairs. Specific tactics to these ends are discussed in later chapters. But such opportunities will not help unless members of these communities themselves recognize the desirability of taking advantage of them, and develop the values necessary to do so.

Hence there are definite limits on how much public policies aimed at improving the quality of life in these areas can accomplish apart from changes in behavior by the residents themselves.

Recognizing this fact should not be construed as "blaming the victims" for discriminatory and exploitative behavior by the rest of society. Nor should it be interpreted as denying the rest of society's responsibilities for changing its own behavior toward residents of concentrated-poverty areas, especially ethnic minorities. Rather, such recognition is an attempt to see clearly what will be truly effective in improving life in those areas.

10

Coping with Poverty

POVERTY is the single biggest cause of neighborhood deterioration and decline. When households are too poor to pay for "decent" housing, urban decay almost inevitably results, unless society is willing to subsidize them. Consequently, large urban areas in the United States have always been plagued by at least some low-quality housing, overcrowding, unsanitary conditions, high crime rates, and other maladies associated with poverty. Only housing abandonment and drug addiction are relatively new ills. Although housing quality in many of the most deteriorated urban neighborhoods has improved substantially over what it was as recently as 1950, urban decay cannot be totally eliminated as long as poverty remains widespread.

The best approach to improving urban neighborhoods would undoubtedly be to reduce poverty. That could be done through national monetary and fiscal policies designed to achieve high levels of employment, special incentives to encourage hiring of structurally unemployed persons (those whose lack of skills keeps them without jobs even during normal prosperity periods), and tax and transfer-payment policies that redistribute income to the poor, especially to those who cannot work. However, detailing such general antipoverty policies is beyond the scope of this book.

This chapter presents only brief discussions of certain specific policies designed to counteract the inner-city concentration of urban poverty. These include redistributing incomes within metropolitan areas, deconcentrating the poor spatially, improving low-income housing, improving the schools serving concentrated-poverty areas, and carrying out several miscellaneous actions. The discussions of these policies included here are not meant to analyze them thoroughly—only to place them in perspective in relation to the major themes of this book.

124

Redistributing Incomes within Metropolitan Areas

As shown earlier, many higher-income households have moved out of central cities as part of the process of socioeconomic segregation, which benefits them but harms central cities and their poor residents. These more affluent suburban households also gain from the operation of the overall metropolitan-area economy, which requires the inputs of many low-income workers living in central cities. Moreover, many poor people cannot earn enough to support themselves or pay for the public services they consume because of the way the economy operates—that is, its markets do not value their services very highly. In a sense, their poverty is generated by the overall metropolitan-area economy; so any public support they receive should be paid for by all those who benefit from that economy.

But a disproportionate number of these poor live in central cities, partly because they are deliberately excluded from suburban communities by the more affluent residents there. In 1977, central cities contained 45 percent of all metropolitan-area households but 60 percent of those earning under $5,000 a year and only 33 percent of those earning $25,000 and over.[1] Therefore, central city governments must pay an unfairly high proportion of the costs of providing these people with public services.

Furthermore, many suburban households use certain facilities located within central cities that serve entire regions nearby, such as stadiums, museums, theaters, medical centers, parks, and transportation facilities. Central city governments also bear a disproportionate share of the cost of providing public services for such facilities. Consequently, it would be both just and socially desirable for most relatively affluent urban residents—including suburbanites—to contribute to the economic support of the central city's government through some type of income redistribution scheme operating within each metropolitan area.

However, in most metropolitan areas, no one general government body encompasses the entire area, and local governments have limited ability to redistribute incomes. Citizens who are heavily taxed by one local government can easily move outside its borders without getting beyond commuting range of their jobs and other activities. Central cities

---

1. Bureau of the Census, *Current Housing Reports*, series H-150-77, *Annual Housing Survey, 1977: United States and Regions*, pt. A, "General Housing Characteristics" (Government Printing Office, 1979), p. 10.

typically tax their residents more heavily than suburbs, thereby creating an incentive for more affluent residents to reside in the suburbs. In 1976, suburban municipalities collected an average of $16.70 in local taxes per $1,000 of local income, compared to $25.80 (54 percent more) collected by cities containing 50,000 or more persons.[2] In multistate metropolises, citizens can even move to another state without changing jobs or sacrificing other urban amenities.

Nevertheless, it is usually inconvenient to escape from state taxes by moving to another state—and extremely costly to leave the United States to escape federal taxes. Thus only broad-jurisdiction federal and state taxing powers can compel suburbanites to pay significant shares of the costs of coping with urban poverty. That is one reason it is appropriate for big-city governments to receive large shares of their total resources through intergovernmental transfers from state and federal governments. In 1977, all cities containing 50,000 or more inhabitants received about one-third of their revenues from state and federal aid, and cities containing 300,000 or more inhabitants (excluding New York City) received almost 40 percent of their revenues from such aid.[3] Even though general governmental budget cutting in the 1980s may slow the growth of both federal and state aids to central cities, it will not alter the basic justice of redistributing significant amounts of resources from other areas to central cities. However, determining exactly how much redistribution should occur, and in what forms (revenue sharing, block grants, or categorical aids), is beyond the scope of this study.

Deconcentrating the Poor

Because many urban problems result from concentration of poor households in inner-city areas, reducing that concentration could improve conditions there. Congress officially recognized this fact in the Housing and Community Development Act of 1974. It states that "the Congress finds and declares that the Nation's cities, towns, and smaller urban communities face critical social, economic, and environmental problems arising in significant measure from . . . the concentration of persons of

2. Department of Housing and Urban Development, *The President's National Urban Policy Report, 1980* (GPO, 1980), p. 7-19.
3. Ibid., p. 11-24.

lower income in central cities."[4] In response, the Department of Housing and Urban Development (HUD) tried to persuade state housing agencies, developers, and local governments to place some federally subsidized housing for low- and moderate-income households outside central city boundaries. These efforts were not very successful, especially since the total number of federally subsidized units declined sharply after 1973. Site selection rules were also adopted that limited the number of subsidized housing units that could be erected near concentrations of poor households. Unfortunately, because suburbanites resisted the location of subsidized housing near them, these rules often halted the addition of subsidized housing anywhere in the areas concerned.[5] This prohibition has subsequently been eased to encourage the building of more subsidized units where low-income households are already located.

State governments have legal authority over the building codes, housing codes, and zoning regulations local governments use to exclude housing for low- and moderate-income households. Most states set minimum standards for the housing covered by such ordinances. But they do not prevent localities from requiring extremely high standards, far surpassing any required to protect the health and safety of the occupants. These standards are clearly designed to keep lower-income households from entering the communities concerned, because residents fear such entry will depress the values of their own homes. Passage of maximum quality and size standards based upon reasonable human needs, rather than desires to exclude the poor, might reduce some of the entry barriers many suburbs have erected.

State governments can also help deconcentrate poor households by financing new subsidized housing outside central cities. Many states have set up housing finance agencies that fund such housing by using both federal housing subsidies and capital from revenue bond issues free from federal taxation. Those bond issues have lower interest rates than conventional mortgage funds; hence housing built with them can have lower rents than conventional housing. When federal subsidies are also used, housing can be built with rents low enough to serve low- and moderate-income households in most of the United States.

4. *Housing and Community Development Act of 1974, Conference Report*, H. Rept. 93-1279, 93 Cong. 2 sess. (GPO, 1974), p. 1. Other causes besides concentrated poverty are also mentioned.

5. See Anthony Downs, *Opening Up the Suburbs: An Urban Strategy for America* (Yale University Press, 1973), chap. 12.

State housing agencies have financed subsidized units both in central cities and in surrounding suburbs. However, many of these suburban subsidized units have been occupied by households who formerly lived in the suburbs; so they have not led to much deconcentration of central city poverty. Nevertheless, at least some such deconcentration has been achieved through state-financed housing. If these efforts continue over many years, they could eventually have a significant impact on poverty concentration, especially in areas where net in-migration of poor households has stopped. This impact would be greater if a certain fraction of all such subsidized units—say, 15 to 20 percent—was initially reserved for households moving out of the nearest central city.

The federal government's experimental housing allowance program provided a housing allowance to renters and buyers, who then find acceptable units in the market.[6] One argument originally advanced in favor of housing allowances compared to construction-oriented subsidies was that the former would allow poor households to move out of concentrated-poverty areas. However, carefully documented experience indicates that this subsidy did not significantly increase socioeconomic or racial integration. Nevertheless, housing allowances could achieve some integration in neighborhoods undergoing gentrification, where rents would otherwise become too high for the initial occupants. Since the section 8 existing housing subsidy is essentially a housing allowance, its continuation can be used for this purpose.

The federal government can also exert pressure upon suburban governments to use their community development block grants to subsidize housing. Such housing could be financed with either construction or rehabilitation funds. Both federal and state government actions aimed at stronger enforcement of antidiscrimination statutes also would help deconcentrate poverty, since many poor central city households are members of minority groups.

Some observers deny that lessening the concentration of poor households would help solve the many severe problems typically found in inner-city poverty areas. They believe voluntary scattering of poor households throughout a metropolitan area would simply spread those problems to more locations. It would also deprive those poor households of easy access to many of the social services they depend upon, including

6. Department of Housing and Urban Development, *Experimental Housing Allowance Program: A 1979 Report of Findings* (GPO, 1979), pp. 41–50.

public transportation and publicly supported medical care. Whether this viewpoint is correct is hard to determine without actually attempting some voluntary dispersal and monitoring its results. Any such attempt should include efforts to deliver to the newly scattered poor households those public services on which they are highly dependent.[7] So far, middle- and upper-income residents of both suburbs and outlying central city neighborhoods have successfully blocked most of these attempts (except for public housing for the elderly).

However, most of those poor households who voluntarily move to scattered locations presumably consider themselves better off than they were in neighborhoods of concentrated poverty, even if their access to public services is worse. If not, why do so many poor households continue to move out of such neighborhoods as soon as they can? Their massive "voting with their feet" suggests that further voluntary deconcentration of poor households out of these areas would certainly benefit those who depart and, less certainly, aid society as a whole by reducing the "critical mass" of problems there.

Improving Access to Housing Credit

In the 1970s, many community groups became incensed at the apparent reluctance or refusal of savings and loan associations and banks to make mortgage loans in many older areas. These groups put strong political pressure on the federal government to change that practice. As a result, Congress passed a law requiring regulated financial institutions to disclose in what areas they receive savings and make loans. This has enabled neighborhood organizations to put enough pressure on many financial institutions so the latter are now more willing to lend money in most older neighborhoods, including those they redlined in the past. (The term *redline* refers to the alleged practice among lending institutions of drawing a line on a map excluding certain neighborhoods from consideration for mortgage loans.)

Moreover, the Federal Home Loan Bank Board and the Department of Housing and Urban Development jointly sponsored a neighborhood

7. An overall strategy and the detailed tactics for deconcentrating urban poverty are set forth in Downs, *Opening Up the Suburbs*.

revitalization program (the neighborhood housing services program) that has been outstandingly successful in 121 neighborhoods in ninety-five cities. (It is discussed in more detail in chapter 12.) Also, the Federal Home Loan Bank Board developed a community investment fund to encourage savings and loan associations to lend money in older city neighborhoods. The combined effect of all these programs has greatly reduced redlining, so they should be continued. In addition, property liability insurance needs to be made more available for city property.

Federal housing subsidies for low- and moderate-income households mentioned in the last section can also be used to improve central city housing. The federal government, in addition, underwrites subsidies for new construction, substantial rehabilitation, low-interest rehabilitation loans, and housing for the elderly. It should also subsidize large-sized units, both new and existing, for poor families too big to be accepted by most private landlords or even by most public housing projects. Local public housing authorities in Rockford, Illinois, and Baltimore, Maryland, have undertaken such programs by purchasing large existing single-family units to be rented at low rates to large, poor households.

As noted in chapter 8, record amounts of new housing production were attained in the 1970s. This massive construction contributed to both the upgrading of many households who moved into better units (whether new or existing), and the partial emptying-out and decay of many older neighborhoods. This production surge was made possible by enormous flows of financial capital into housing. Strong demands for additional housing units will probably continue in the 1980s. Whether they will be met through massive construction, rehabilitation of existing units, or more crowding in existing units depends in part upon how much capital will be available to finance housing construction. Many politically powerful sectors will be competing for available capital. It is impossible to predict how defense spending, investments in conserving energy and developing new energy sources, spending on new federal health-care programs, and so on, will affect the amount of capital available for housing.

If housing construction absorbs massive amounts of capital, suburban growth will continue, further undermining many central city housing markets and weakening revitalization. However, if federal policies and other factors shift so much capital to other activities that housing construction is greatly restricted, pressure for revitalizing older, central city neighborhoods could increase sharply.

Improving Public Schools

Many big-city public school systems are failing to serve urban children and parents effectively.[8] Evidence supporting this conclusion includes increasing violence within schools, declining achievement scores over time, high absenteeism levels, and greater shifting of relatively bright students from public to private schools.[9] This situation has four tragic consequences. First, children from the poorest households receive the worst education, even though they need education's assistance more than most others. Second, society loses these children's potential talents and capabilities. Third, society must cope with the consequent unemployment, crime, poverty, and other social maladies. Finally, many middle- and high-income households leave central cities to escape such schools.

The failings of big-city public schools have such complex causes that no brief analysis or single set of recommendations can effectively cope with them. Nevertheless, some feasible changes have an excellent chance of improving the present situation; they are discussed below.

Many people believe that a school attended primarily by children from impoverished homes, especially minority-group homes, cannot effectively educate those children.[10] Recent studies, however, have discovered many schools attended mainly by such children with achievement levels at or above national norms.[11] Ronald Edmonds concludes that all these schools exhibit traits that appear to be responsible for their effectiveness: strong leadership from the principal, high expectations of the students' performance, a disciplined, orderly atmosphere, emphasis upon improving reading, and constant assessment of student performance. He concludes

8. Much of this section closely parallels a similar section in Katharine L. Bradbury, Anthony Downs, and Kenneth A. Small, *Urban Decline and the Future of American Cities* (Brookings Institution, forthcoming).

9. See "Why Public Schools Fail" and "Bright Flight," *Newsweek*, April 20, 1981, pp. 62–65, 66–73.

10. This belief is based on the premise that educational achievement is rooted in the child's socioeconomic and parental background. See Christopher Jencks and others, *Inequality: A Reassessment of the Effect of Family and Schooling in America* (Basic Books, 1972); see also Gary Orfield, *Must We Bus? Segregated Schools and National Policy* (Brookings Institution, 1978), p. 69.

11. Ronald Edmonds, "A Discussion of the Literature and Issues Related to Effective Schooling" (Harvard University, Center for Urban Studies); Michael Rutter and others, *Fifteen Thousand Hours: Secondary Schools and Their Effects on Children* (Harvard University Press, 1979), pp. 180–205.

that "all children are eminently educable, and . . . the behavior of the school is critical in determining the quality of that education. . . . In and of itself, pupil family background neither causes nor precludes elementary school instructional effectiveness."[12] Whether such school performance can be repeated on a large scale within big-city school systems remains to be proven, but Edmonds's analysis indicates such systems have the *potential* of working well.

Federal and state governments have vital interests in this situation. States provide a major share of public elementary educational funding. The federal government furnishes public schools with funds for children from low-income households. Moreover, it pays welfare, unemployment compensation, and categorical-program costs that arise from the failure of public schools to prepare students for productive lives. The federal government has sponsored many programs to improve the performance of these schools. State governments have also increased their funding of big-city schools through transfers of revenues. None of these efforts has remedied the deficiencies of big-city school systems, yet improvement of the public schools is essential to the improvement of many urban neighborhoods.

The federal government and state governments must continue to explore new avenues. For example, states should permit public schools to suspend or expel disruptive students. No teacher can run an effective classroom without order, which is impossible if disorderly students—and especially violent students—cannot be put out and kept out. Properly drawn statutes—perhaps even exempting children who are repeatedly disruptive from compulsory school attendance—could correct the situation without jeopardizing the rights of young people.

Many private city schools provide better education at lower cost per pupil than public schools. Using public funds to provide at least some support to privately run schools would enable some students now attending public schools to switch to private ones. One way to do that is through tax credits or refunds to parents of children attending qualified private schools. Or local governments could give parents vouchers and let them decide which schools received their shares of public educational funds.[13] Any funding methods used for this purpose must be designed to

12. Edmonds, "Effective Schooling," pp. 28–29.
13. The use of vouchers is a complex subject involving many controversial issues. The exact structure of any voucher program crucially affects how well it would serve public and private education goals. Financing arrangements, regulations on such particulars as

keep private-school tuition at the public-funding level so affluent parents cannot create high-cost schools that poor students could not afford. Moreover, both tax credits and vouchers should be used only with strict minimum educational standards (including some guarantee of academic freedom) and prohibition of discrimination by race and income.

An argument against public support for private schools is that the most capable public school students will enroll in them and the least able students will not, leaving the latter in even worse educational surroundings than before. However, students in some big-city schools are already in such educationally terrible surroundings it is hard to imagine their being worse off. These schools are marked by robberies, assaults, drug dealing, disorderly classrooms, student absenteeism, and lack of teaching materials. Compelling able students, whether from poor or nonpoor families, to attend such schools unfairly penalizes both them and society in the hope of benefiting less able students. Yet that hope will remain in vain as long as such conditions prevail there. Certainly most big-city public schools are not in such awful condition; many provide excellent educations. But enough fit this description to call for drastic remedies.

However, bureaucracies—including big-city school systems—seldom reform themselves. Reform usually occurs only when outside pressure threatens the survival of the system or its leaders.[14] Therefore, unless pressured from outside the system, most big-city schools serving low-income areas will not adopt the characteristics of school effectiveness identified by Edmonds. If parents organized themselves effectively they might create such outside pressure. But many children in very poor neighborhoods come from single-parent households plagued with multiple problems, starting with poverty. It is unrealistic to expect the households in most such neighborhoods to effectively pressure their public schools to change, even though that happens occasionally.

However, federal and state officials, because they provide so much money to big-city public school systems, could threaten those systems seriously enough to compel them to change. The possibility that sizable parts of federal or state school funding might be available to private

---

attendance and curriculum, and the information furnished to parents, can vary tremendously, with quite different effects on both participating children and society in general. See Henry M. Levin, "Educational Vouchers and Social Policy," Program Report 79-B12 (Stanford University, Institute for Research on Educational Finance and Governance, July 1979).

14. For a detailed discussion of change in bureaucracies, see Anthony Downs, *Inside Bureaucracy*, a Rand Corporation Research Study (Little, Brown, 1967), especially chap. 16.

schools would be a dire threat, and a credible one, given the political support it would have. Even a small shift in funds of this type might create an atmosphere in which public schools would improve, perhaps eliminating the need for transferring large amounts of resources.

Besides giving impetus to an improved public school system, some public support of private schools would also strengthen the latter. These schools already play crucial roles in the upgrading of many urban neighborhoods, expanding the market for rehabilitated housing to households with school children. In New York City, Chicago, Washington, D.C., and many other cities, private schools form the nuclei for many revitalizing neighborhoods. Competition for entry into some big-city private schools is so keen that parents register their children at birth to ensure them a place. Other parents have established new private schools in their neighborhoods. In view of the role these schools are already playing in neighborhood revitalization, the use of some public funds to strengthen them and make them available to more children seems logical—as long as it is accompanied by regulations that prevent racial or economic segregation. At the very least, a significant number of demonstration projects involving such funding should be undertaken with careful evaluation of the results.

True, many thorny constitutional questions would be involved in such an effort. These and other controversial aspects of this proposal cannot be fully explored within the scope of this book. But the immense importance of improving the quality of schools serving big-city poverty neighborhoods justifies major efforts at changing the existing situation.

Additional Recommendations

Hundreds of other federal policies related to poverty affect urban neighborhoods. The following recommendations concern a few of them:

Including regional cost-of-living allowances in federal income transfer programs. No income transfer programs (except some housing subsidies) now include differential payments to compensate for regional variations in living costs. If such differentiation were adopted, average federal payments would rise in the Northeast and decline in the South. That might reduce current higher local tax burdens in the Northeast relative to those in the South, thereby decreasing the comparative advantage of the latter for high- and middle-income households who pay most local taxes.

Providing full federal funding of welfare. Such funding would raise transfer payments in the South, making them more nearly equal payments in the North and West. Since living costs are lower in the South, this might motivate some welfare households in the South to remain there, and some in the North and West to move to the South.

Making federal sewer and water facility funds usable for repairs of existing systems. Most such funds have been used for new systems, mainly in the suburbs, while existing facilities in many cities decayed through lack of maintenance. Making these funds applicable to repair of existing facilities would help big cities increase their residential attraction relative to their suburbs.

Providing some federal incentives for firms to locate in large cities. Tax credits for hiring unemployed workers and investment credits for locating in cities encourage businesses to remain or to locate there. Up to 1980, Congress had not adopted any such incentives strong enough to notably improve the economies of these cities. However, several proposals to create "enterprise zones" within poverty neighborhoods were being weighed by Congress and the administration in early 1981. Such incentives probably cannot halt the overall loss of jobs in cities that have suffered prolonged economic declines. But they might generate some added jobs for the most deprived residents of concentrated-poverty areas in those cities, if their incentives are targeted to that group.

Restricting or eliminating state and local revenue bonds to finance new business facilities. Tax exemptions for local and state industrial bonds should be eliminated except in communities with high unemployment rates or other signs of economic distress. Such bonds have in recent years subsidized construction of all types of new industrial and commercial properties, often in affluent suburbs competitive with older existing commercial districts in nearby cities. This amounts to deliberately encouraging further economic decline in large cities at the expense of federal taxpayers. Since Congress has been unwilling to place reasonable geographic limits on use of such subsidies, it should abolish them altogether.

11

Balancing Suburban Growth and Central City Revitalization

EARLIER chapters show that the rate of suburban growth in relation to changes in population within each metropolitan area has important effects upon its central city. In some situations, rapid suburban growth benefits the central city by relieving overcrowding. In others, such growth undermines the demand for existing housing in the central city, thereby discouraging revitalization. This chapter explores the need for policies that pursue an appropriate balance of both suburban growth and central city revitalization under different circumstances.

Effects of Suburban Growth upon Central Cities

When new housing units (net of removals) are being added to the suburbs faster than the net growth of households within the entire metropolitan area, many households are attracted to the suburbs out of older central city units. Under all circumstances, such *net dispersive* suburban housing growth benefits low-income households as a whole, most of whom are renters. It expands the overall supply of housing relative to demand, thereby reducing rents and prices compared to what they would otherwise be. If the central city is overcrowded or experiencing rapid in-migration of poor households, such growth also benefits most other central city residents by relieving congestion there.

But if the central city is not overcrowded, especially if it has already lost a lot of households, rapid suburban growth creates an overall housing surplus. Excess vacancies trickle down through chains of moves to neighborhoods in the poorest physical condition (stages 4 or 5 described

136

in chapter 5). The housing in these neighborhoods is old and somewhat obsolete in relation to consumer desires. Since most such neighborhoods are in central cities, this process undermines the market for housing there and reduces property values compared to what they would otherwise be. That injures property owners and harms central city taxpayers generally by reducing assessed values. If the city's population falls far enough, housing abandonment may appear and revitalization of older structures and neighborhoods will be discouraged. Many large U.S. cities have recently lost enough population so that continued net dispersive suburban growth is probably undesirable to most of their residents and their local governments. From 1970 to 1975, among the 121 largest central cities in the United States, 77 decreased in population, including 34 that decreased in both population and households.[1]

Most people in such cities would benefit from *net compressive* suburban growth. Then the demand for central city housing increases, because net additions to the suburban housing inventory are smaller than net additions to the number of households in the entire metropolitan area. But the home building industry has built enough new suburban units to cause net dispersive suburban growth nearly everywhere. True, during some years when housing credit was extremely tight, the number of new suburban units added in some metropolitan areas was smaller than the number of households added there. But over any three- or four-year period since the mid-1960s, net dispersive suburban growth has predominated in almost all metropolitan areas.

Table 11-1 shows the relation between changes in population and households and varying levels of net metropolitan-area housing construction. Those metropolitan areas that lost population from 1970 to 1975— even excluding New York City—gained over twice the number of new housing units as additional households. Those that gained population added only about a third more new housing units than new households. Central cities in the first group had major population losses, but most of those in the second group gained population. Informal observation of real estate markets shows that housing abandonment and neighborhood decline are also greater in the central cities of shrinking metropolitan areas than in those of growing ones. The total assessed value of residential property in such central cities often falls in real terms, perhaps even in current dollars. Moreover, cities that lose households typically lose

1. See Katharine L. Bradbury, Anthony Downs, and Kenneth A. Small, *Urban Decline and the Future of American Cities* (Brookings Institution, forthcoming).

Table 11-1. *Housing Construction and Changes in Population and Households, Twenty Metropolitan Areas, 1970–75*

Metropolitan area	Population change		Household change		New housing units	Ratio of new housing to new households	Percent of new housing in suburbs	Central city population change
	Number	Percent	Number	Percent				
Losing population								
New York	-412,627	-4.1	-58,215	-1.5	197,737	-3.397	32.8	-5.2
Cleveland	-97,004	-4.7	26,315	4.0	51,247	1.947	88.0	-14.9
Pittsburgh	-79,138	-3.3	28,478	3.8	48,305	1.696	91.0	-11.8
Newark	-58,443	-2.8	-978	-0.2	30,731	-31.422	91.5	-11.1
Los Angeles	-54,992	-0.8	109,511	4.5	208,874	1.907	63.1	-3.0
St. Louis	-44,342	-1.8	29,954	4.1	73,086	2.440	95.5	-15.6
Buffalo	-22,363	-1.7	9,562	2.3	34,704	3.629	93.8	-12.0
Seattle	-17,859	-1.3	42,985	9.1	44,554	1.037	81.7	-8.2
Philadelphia	-17,109	-0.4	44,500	3.0	144,828	3.255	85.9	-6.9
Paterson	-8,350	-1.8	4,900	1.1	16,882	3.445	86.4	-6.0
Total or average	-812,227	-2.3	237,012	3.0	850,948	3.590	81.0	-9.5
Gaining population								
Houston	286,931	14.4	130,477	21.4	121,028	0.928	23.9	8.3
Orange County	278,433	19.6	144,711	33.2	142,540	0.985	80.9	16.4
Phoenix	251,989	26.0	139,456	46.1	146,853	1.053	57.4	12.9
San Diego	226,729	16.7	115,400	27.3	145,111	1.257	58.9	11.0
Atlanta	194,611	12.2	76,700	17.9	163,950	2.138	89.3	-11.9
Denver	173,841	14.0	97,562	24.9	144,377	1.480	78.1	-5.9
Miami	171,689	13.5	81,800	19.1	155,383	1.900	84.0	9.0
Dallas	149,601	6.3	97,533	19.8	140,894	1.445	62.8	-2.6
Orlando	129,394	28.5	43,756	32.6	75,250	1.720	81.0	14.1
Washington	112,446	3.9	100,833	11.2	163,393	1.620	95.9	-6.0
Total or average	1,975,664	15.5	1,028,228	25.3	1,399,049	1.361	71.2	4.5

Sources: Based on Bureau of the Census, *Current Housing Reports*, series H-170-76, *Annual Housing Survey, 1976: United States and Regions*, "Housing Characteristics for Selected Metropolitan Areas" (Government Printing Office, 1976), table 1; ibid., series H-170-77 (GPO, 1977); and ibid., series H-170-78 (GPO, 1978); Bureau of the Census, *Construction Reports—Housing Authorized by Building Permits and Public Contracts, 1970–75* (GPO, 1971–76), table 3.

employment, too; so their real nonresidential tax bases often shrink. As a result, these cities have fewer resources for combating decay.

Stimulating Central City Revitalization by Limiting Suburban Growth

These relationships suggest that any policies affecting suburban growth may also affect central city revitalization. Thus, in theory, one way to revitalize central cities would be to put stringent limits on future growth in surrounding suburbs. Eleven specific forms that such growth limits might take are shown in table 11-2. The first eight are all now in use in at least one U.S. suburban community. If such limits cut net suburban housing construction below the net number of households being added to the metropolitan area, that might generate added demand for housing in older central city neighborhoods. True, there is some risk that such limits would deflect potential growth of the entire metropolitan area either to locations beyond the growth limits or to other metropolitan areas altogether.

Nevertheless, if such growth limits were feasible, they would probably increase central city growth at least somewhat. Projections for household growth in the Cleveland metropolitan area, for example, both with and without strong limits on suburban growth, show the following:[2]

Household changes, 1980–90

	City of Cleveland		Suburbs of Cleveland	
Simulation	*Number*	*Percent*	*Number*	*Percent*
Without suburban growth limits	−23,474	−10.9	50,091	10.4
With suburban growth limits	−13,443	−6.2	37,536	7.8
Result of limits	+10,031	+4.6	−12,555	−2.6

Thus, policies limiting suburban growth in the 1980s to three-fourths of what it would otherwise be probably would keep the city of Cleveland's household loss to 57 percent of what it otherwise would be.[3]

2. Katharine L. Bradbury, Anthony Downs, and Kenneth A. Small, *Futures for a Declining City: Simulations for the Cleveland Area* (Academic Press, forthcoming).

3. Limits on suburban growth are practiced in a few European cities. Stockholm, for example, bans suburban shopping centers except at rapid transit stops, on land owned by the city. City shopping centers prosper and downtown Stockholm remains vital. Many German cities similarly support their downtown commercial districts, and also create traffic-free pedestrian zones, subsidize downtown parking and public transit, and heavily tax

Table 11-2. *Possible Means of Limiting Suburban Residential Growth in Order to Stimulate Inner-City Housing Demand*

1. Limiting new sewer and water systems
2. Establishing yearly maximum permits for new housing units in the entire metropolitan area, with quotas for each part of the area
3. Enforcing very low-density zoning in most vacant, undeveloped land to reduce the number of new housing units potentially competitive with those in the central city
4. Using Environmental Protection Agency regulations for air and water pollution to prohibit or limit growth in environmentally fragile (and other) portions of the metropolitan area
5. Creating green belts (forest preserves or other open space) of vacant suburban land to keep it from being urbanized
6. Purchasing development rights to agricultural land to keep it agricultural
7. Purchasing scenic or other land outside the city with public funds and holding it as open space
8. Shifting the financing of new infrastructures (such as roads, streets, sewer and water systems, street lights, and schools) from general property taxes to building permit fees, development fees, and land contribution requirements charged against the new developments that would use these infrastructures
9. Creating a federal or state building permit tax charged against every new suburban housing unit within those metropolitan areas with significant central city housing surpluses
10. Requiring local governments, through state rules, to develop future land-use and urban development plans for all land within each of their metropolitan areas by using some areawide planning body given the power to execute such plans, at least for transportation facilities, sewer and water systems, and housing
11. Requiring every suburban housing or other developer to prepare and file detailed environmental and urban impact statements concerning the effects of any proposed project before it could be built

Sources: Joanna Hirst and Thomson Hirst, "Capital Facilities Planning As A Growth Control Tool and A Case Study of Metropolitan Washington, D.C.," and Malcolm D. Rivkin, "Sewer Moratoria As A Growth Control Technique," in Randall W. Scott, ed., *Management and Control of Growth: Issues, Techniques, Problems, Trends,* vol. 2 (Washington, D.C.: Urban Land Institute, 1975), pp. 461–72, 473–82; Marjorie W. Macris, "New Growth Management Underway in Marin County," John V. N. Klein, "Preserving Farmland on Long Island," and Donald V. H. Walker, "Boulder Preserves Open Space," in Frank Schnidman, Jane A. Silverman, and Rufus C. Young, Jr., *Management and Control of Growth: Techniques in Application,* vol. 4 (Washington, D.C.: Urban Land Institute, 1978), pp. 58–64, 144–46, 147–50.

The response of housing markets to limits on suburban housing construction can be seen to some extent by observing what happened when tight housing credit cut back such construction greatly in 1974 and 1975. New housing starts (excluding mobile homes) plummeted from 2.4 million in 1972 and 2.0 million in 1973 to 1.3 million in 1974 and 1.2

---

automobiles and gasoline. But in Paris and London many planned suburban communities have been built, encouraging jobs to move outside the cities. See *Successes Abroad: What Foreign Cities Can Teach American Cities,* Hearings before the Subcommittee on the City of the House Committee on Banking, Finance and Urban Affairs, 95 Cong. 1 sess. (Government Printing Office, 1977), pp. 2–11.

million in 1975.[4] This sharp slowdown in new suburban building was accompanied by a remarkable increase in spending on renovation and maintenance of older homes in all central cities.[5]

However, in practice, it is extremely difficult to limit new suburban housing construction throughout a metropolitan area as a deliberate means of stimulating central city revitalization. Intense opposition to such a strategy would arise from the home building industry, suburban realtors, suburban landowners, and even central city residents hoping to upgrade themselves in the future. In addition, governmental control over land use in most metropolitan areas is fragmented among many small jurisdictions. Hence imposing effective growth limits over an entire area is almost impossible. Moreover, in areas where many suburbs have limited growth, much growth moves farther out into unregulated territory, where land is inexpensive, rather than back into the central city, where land is costly.

Even so, housing demand in central cities is likely to be increased somewhat by any factors that slow suburban growth, such as higher gasoline and capital costs.

Achieving Fairer Distribution of the Social Costs of Suburban Growth

Because of the above relationships, the social costs associated with suburban growth are likely to be distributed in ways that unfairly benefit suburbanites and penalize central city residents. The typical departure of any household from the central city to a suburb causes a fall in actual or potential taxable resources in the central city. This is true even when the household is replaced by another, since those who move out usually have higher incomes than those who move in. If the household is not replaced, local government costs will not decline commensurately, since they include large fixed-cost elements. Thus, central city government cost per household rises with each loss of a household.

How could this situation be improved? In theory, a one-time nationwide

4. Council of Economic Advisers, *Economic Indicators: March 1980* (GPO, 1980), p. 19.

5. Franklin J. James, "The Revitalization of Older Urban Housing and Neighborhoods," in Arthur P. Solomon, ed., *The Prospective City: Economic, Population, Energy, and Environmental Developments Shaping Our Cities and Suburbs* (Massachusetts Institute of Technology Press, 1980), pp. 132–36.

sales tax could be placed upon every new housing unit built in the suburbs. Not only would it serve to slow suburban growth, but the revenue it raised would compensate central city governments and property owners for the weakening of their tax bases from loss of high-income households. Imposing such a tax at the time of construction would allow it to be part of the initial purchase cost, permit it to be spread over the lifetime of the mortgage, and reduce its burden on the first occupant. If a $1,000-a-unit tax had been applied nationwide in 1977, $750 million would have been raised even if suburban housing starts had dropped from about a million to three-quarters of a million.

However, in reality, such a tax would be complex and controversial. It should not apply, even in theory, to suburbs in areas where central city housing demand is growing. Furthermore, Congress and state legislatures are not likely to adopt such a tax. Suburbanites greatly outnumber central city residents, and would surely oppose it.

Nevertheless, the above analysis provides reasonable justification for certain other policies that would increase costs borne by those who move into new suburban housing—especially if they are coming from central cities that are losing many households. For example, from the viewpoint of pure equity, the capital costs of streets, sewer and water systems, parks, and other infrastructures in new suburban subdivisions should usually be paid for by residents of those subdivisions themselves. (However, where severe overcrowding exists in the central city, the costs should be borne by general property taxes so as to encourage out-migration to the suburbs.) Local governments could pay for the facilities initially, since bond interest rates are lower for tax-free public-sector financing than for taxed private-sector financing. But such bonds should be financed through special assessments on the subdivisions served. In addition, local governments could get developers to defray some costs by charging them substantial building permit fees and requiring them to build the necessary infrastructures and to provide land for parks and schools. Those costs would then be passed on to the purchasers of new homes.

Home builders and other housing advocates have opposed such cost shifts because they increase the prices of new suburban housing, making it less available to households with modest or even middle incomes. Yet precisely such price increases also shift some demand from new suburban housing to older housing in both the suburbs and central cities.

Other policies influencing suburban growth that should be changed to encourage central city revitalization involve "biases" favoring the former at the expense of the latter. Federal tax laws, for example, favor new construction over rehabilitation, expensive homes over less expensive ones, and home ownership over renting. In all these ways, they favor suburbs over central cities. The federal government should allow as rapid depreciation write-offs for housing rehabilitation as for new construction. Many proposals for fast depreciation write-offs on new investments to counteract inflation do not extend similar advantages to renovation of older properties. Enacting them without modification would therefore unwisely perpetuate existing biases against city revitalization.

The present deductibility of mortgage interest payments and local property taxes from federally taxable income should be replaced by an income tax credit. Every taxpayer would compute the credit by multiplying interest and property tax by a single percentage (perhaps the marginal tax rate paid by the average household). At present, tax advantages are proportionally greatest for home owners in high tax brackets and greater for those who make large interest and property tax payments. If the standard deduction were reduced for home owners and they were allowed to use it *along with* a tax credit, the relative tax advantage of owning a costly home would be the same as that of owning a less costly one. This would reduce the bias favoring investments in high-priced homes, which creates an incentive to live in the suburbs rather than in most city neighborhoods. It would also redistribute the tax advantages of home ownership from high-bracket households to low-bracket ones, thus increasing relative income flows into central cities. To make this change politically palatable, it could be phased in on a hold-harmless basis, which would require that home owners use the new method only when they move to different dwellings.

Tax-exempt municipal bonds for financing home mortgages should be limited to aiding low- and moderate-income households or residents of city neighborhoods where conventional mortgages are hard to obtain. Tax-exempt bonds that aid home buyers regardless of income and location are subsidies from the general taxpayer to home owners. Any policy subsidizing home ownership in general over rental creates incentives to locate in suburbs. In 1977, only 49 percent of all occupied housing units in central cities were owner-occupied, compared to 71 percent in the suburbs.[6]

State and federal governments once were active in aiding land assembly

---

6. Bureau of the Census, *Current Housing Reports*, series H-150-77, *Annual Housing Survey, 1977: United States and Regions*, pt. A, "General Housing Characteristics" (GPO, 1979), p. 1.

for urban renewal. Reactivation of these programs would help local governments make large parcels of land in older neighborhoods available for private development. At present, the easier availability of vacant land in suburban areas makes development costs there lower than in many older cities.

All laws prohibiting racial and ethnic discrimination in the sale or rental of housing should be much more vigorously enforced. Minority groups typically form larger percentages of the population of central cities than of the suburbs, and these residents generally have lower incomes than whites. Therefore, racial and ethnic discrimination by realtors and home owners tends to keep low-income households in older neighborhoods.[7] Moreover, it makes suburban communities more attractive than central cities to middle- and upper-income whites who prefer segregation.

Providing More Accessible Mortgage Financing for City Revitalization

Another key issue connecting suburban growth and central city revitalization involves the spatial allocation of mortgage funds by thrift institutions and other mortgage lenders. Some observers have blamed big-city neighborhood decline mainly on urban banks and savings and loan associations. They contend those institutions often refused to make loans in older neighborhoods, or made them only with adverse terms (redlining). These critics further accuse such institutions of "neighborhood disinvestment"; that is, taking more dollars out of older neighborhoods in savings than they put into those neighborhoods in mortgage loans.[8] The institutions typically invested those dollars in financing sales of new and existing housing in fast-growing suburban areas.

When conventional mortgages are unavailable in older areas, sales must be financed by mortgages with Federal Housing Administration (FHA) or Veterans Administration (VA) guarantees. These loans require

7. For evidence that such discrimination is still an important factor in housing markets, see Ronald E. Wienk and others, *Measuring Racial Discrimination in American Housing Markets: The Housing Market Practices Survey,* Department of Housing and Urban Development, Office of Policy Development and Research (GPO, 1979).

8. For an example of such criticism, see Karen Kollias and others, *Disclosure and Neighborhood Reinvestment: A Citizen's Guide* (Washington, D.C.: National Center for Urban Ethnic Affairs, October 1976).

lower down payments than most conventional loans and often have less stringent credit standards. Hence households with much lower incomes than those who would borrow in the conventional loan market can buy homes. Some of these newcomers do not have enough resources to maintain their properties or are first-time home owners unaccustomed to doing so. Thus, according to those who believe redlining is the major cause of neighborhood change, a shift from conventional to FHA and VA financing can change the character of residents, lower the level of housing maintenance, and start neighborhood decline.

But such behavior by financial institutions is not necessarily wrong or socially undesirable. The demand for mortgage loans in new-growth areas is normally much higher per household than in older neighborhoods, and savings and loan associations are supposed to help society meet such demands wherever they arise. Hence shifting savings from older areas to new ones is beneficial, unless there are biases in favor of new-growth areas and against older neighborhoods—more stringent credit standards in older areas, for example. In addition, low-down-payment FHA and VA loans have enabled thousands of moderate-income households—white and black—to attain home ownership. Most of these households subsequently maintained their homes in good condition.

Redlining can be put in proper perspective by distinguishing its use in different types of neighborhoods. Neighborhoods in stage 2, for example, have begun to decline (see chapter 5), but most housing is in good condition and most residents—existing and potential—are good mortgage credit risks. Withholding conventional mortgages from such areas, or imposing more stringent credit terms there than elsewhere, is undesirable and unnecessary, and could be called *irresponsible redlining*.

At the other extreme are neighborhoods in stages 4 and 5, where abandonment and vandalism are rampant. Property values are low and falling; many residents cannot afford to repay conventional mortgages or to pay high enough rents so landlords can repay them. Recently, financial institutions have been under social and legal pressure to make conventional loans in these areas if the particular properties and borrowers are sound. Some states have laws against lenders taking neighborhood condition into account in mortgage loans. Nevertheless, making long-term loans under such circumstances is probably unwise unless society assumes some of the risks. The area may decay further; buyers with reasonable incomes may not purchase these units when the present owners must move out. Financial discrimination in these conditions protects the depositors of the lending institutions, and could be called *responsible redlining*.

Between these two extremes are neighborhoods in stage 3, where decline is clearly under way. Many residents can afford to support "decent" property standards, but there is great uncertainty about the areas' futures. Redlining in these neighborhoods can contribute to decline, and should be prevented. But the goal is to reduce the uncertainty regarding these neighborhoods, not to force lending institutions to stop what for them is a rational and necessary exercise of their fiduciary responsibilities to depositors. Assuring such a neighborhood's vitality requires the cooperation of many local actors. If all lenders serving such an area agree to service normal loan demands meeting specific criteria, and all contribute to a single pool to service higher-risk loans, their collective behavior can eliminate the undue risk that each would face if it acted that way alone. Such cooperation is the essential ingredient in the remarkable success of the neighborhood housing services program.[9] This coordinated approach by local financial institutions, the local government, and community organizations can eliminate redlining in these neighborhoods by "managing the market" so as to minimize joint risk.

Balancing Neighborhood Revitalization and Displacement

Within cities, encouragement of neighborhood revitalization must be balanced with sensitivity to the resulting displacement of households. Gentrification inevitably displaces some poor original residents, and even incumbent upgrading often does so. Displaced persons with three characteristics usually endure the greatest hardships: they are poor, they would not have moved except for rising occupancy costs caused by revitalization, and they have lived in the area for several years. They often suffer intangible costs, like the loss of established social networks. And they may have difficulty finding accommodations elsewhere comparable in price, quality, and convenience to those they leave. Some form of public policy intervention is often warranted to protect their interests, since normal market processes may fail to do so.

Some urban analysts argue that all households have an inherent right to continue occupying their current housing units, regardless of their ability to pay. This right is supposedly implied by Congress's repeated

9. For a description of the program see Roger S. Ahlbrandt, Jr., and Paul C. Brophy, *Neighborhood Revitalization: Theory and Practice* (Lexington Books, 1975), chap. 9.

declaration of the goal of "a decent home and a suitable living environment for every American family."[10] However, who will bear the costs of making this "right" available to everyone? American society has recognized that government should ensure some rights for everyone—such as the right to a fair trial, the right to an elementary education, and perhaps the right to minimum health care. But I do not believe society has accepted everyone's right to live in whatever home or neighborhood he or she chooses, regardless of ability to pay. Therefore, when occupancy costs in an area rise because of revitalization, not all the initial residents should expect to remain living there. Nevertheless, it is reasonable to consider the interests of households with the three traits mentioned above in all policies concerning neighborhood revitalization.

This means all such policies must be designed to pursue simultaneously both the revitalization of neighborhoods and the protection of initial residents. The specific goals of revitalization are upgrading deteriorating neighborhoods, providing every household with a decent housing unit in a suitable neighborhood environment, raising the average income level of central city residents by increasing incomes of existing residents and by attracting affluent households to the city, and achieving a mixture of income groups in revitalized neighborhoods. These goals should be sought within the constraints of protecting poor initial residents from undue displacement costs, preserving the rights of private property owners, and conserving public fiscal resources. This balanced approach recognizes that displacement and revitalization are inseparable; so policies concerning both must be formulated together. This is true even though most involuntary displacement of poor households in big cities is caused by demolition and abandonment of older structures, not by revitalization.[11]

Relative priorities awarded to the above goals and constraints should

10. This goal was first stated in the Housing Act of 1949 (63 Stat. 413). See House Committee on Banking, Currency and Housing, *Basic Laws and Authorities on Housing and Community Development, Revised Through July 31, 1975*, Committee print, 94 Cong. 1 sess. (GPO, 1975), p. 1. For a defense of this "right," see Chester W. Hartman, *Housing and Social Policy* (Prentice-Hall, 1975), Introduction and pp. 76–84.

11. See Howard J. Sumka, "Neighborhood Revitalization and Displacement: A Review of the Evidence," and Sumka, "The Ideology of Urban Analysis: A Response to Hartman," in *Journal of the American Planning Association*, vol. 45 (October 1979), pp. 480–87 and 491–94. Chester W. Hartman presents a different view in "Comment on Neighborhood Revitalization and Displacement: A Review of the Evidence," ibid., pp. 488–91. The conclusion that displacement caused by revitalization is a small part of total displacement is also reached by George and Eunice Grier, "Urban Displacement: A Reconnaissance," Memo Report prepared for the Department of Housing and Urban Development, Office of the Secretary, revised March 1978.

vary, depending upon local circumstances. The key factor should be the balance of supply and demand in the surrounding housing market.

In relatively loose housing markets with low in-migration of poor households, suitable accommodations can presumably be found nearby for poor displaced households. Hence both gentrification and incumbent upgrading should be encouraged by making mortgage financing and home insurance readily available. Public subsidies are often needed for incumbent upgrading to supplement the housing purchasing power of low-income households. Under such circumstances, local governments should not try to prevent all displacement in deteriorated neighborhoods whose residents have very low incomes. Neighborhoods that cannot be revitalized through purely incumbent upgrading will require some gentrification.[12]

Under these conditions, it is appropriate to provide moving-cost compensation to those low-income displaced households described earlier. Where the incoming households are likely to reap large capital gains from either upgrading single-family units or condominium conversion, they can justifiably be compelled to pay moving costs directly to those they displace. Where displacement is caused by public-sector actions, the local government should furnish such compensation.

In very tight housing markets it may be difficult to find convenient alternative accommodations that displaced low-income households can afford. If market forces are allowed to operate, households with higher incomes will outbid those with lower incomes for substandard units and then convert them to standard units. Many displaced residents will be forced to occupy even lower-quality housing or to live more crowded together unless they receive public subsidies. If such subsidies are big enough to raise their purchasing power to that of the potential newcomers, they can upgrade their initial housing units and remain in the area. More likely, any subsidies will enable them merely to move to housing elsewhere similar in quality to their initial units. In the absence of subsidies, their housing quality will be lowered. The only long-range

12. Gentrification raises the central city's average income level above what it otherwise would have been, even though many of the newcomers to revitalized neighborhoods have lower incomes than those who move to the suburbs. See Joseph C. Hu, "Who's Moving In and Who's Moving Out—and Why," *Federal National Mortgage Association, Seller/ Servicer*, vol. 5 (May-June 1978), p. 21; and John D. Hutcheson, Jr., and Elizabeth T. Beer, "In-migration and Atlanta's Neighborhoods," *Atlanta Economic Review*, vol. 28 (March-April 1978), pp. 8–9.

solution that does not require subsidies is expansion of the total supply of decent housing in the area. But that is clearly beyond the powers of any one neighborhood or local government.

Thus, if the local government does not have sufficient public subsidy funds to enable the existing low-income residents of a revitalizing area to occupy decent housing, it must choose between two courses of action, both undesirable. One is allowing gentrification to proceed. This aids the city government and upgrades the neighborhood but imposes heavy costs upon many poor displaced households. It may be unpopular politically, even if the government requires payment of moving-cost compensation to displaced households.

The second course is trying to prevent revitalization. This can be done by refusing to issue building permits for rehabilitation or charging exorbitant fees for them, encouraging tenants to resist eviction, adopting rent controls, restricting condominium conversions, and otherwise exerting a heavy regulatory hand in residential property markets.

This policy is really *slum preservation*, though local officials would never admit that conclusion. Yet, by neither allowing gentrification nor subsidizing incumbent upgrading, they in fact support maintaining substandard neighborhoods in their present condition. This policy is more common than most people realize, for it is usually obscured by rhetoric about protecting the housing choices of the poor and the need for more federal housing subsidies. Local officials rationalize their opposition to present upgrading of substandard neighborhoods through gentrification by "demanding" infusion of enough added federal subsidies to permit incumbent upgrading. Such infusions would allow neighborhood revitalization without much displacement of poor residents. But the federal government has never provided enough housing subsidies to meet all needs for them, nor will it do so in the foreseeable future. In fact, the likelihood of such subsidies has recently fallen sharply because of pressure on all levels of government to cut spending.

Therefore, completely opposing gentrification until enough federal subsidies are available to avoid all involuntary displacement amounts to indefinitely postponing most revitalization. In effect, such a policy blocks the single most powerful housing upgrading force now operating within central cities. Consequently, prolonged opposition to all gentrification is a short-sighted policy in relation to the long-range fiscal, physical, and social needs of central cities.

Encouraging Suburban Growth to Reduce Housing Prices

An entirely different type of balance between suburban growth and central city revitalization needs to be attained in metropolitan areas without any surpluses of central city housing. If there is a housing shortage within the central city and not much vacant land there, rapid suburban growth should be encouraged rather than limited. If housing supply and demand within the central city are rather well balanced, it is still in the interest of society to encourage suburban development that will produce at least some relatively low-priced new housing. That will enable more households to attain home ownership and increase the overall supply of units available to low- and moderate-income households.

The higher the prices that suburban developers must pay for land, the higher the long-run cost of creating additional housing. Except in periods of exceptionally strong housing demand or limited housing supply, lower land prices to developers ultimately express themselves as lower housing purchase costs. Therefore, it is socially desirable to keep the price of land available for urbanization as low as feasible, other things equal.

One way to do this is by maintaining an inventory of vacant land ready for development several times as large as the amount the market is likely to absorb in the very near future. In fact, only if some such excess supply exists will there be enough competition among landowners to reasonably restrain the prices they charge developers. This large inventory must be supplied with utilities and infrastructures and be appropriately zoned.

However, suburban governments, owners of existing suburban homes, and owners of vacant land ready for development all benefit from restricting the inventory of developable land. Suburban governments usually have to pay for the public infrastructure on vacant land in advance of development. Hence the larger the inventory of land ready for development but not yet urbanized, the more front money they must supply. This money is usually raised from taxes on existing residents. Moreover, tighter supplies of developable land raise housing prices (a benefit to owners) and raise the assessed values of existing housing (a benefit to local governments). The owners of developable vacant land also want the highest possible prices.

It is unfair for the residents of individual suburbs to bear the costs of providing public infrastructure for large amounts of vacant land so as to hold down the long-run cost of new housing for society as a whole. In the past, the federal government has paid some of these costs through water and sewer grants to suburban governments. If these programs are curtailed, state governments ought to help local governments provide these infrastructures in advance of immediate need.

Some states have adopted urban growth-control laws that require local governments to designate certain areas as suitable for future growth and others as unsuitable. Advocates of these laws are trying to protect environmentally sensitive land (such as marshes and river fronts) or keep croplands in agricultural use. But they have not paid much attention to the impacts of such laws on the trade-off between suburban growth and central city revitalization or upon prices of urban land and housing.[13] The more such laws reduce the excess supply of developable land, the higher they drive land and housing prices. However, no one knows precisely how large such a surplus needs to be in relation to current absorption rates in order to help restrain price increases.

Conclusion

The preceding discussion illustrates the difficulty of designing uniform urban growth policies for the entire nation, or even for an entire state. Programs aimed at helping fast-growth areas would have to exclude slow-growth areas in order to avoid aggravating central city housing abandonment. Regulations aimed at restricting suburban growth to bolster central city housing demand would have to exclude fast-growth areas to avoid aggravating housing shortages there. But it is difficult to get political support for policies that so precisely target funds or regulations. This is especially hard when the programs involve large amounts of money. Legislative representatives from areas that would not qualify for targeted funds are often willing to support such programs only if they are part of some larger program which provides them with other benefits offsetting the unequal effect of targeted spending.

Therefore, policies at all levels of government affecting the trade-off between suburban growth and central city revitalization should be designed so they can be adapted to conditions prevailing within each

13. For a discussion of state land-use policies, see Edward C. Rochette, "Statewide Land Use Control: The Oregon Experience," *Zoning and Planning Law Report*, vol. 2 (April 1979), pp. 129–35. Also see the Department of Housing and Urban Development, *The President's 1978 National Urban Policy Report* (GPO, 1978), pp. 35–36.

metropolitan area. Since there are few effective governments at the metropolitan-area level, many of these policies may have to be applied by federal and state officials. They need to be acutely aware of the basic trade-off described in this chapter and its varying implications within each metropolitan area across the nation.

12

Physically Improving Central City Residential Neighborhoods

THE PHYSICAL condition of a city's residential neighborhoods, which contain much of its territory and most of its population, has an important bearing on the overall health of the city. The key elements involved in improving that physical condition include coping with deteriorated housing, providing certain services (such as fire protection, housing code enforcement, assessment, and trash collection), investing in certain public improvements (such as streets, street lighting, parking lots, and some public buildings), managing traffic flows, and maintaining certain amenities (such as parks and open space). These elements reflect relatively broad conceptions of *physical condition* and *residential neighborhoods*. The conceptions are necessarily arbitrary. This chapter explores the possibility of a city government's approaching all these elements through a single, relatively coherent overall strategy. That is an optimistic goal, but the analysis herein can help local officials achieve it to varying degrees, depending upon local circumstances.

Available Resources

The appropriate overall strategy for improving these elements—especially housing—depends upon the total resources a city has compared to the total required for completely renovating the entire city within some reasonable time, say two decades. Although the overall strategy discussed here must be formulated by the city government, it involves resources from both the private and public sectors. Hence it should

153

probably be developed through cooperative planning by key people in both sectors.

Private resources include capital for investment in building new structures and upgrading and maintaining existing ones, plus household incomes out of which occupancy costs can be paid. There must be enough such resources available to bring the privately owned parts of the city into good physical condition within the required time period. Moreover, these resources must be owned by the households who have plausible incentives for spending them on creating, maintaining, or occupying the city's private structures in accordance with normal behavior patterns. There may be a few wealthy households in a severely deteriorated city whose resources could upgrade it to the required degree if they spent them all for that purpose. However, it is unreasonable to expect such behavior on their part. If the necessary resources are distributed so that normal investment and spending behavior by the citizenry will improve and maintain the privately owned portions of city to the required degree, then it has "adequate" private resources, as discussed further below. The larger the concentrations of very low-income households within a city, the lower the probability that this "adequate" condition will exist.

Public resources are city government funds necessary to maintain the publicly owned structures within the city, provide adequate minimum levels of normal public services to all citizens, and furnish some subsidies to help low-income households pay their housing occupancy costs. If the city government is fiscally strapped, it may be unable to meet this definition of adequate public resources.[1]

The standard of urban resource "adequacy" defined above may seem impossibly high—what city could meet it? However, it is met every day by thousands of suburban communities, and even by some central cities. In fact, in 1977, 81 percent of all owner occupants in central cities and 64 percent of all renters rated their neighborhoods as "excellent" or

---

1. For example, Cleveland's "city-owned water system, which serves most of the metropolitan area, needs $250 to $500 million in replacements and renovation. One treatment plant is in hazardous condition, and clogged and corroded pipes have reduced the system's capacity to deliver water at acceptable pressures. The condition of 30 percent of the city-owned bridges has been rated as unsatisfactory or intolerable, and in need of more than $150 million in major repairs. The city's sewer collection system is plagued with frequent overflows and basement floodings; an estimated $340 million would be needed to alleviate floodings alone." Nancy Humphrey, George E. Peterson, and Peter Wilson, *The Future of Cleveland's Capital Plant* (Washington, D.C.: Urban Institute, 1979), p. xv.

"good."[2] However, only 24 percent of central city owner occupants and 19 percent of renters thought their neighborhoods had no bothersome characteristics (analogous percentages were only slightly higher in suburbs). So considerable improvement would be required to bring all neighborhoods up to acceptable minimum standards, even over twenty years.

Cities can be roughly classified into three groups concerning the amount of these resources they have available: *adequate, somewhat inadequate*, and *grossly inadequate*. These categories are very crude and imprecise; yet in practice, it is likely to be fairly clear into which category any given city falls. Cities with large overall housing surpluses are likely to be in the third group, or perhaps the second, but almost never the first.

Cities with grossly inadequate resources cannot carry out certain strategies possible for those with adequate resources, and perhaps for a few with somewhat inadequate resources. In particular, the meeting-all-needs strategy (explained later) is never possible for cities with grossly inadequate resources. It is rarely possible for cities with somewhat inadequate resources. Yet this strategy is often rhetorically advocated by city leaders unwilling to confront the hard decisions inherent in having too few resources to renovate the entire city. This issue is discussed further below.

Classification of cities by the amount of resources available can be achieved through a very rough measurement of those resources. Even crude estimates are sufficient for purposes of this analysis. Consequently, there is no point in trying to define precisely either the amount required to fully renovate each city within twenty years or the exact amount actually available.

Strategies for Spatially Allocating Resources

Every city's public officials and other leaders have some influence over where certain public and private resources will be used. These resources include local tax funds, some intergovernmental aid flows, and

2. Bureau of the Census, *Current Housing Reports*, series H-150-77, *Annual Housing Survey, 1977: United States and Regions*, pt. B, "Indicators of Housing and Neighborhood Quality" (Government Printing Office, 1979), pp. 15–17.

some private investment. They also include certain normal city government services that can be moved about the city, such as police traffic patrols. The way these discretionary resources are allocated spatially is a key element in a city's neighborhood strategy. There are infinite ways they could be spread across a city. Narrowing them to a small set of clearly defined strategies requires drastic oversimplification, but is helpful in illustrating the possibilities.

All strategies involve spending some discretionary resources in almost every neighborhood, in addition to basic services. Under the "law of political dispersion," every elected official tries to provide some benefits to all parts of his or her constituency. Yet a small amount of a city's resources can be spread in a highly visible manner in every neighborhood, while most of its discretionary resources are spent in certain areas.

Each of the following eight strategies could effectively serve several different goals. However, each implies its own relative priorities. For example, strategy 1 clearly puts the highest priority on directly serving the city's lowest-income citizens. Strategy 3 puts the highest priority on encouraging active neighborhood organizations, regardless of what income groups they represent.

1. *Focusing on intense needs*. Most discretionary resources are concentrated where deterioration and social disorganization are greatest. This includes stage 4 or stage 5 neighborhoods in cities with large housing surpluses. If the city has grossly inadequate resources, all deteriorated neighborhoods cannot be fully renovated and any resources be left for other purposes. In fact, those neighborhoods probably cannot be fully renovated even if all discretionary resources are spent there. Cities with adequate resources are not in this bind; cities with somewhat inadequate resources may or may not be.

2. *Focusing on preservation*. Most discretionary resources are concentrated in neighborhoods where decay is marginal and the housing market is still strong. Resources expended in these neighborhoods have a much better chance of achieving full renovation than those expended in highly deteriorated areas. Money spent in the former produces more direct positive effects and attracts more private investment per public sector dollar. Hence this strategy is far more efficient than the preceding one in terms of physical results obtained per dollar spent. However, it gives less aid to people in the greatest need.

3. *Responding to local initiative*. This approach focuses discretionary resources upon those neighborhoods that establish a strong local orga-

nization, identify specific needs, and start their own actions. Baltimore has used this approach to some extent in allocating resources to neighborhood organizations. It rewards initiative and gives resources to those most likely to use them effectively. But this strategy may favor middle-income neighborhoods over really poor ones, since the former are usually better self-organizers.

4. *Focusing equally everywhere*. Most discretionary resources are allocated in proportion to neighborhood population or some other measure independent of condition. An example is dividing resources equally among city districts, even though they vary widely in needs for renovation. This strategy assumes that no truly fair way to measure different neighborhood needs can be devised; so resources should be divided in proportion to population. Few cities follow this procedure unless their neighborhoods are all in about the same condition.

5. *Focusing on opportunity*. Most discretionary resources are allocated to specific projects that will improve the city's economic base, or upgrade some part of it, regardless of where they are located. This approach makes sense in a city with grossly inadequate resources. It could not successfully upgrade all of either its worst or marginal areas even if it focused all its discretionary resources in either type. Rather than spending them there for few long-term benefits, the city could concentrate them on whatever positive opportunities for improvement appeared anywhere. Those opportunities would be selected by likely project effectiveness in creating jobs or physical upgrading. For example, Detroit's downtown Renaissance Center represented a unique opportunity, even though it did not directly upgrade any deteriorated residential neighborhoods.

6. *Meeting all needs*. If a city has enough discretionary resources to fully renovate all its neighborhoods within a reasonable period, it does not have to make difficult allocation decisions that necessarily disappoint some areas. This strategy is possible only in those cities with adequate resources. However, it is often advocated rhetorically in cities that cannot actually achieve it, since its proponents can avoid explicitly identifying the areas where they will not meet pressing needs.

7. *Combining focusing on opportunity and one other strategy*. A certain fraction of funds is set aside for especially promising project opportunities, regardless of their location, before discretionary funds are allocated by some other strategy.

8. *Focusing on both intense needs and preservation*. Job creation, social services, and income supplements are focused where the lowest-

income households live, whereas physical upgrading resources are concentrated where deterioration is not yet advanced. This mixture provides residents of very deteriorated areas with what they need most—better jobs, more income, and more social services. Yet infrastructure improvements, rehabilitation loan funds, and improved access to mortgage funds are placed where they will have the greatest long-run impact. This strategy avoids the undesirable extremes of ignoring the neediest neighborhoods or of pouring all available resources into them without any lasting effects. Also, it attracts private resources into the revitalizing neighborhoods.

The following table shows the strategies appropriate to the three levels of central city resources:

Adequate resources

Strategy 2—Focusing on preservation
Strategy 4—Focusing equally everywhere
Strategy 6—Meeting all needs

Somewhat inadequate resources

Strategy 1—Focusing on intense needs
Strategy 2—Focusing on preservation
Strategy 3—Responding to local initiative
Strategy 5—Focusing on opportunity
Strategy 7—Partially focusing on opportunity

Grossly inadequate resources

Strategy 1—Focusing on intense needs
Strategy 2—Focusing on preservation
Strategy 3—Responding to local initiative
Strategy 5—Focusing on opportunity
Strategy 7—Partially focusing on opportunity
Strategy 8—Focusing on both intense needs and preservation

Sometimes a city's leaders resort to a *rhetorical revival strategy*. They deny there has been or will be any drop in housing demand or any neighborhood deterioration, or they admit these things have begun but assert that "attracting more middle-class households back into the city" will counteract them. In large cities experiencing major population declines, this strategy is wishful thinking that prevents city officials from responding effectively to decline-related problems. But in cities with no severe deterioration, where the number of households is still rising, this strategy can be appropriate, since it avoids negative self-fulfilling prophecies. Official optimism in uncertain conditions encourages positive expectations, which in turn encourage positive actions. But ignoring real needs until deterioration becomes widespread does no service to a city's residents.

Treatment by Neighborhood

Another dimension of each city's neighborhood physical-condition strategy consists of the way it treats individual neighborhoods, or groups of neighborhoods with similar characteristics. Eight prototype treatments have been identified from actual experience.

1. *Normal upkeep*. This applies to neighborhoods in excellent condition; it is designed to keep them that way. It involves maintaining normal public services and vigorous housing code enforcement but little additional public investment.

2. *Low-intensity preservation*. This is designed for neighborhoods in good condition that show a few signs of decay, or for neighborhoods in moderate condition where an indication of government concern will encourage private investment to restore them to good condition. For example, the streets in some southern and western cities were originally built without curbs or gutters. Installation of these improvements may convince residents they can improve their properties and fully recapture their investments at time of sale. Low-intensity preservation involves small investments of public funds per household and no special mortgage financing or subsidies.

3. *High-intensity preservation*. This is appropriate for neighborhoods experiencing significant decline but still in basically sound condition. However, the market has begun to lose confidence in their future—mortgage credit is difficult to obtain, and owners hesitate to make major improvements. The goal is to stabilize property values by preserving the sound housing stock, mainly through incumbent upgrading. Major efforts are needed to restore full access to mortgage credit, to help nonqualifying property owners get rehabilitation loans, and to improve public infra-structures. A cooperative venture uniting the city government, local real estate financial institutions, and local property owners is an effective approach.

4. *Revival*. This differs from preservation because its goal is upgrading through gentrification. Incoming households buy and renovate older homes, which improves the neighborhood physically but raises housing

prices and rents. This may displace many initial, lower-income residents. Revival usually occurs through private efforts with relatively little local government intervention. If society wishes to preserve a socioeconomic mixture in reviving areas, it must subsidize some low-income residents so they can remain in spite of higher occupancy costs. That is quite expensive.

5. *Stabilization.* This aims at stopping further decline where major deterioration and demolition have already taken place. Most deteriorated structures may already have been removed. As a result, the area may contain far more vacant land than where preservation is appropriate. Code enforcement in stabilization areas should be closely linked with provision of counseling and financial assistance. Its goals should be removal of irremediable buildings and upgrading of all those that can be saved, rather than punishment for violations. Such selective code enforcement should tolerate minor violations that do not endanger occupants.

6. *Emptying out.* This seeks to help those residents left in a heavily abandoned neighborhood move somewhere else; then the area can be completely cleared for eventual recycling. It deemphasizes rehabilitation or other investment, stresses relocation assistance and further demolition, but also maintains adequate levels of basic city services for the remaining residents. Such treatment may be advisable even when there are no immediate uses for the cleared land. Such uses will emerge at some future time, when the city will benefit from having vacant land available.

7. *Redevelopment.* This consists of building entirely new structures on land cleared of its former uses. Some demolition may be required to remove a few remaining structures.

8. *Inaction.* This is doing as little as possible, even reducing normal public services. It is not recommended but has been included because some cities strapped for resources may resort to it in very deteriorated areas (though they rarely admit to doing so).

The following table shows the treatments appropriate to the five stages of neighborhood decline (defined in chapter 5):

Stage 1: Stable and viable
Treatment 1—Normal upkeep

Stage 2: Minor decline
Treatment 2—Low-intensity preservation
Treatment 3—High-intensity preservation
Treatment 4—Revival

Stage 3: Clear decline
Treatment 3—High-intensity preservation
Treatment 4—Revival
Treatment 5—Stabilization

Stage 4: Heavily deteriorated
Treatment 4—Revival (occasionally appropriate)
Treatment 5—Stabilization
Treatment 6—Emptying out

Stage 5: Unhealthy and nonviable
Treatment 6—Emptying out
Treatment 7—Redevelopment

The levels of resources required for each treatment are described in table 12-1. These descriptions are approximate; other ingredients not shown in the table may also be involved. Dozens of programs for preserving neighborhoods have been developed by local governments and private interests; only a few are shown in the table. Moreover, the amount of each resource indicated for each treatment may vary from city to city and from neighborhood to neighborhood. For example, the revival treatment indicates a use of major relocation aid. This assumes that many initial residents cannot afford to remain. However, if the initial residents are home owners, they will profit from rising values if they sell and will not need any relocation aid. Elderly owners with low incomes may be compelled to sell because they cannot pay the increased property taxes resulting from higher assessed values, but most evidence indicates this type of displacement is rare.[3]

Neighborhood treatment includes coping with commercial blight. Deterioration of a nearby shopping district and industrial decay in mixed-use neighborhoods can precipitate housing blight. There are several ways to deal with deteriorating commercial property: (a) reduce the commercial space in a shopping district as the incomes of surrounding residents decline and move the surviving stores from the strips between intersections to clusters of sites near the intersections; (b) convert vacant stores

3. Ann B. Schnare, *Household Mobility in Urban Homesteading Neighborhoods: Implications for Displacement*, prepared for the Department of Housing and Urban Development, Office of Policy Development and Research (GPO, 1979). She states that "it seems reasonably safe to conclude that owner-occupants in homesteading neighborhoods have not become the victims of displacement. . . . The households most susceptible to displacement—the elderly and the poor—tended to be the least likely to move" (p. ii). See also Department of Housing and Urban Development, *Final Report on Housing Displacement* (GPO, 1979).

Table 12-1. *Level of Resources Required for Eight Types of Neighborhood Treatment*

Resource[a]	Normal upkeep (1)	Low-intensity preservation (2)	High-intensity preservation (3)	Revival (4)	Stabilization (5)	Emptying out (6)	Redevelopment (7)	Inaction (8)
Public services								
Job creation	none	none	moderate	none	major	none	none	none
Social services	minor	minor	major	moderate	major	moderate	moderate	none
Protective services and trash removal	moderate	moderate	major	major	moderate	moderate	moderate	minor
Education	moderate	moderate	moderate	moderate	moderate	moderate	moderate	moderate
Private investment								
Housing rehabilitation	minor	major	major	major	major	minor	none	none
Housing construction	minor	minor	minor	minor	none	none	major	none
Conventional-mortgage pooling	none	none	major	minor	moderate	none	none	none
High-risk mortgage pooling	none	none	major	minor	major	none	none	none
Conventional mortgages	major	major	major	major	moderate	none	major	moderate
Energy-saving home improvements	minor	minor	major	major	major	none	major	none
Public investment								
Demolition	none	none	minor	minor	major	major	none	minor
Housing code enforcement	major	major	major[b]	moderate[b]	major[b]	major	major	minor
Vacant land maintenance	none	none	minor	none	major	minor	major	none
Infrastructure improvement	moderate	major	major	minor	moderate	none	major	none
Resident relocation	none	none	none	major	none	major	minor	none
Financial subsidies								
Tax abatement for rehabilitation	minor	major	major	major	major	none	none	none
Tax abatement for new construction	none	none	none	none	none	none	major	none
Low-interest rehabilitation loans	none	minor	major	minor	major	none	none	none
Financial counseling	none	minor	major	major	major	major	minor	none
Low-income rental assistance	none	none	moderate	major	major	major	major	none
Tax write-off for rehabilitation	none	none	major	major	minor	none	none	none
Total resources	minor	minor	major	minor	moderate	minor	major	minor

a. The measures of resources are none, minor, moderate (or normal), and major.
b. Enforcement should be selective.

to residences, storage, light manufacturing, or crafts; (c) demolish vacant stores and use the sites for parking or recreation; and (d) transform industrial and commercial buildings and sites into artists' studios (such as Alexandria, Virginia's, Torpedo Factory) or into galleries of boutiques and restaurants (such as San Francisco's Ghirardelli Square and Cannery, Boston's Faneuil Hall, and Chicago's Old Town and New Town areas).

Coping with Housing Deterioration

A key element in any city's strategy for physically improving its residential areas involves how it copes with deteriorated housing. Whether highly deteriorated housing should be demolished or eventually rehabilitated depends partly on its construction. Brick housing can often be salvaged and successfully marketed, especially if it originally had large rooms, fireplaces, or other architecturally desirable traits. Old frame housing is harder to rehabilitate. It often decays drastically if left vacant over a severe winter. Hence neighborhoods where most housing was originally brick have better rehabilitation prospects than those where it was frame.

Deteriorated housing in any city with an overall housing surplus probably will not be rehabilitated spontaneously. If the city's housing supply is reduced, remaining housing will be in greater demand and more likely to be upgraded. There are three ways to remove some of a city's deteriorated housing. *Concentrated demolition* is the removal of all abandoned and highly deteriorated housing from each stage 4 and stage 5 neighborhood. It should be part of the stabilization, emptying out, and redevelopment treatments. *Spread-out thinning* is the removal of some substandard housing from many neighborhoods but does not clear any one neighborhood. In Akron, many neighborhoods of single-family homes had dwellings in converted garages along the alleys. By demolishing these, Akron reduced its housing surplus, increased its open space, and avoided creating excessive vacancy in any one neighborhood. This tactic works best where housing demand will sustain housing values and market activity throughout the city, and where housing suitable for removal is easily identified. Then households in standard housing are not fearful of having their homes demolished or of being left stranded in semidemolished neighborhoods. *Spot clearance* is the removal of only those buildings in the worst condition, wherever they are located.

Housing Code Enforcement

Enforcement of a city's housing code is a crucial element in its housing strategy. Every local housing code specifies minimum conditions required for health and safety in all dwelling units. How should the city government enforce such ordinances in its many diverse neighborhoods? In nearly all cities, two basic approaches are applicable: *selective or differential enforcement* by neighborhood, and *building positive expectations* among property owners through various programs founded on code enforcement.

Legally, the housing code is supposed to be enforced vigorously and equally in all neighborhoods, compelling immediate removal of all deficiencies. But few cities have the resources to inspect their housing often, or even to investigate all complaints. Furthermore, compelling compliance through court action is complex and time consuming, especially since local judges often favor property owners, even habitual code violators. Besides, the primary purpose of housing code enforcement should be maximum maintenance and upgrading of the city's housing inventory, not punishment of violators.

Therefore, selective enforcement makes sense for most cities. That is, housing codes should be enforced to different degrees in different neighborhoods, or under different circumstances—not uniformly enforced everywhere. The basic law should ensure that conditions which endanger life are alleviated promptly in all neighborhoods, and it should be applied uniformly without corruption. But its administrators should recognize that old housing cannot be economically maintained in the same condition as new housing, and that housing in low-income neighborhoods cannot be kept to the standards of housing in high-income neighborhoods. Neither would the minimum standards appropriate for neighborhoods in the poorest condition work for those in the best condition, because residents of the latter demand very high minimum standards.[4]

Ideally, the code enforcement program should assist property owners in maintaining or upgrading their housing. To this end, it should provide information on loans and advice on renovation and maintenance. Inspectors should be trained to provide some rehabilitation counseling to

4. Ironically, the conversion of old loft buildings into luxurious apartments in the Soho district of Manhattan highlights the need for differential housing codes. Pressured by the affluent owners and developers of these units—which flagrantly violate existing codes— New York City is legally recognizing a condition prevalent in low-income neighborhoods for decades. It is modifying existing codes to allow such conversions, while maintaining different legal standards in more traditional residential areas.

property owners, and more complete counseling follow-up services should be part of the program.

As pointed out in chapter 9, the mutual interdependence of expectations among property owners can lead to neighborhood deterioration. Most owners will invest in maintaining their properties only if they expect that owners of nearby properties will also keep the latter in good condition. Thus, if many owners develop negative expectations, or just great uncertainty, about the future maintenance behavior of their neighbors, they will reduce their own maintenance, and deterioration will soon become widespread. However, such uncertainty can be greatly reduced, and positive expectations can be created, by policies of local government built upon certain methods of housing code enforcement. Housing codes are designed to improve housing quality both directly (by pressuring owners to conform to code standards) and indirectly (by influencing owners' mutual maintenance expectations).

As noted above, most cities enforce their codes differentially—rigorously in high-income areas, less so in most middle-income areas, and not rigorously in low-income areas, especially where major deterioration has occurred. However, differential code enforcement may work against marginally deteriorated neighborhoods. Residents there need to build positive expectations or the neighborhood will decline. Moreover, rigorous enforcement is politically feasible in this type of neighborhood, which has few very poor residents. However, it is likely to occur only if someone constantly pressures the city government to do it. That can be a strong neighborhood organization, a large institutional owner of many parcels (such as a university), or a small group of vigilant residents.

Some small, relatively undeteriorated cities have adopted certificate of inspection or certificate of occupancy programs. These certificates document that properties conform to local codes. They must be obtained before the properties can be sold or rented to new occupants. These programs pressure all owners to maintain their properties, thereby creating a climate of positive expectations that further encourages good maintenance.[5]

5. Few large cities have adopted such programs because those cities usually contain some very deteriorated neighborhoods in which it would be unreasonable to expect property owners to bring units up to code before selling or renting them. That would require large investments which those owners could not recover by raising rents, since residents of such areas are usually quite poor. Hence these programs have usually been adopted only in cities where most of the housing stock is in relatively good condition. Then the overall demand for housing is strong enough to support rents that will pay for maintaining properties up to code standards.

The neighborhood housing services program involves cooperation among local real estate lending institutions (mainly savings and loan associations), neighborhood organizations, and the local government in improving selected neighborhoods. The financial institutions provide conventional mortgages to residents who meet normal underwriters' criteria. They also contribute to a pool of loan funds to help high-risk borrowers. The local government improves visible amenities such as streets, street lights, curbs, and gutters, and pledges services such as frequent garbage removal and adequate police patrols. The neighborhood organizations inform the area's property owners about these opportunities and encourage them to maintain their properties in good condition.

This cooperative venture has two main aims: to provide resources for neighborhood improvement and to raise the expectations of property owners. When they see public and private institutions making strong efforts to improve their neighborhoods, they will be reassured that their investments will not be undermined by future deterioration. Thus, the program seeks to remove destructive uncertainties by *managing the whole local housing market* through cooperative action. Such cooperation among financial institutions might be considered a violation of antitrust laws under other circumstances. But in these conditions, it is encouraged by the government regulators of these institutions.

Another means to the same end would be a neighborhood maintenance service that contracts with owners to keep their buildings in good condition. This service could be operated by a neighborhood organization. It would help absentee owners, the elderly, and others who find it hard to keep up their properties themselves. It would also cultivate sources of financing for property improvements not easily accessible to individual owners.

In some neighborhoods so many absentee owners fail to maintain their properties that such a voluntary approach would not work. There the local government could create a property management corporation run by neighborhood residents and legally responsible for maintaining all the residential properties within certain boundaries. Neighborhood organizations with access to community development block grants might undertake such a corporation. The corporation would manage only those properties whose owners failed to keep them up to code, leaving all others in the hands of their present owners. It would collect rents from tenants and use them to bring the properties up to code standards. It would also decide the occupancy of those properties it managed, thereby controlling somewhat the percentage of welfare or destitute households in the neighborhood. Such a corporation might develop and manage subsidized housing after it had gained management expertise. This as-yet-untried concept raises the legal question of whether a semipublic, semiprivate organization can take over private properties without the consent of their owners. However, local governments already can expropriate properties whose owners fail to pay their property taxes and assign the properties to private parties to manage them.

Collective management by any method cannot compensate for the basic problem in many deteriorating neighborhoods—lack of income. If occupants are too poor to pay enough rent for adequate maintenance, no properties can be kept in good condition without public subsidies to either the owners or the tenants.

Because of tax delinquency, local governments often take possession of older housing units, many of them in deteriorated neighborhoods. For example, in 1974, 7 percent (11,000) of all parcels in Cleveland were tax delinquent. About 70 percent of these delinquent parcels were in declining neighborhoods; over half were in areas in advanced stages of decline. Forty-two percent of these units were vacant, but many were still occupied. In one neighborhood (West Hough), 32 percent of all parcels were delinquent.[6]

Nearly all tax-delinquent units are in violation of housing codes. Hence the local government faces the same dilemma that caused the former owners to abandon ownership. Making the repairs necessary to remove all violations is not economically feasible, since the tenants cannot pay high enough rents to provide a reasonable return on the required investment. Yet the city government does not want to become a slum landlord by keeping occupied properties without removing their code violations.

There are several possible responses to this dilemma. (a) Occupants could be evicted and the housing demolished. This is expensive, and in cities with tight housing markets with a shortage of low-rent housing, eviction arouses substantial political opposition. (b) The city could use federal funds, particularly community development block grants, to improve the properties. In essence, this converts such funds to a new federal housing subsidy. (c) The city could encourage residents to upgrade these units themselves. For example, the city might sell the units to

6. Susan Olson and M. Leanne Lachman, *Tax Delinquency in the Inner City: The Problem and Its Possible Solutions* (Lexington Books, 1976), pp. 129–30, 148.

residents for a few dollars, with the requirement that the new owners rehabilitate them within a certain period (urban homesteading). Second, they might allow poor households to earn ownership in cooperative arrangements by working to improve the properties (sweat equity). (d) The city could forgive all or portions of the delinquent taxes of owner occupants, thus keeping households in the units and preventing vandalism. (e) The city could sell the units to developers to rehabilitate them and resell them. However, most units thus sold are rarely returned to good condition (unless they are in stable neighborhoods), and when the developers resell them, the units are soon delinquent again.

None of these tactics is likely to produce satisfactory results; some may not work at all. The basic problem is an irreconcilable conflict between two harsh realities: the high cost of maintaining housing in good condition, especially in deteriorated areas, and the low incomes of existing or potential tenants of properties in those areas.

Assessment Practices

Real estate assessment procedures directly affect property values, thereby influencing owners' incentives to maintain or renovate their properties. Hence those procedures are a key part of each city's strategy for physically improving its neighborhoods. Assessed values may lag far behind changes in market values. Where market values fall and assessments do not decline proportionately, assessed values impose unfairly high property taxes. Where property values rise rapidly, lagging assessed values unfairly benefit property owners. These distortions discourage investment in older areas with stable or declining property values. Frequent reassessment should reduce these disparities and encourage investment in older neighborhoods.

Furthermore, classification of property affects assessment value. In many areas, all property is assessed at the same ratio to market value. This may be required by local ordinance or even the state constitution. However, in recent years the market values of single-family homes have risen much faster than those of most other types of real property, making their property taxes rise faster. Owners of single-family homes—who vastly outnumber owners of other types of property in nearly every community—are organizing to resist these tax rises.

In response, some cities have begun to classify property by type. They use a much lower ratio of assessed value to market value for single-family homes, and perhaps other residential properties, than for commercial and industrial properties. This tactic provides relief only once, unless the ratio for single-family homes is continually adjusted downward as the market values of housing increase. Moreover, owners of industrial and commercial property, whose taxes go up commensurately, usually oppose such differential classification.

Circuit breakers are another form of tax relief that enhances the attractiveness of older residential neighborhoods by keeping property taxes on homes relatively low. They limit the property tax to a percentage of current household income regardless of the market value of the property. Such tax limits are usually confined to specific population groups, like the elderly.

Local real estate taxes also should not penalize housing rehabilitation. Property tax increases on revitalized property could be deferred until resale, for example, or phased into effect gradually.

Traffic and Transportation

Over the long run, transportation facilities and their operation have major impacts upon the physical condition of each city's residential neighborhoods. Hence policies concerning them should be at least partly incorporated into the city's overall strategy for improving those neighborhoods.[7]

For example, heavy automotive traffic flows on urban streets have many negative physical effects upon the surrounding environment. These include fumes, noise, traffic hazards, vibration, blockage of sunlight, and unsightly appearance. Such disamenities sometimes affect a neighborhood's social cohesion as well as its physical environment. One study analyzed three city blocks in San Francisco which were matched in most respects except amount of street traffic.[8] Residents on the heavily traveled streets spent less time on the sidewalks, knew fewer neighbors, and were

7. This section is taken largely from Kenneth A. Small, "Transportation and Urban Development."

8. Donald Appleyard and Mark Lintell, "Environmental Quality of City Streets: The Residents' Viewpoint," *Highway Research Record*, no. 356: "Social, Economic, and Environmental Factors of Transportation" (National Academy of Sciences–National Academy of Engineering, Highway Research Board, 1971), pp. 69–84.

less satisfied with the quality of their neighborhoods than those on less-traveled streets.

In recognition of these effects, the city of Berkeley, California, began an experiment in 1975 designed to manipulate street traffic patterns.[9] Barriers were set up to discourage through traffic on most residential streets. Most motorists were outraged; many citizens complained about the aesthetics and safety of the barriers; others worried about emergency vehicles getting through; and the residents of nonbarriered through streets, which became much more heavily traveled, objected vehemently. Nevertheless, a referendum in November 1977 showed that Berkeley voters believe the benefits outweigh the negative effects.

Major transportation arteries, like expressways and railroads, often act as the boundaries to neighborhoods and sometimes seriously disrupt them. Such arteries provide benefits for many persons scattered over large areas but concentrate their direct physical costs upon a small number of persons living nearby. Whenever any major artery is built through the middle of a neighborhood its former unity is often destroyed. To prevent this, residents of neighborhoods in the planned paths of interstate highways in Washington, D.C., New York City, San Francisco, Baltimore, and Chicago have permanently blocked their completion. Traffic plans in these cities have had to be redesigned. To avoid such outcomes, authorities should take account of the neighborhood-disrupting impacts of transportation arteries in the planning stages, in consultation with local residents. They should also recognize that bus stops, subway stations, and expressway interchanges become places where people or vehicles congregate, with major impacts upon the immediately surrounding territory.

If public transportation funds are to have maximum physical upgrading impacts upon a city's residential neighborhoods, those funds should be concentrated upon improving movement within the city, rather than movement between the city and the suburbs. The former increases the accessibility of city housing to downtown and within the city generally, thereby raising demand for such housing. In contrast, improved public transit links between the city and the suburbs make it easier for downtown workers to commute to suburban homes, thereby reducing the demand

9. See Donald Appleyard, *Livable Urban Streets: Managing Auto Traffic in Neighborhoods*, Monograph 24, University of California at Berkeley, Institute of Urban and Regional Development, prepared for Department of Transportation, Federal Highway Administration, DOT-FH-11-8026 (GPO, 1976), pp. 239–56.

for city housing. Further, by concentrating some public transit improvements upon a few neighborhoods that would be attractive to transit-oriented households, cities will encourage even more such households to live there. If transit patronage there is consequently raised, transit service to these areas may become more efficient, perhaps self-supporting. These neighborhoods should include some low-income neighborhoods, since poor households are highly transit-oriented because of their limited purchasing power.

City governments can adopt other transportation policies to improve the condition of central city neighborhoods, such as removing legal obstacles to shared-ride taxi service, like jitneys. This might require eliminating or modifying monopolies now granted to local taxi and bus companies.

Conclusion

It would be unrealistic to expect any city government to create a completely consistent strategy for physically improving its residential neighborhoods from the many diverse elements discussed above. However, city officials can at least recognize the close linkages among them and relate them to each other in terms of some overall strategic perspective they all share—presumably after hammering it out together. Doing so should greatly improve the net effectiveness of these elements in maintaining and revitalizing the city's neighborhoods.

Of course, many urban neighborhoods need improvements in their nonphysical characteristics even more than physical upgrading. Examples are levels of crime and security, and the quality of education available to local residents. Policies concerning some such characteristics—such as public schools—are discussed in other chapters of this book. However, they have not been included in this strategy analysis. It would be unreasonable to expect any city government to develop a completely comprehensive neighborhood strategy covering all aspects of life. Policies concerning certain other vital nonphysical characteristics—such as crime and security—are not discussed in this book. That is both because they are immensely complex subjects in themselves and because no one has clear ideas what to do about them.

13

Focusing on Activities within Neighborhoods

BECAUSE the major forces, trends, and government powers affecting neighborhoods have their roots in larger areas, most policies concerning neighborhoods must be established and carried out at broader geographic levels. Moreover, this book is mainly about relationships between neighborhoods and overall urban development; so it does not deal in detail with social structures and activities *within* neighborhoods. However, this final chapter discusses certain aspects of activities and organizations within neighborhoods relevant to their relationships with the rest of society.

Some Attitudes of Neighborhood Residents and Their Implications

Relationships between most neighborhoods and the larger society are greatly influenced by certain typical attitudes of neighborhood residents. No matter what their income level or ethnicity, most such residents are both *parochial* and *conservative* regarding any changes in local conditions.

They normally promote the interests of their own neighborhoods over the interests of other areas. For example, each tries to get his or her area awarded the highest priority on every resource-allocation schedule, regardless of its relative merits or needs as measured objectively. This perfectly natural bias has two implications for public policy. First, persons developing policy must realize that local residents often exaggerate the severity of their own needs and their ability to use aid effectively. Hence allocations of scarce resources should not be made by residents of any

172

one neighborhood acting parochially. True, all officials live somewhere; but they all should be able to differentiate the perspective appropriate in their public roles from that appropriate in their narrower, purely residential, roles.

Second, their natural partisanship makes neighborhood residents effective critics of both public and private agencies that provide services throughout the city. Many such agencies—especially public ones—have monopolies over the services they provide; so they often exhibit the faults of most monopolists. As noted earlier, these faults are unwillingness to work hard, insensitivity to the needs of individual customers, and a tendency to suit their own convenience rather than that of those they serve. To overcome these shortcomings, citywide agencies need pressure to increase their responsiveness to customers, analogous to the forces of competition in a free market. Neighborhood residents form the most likely source of such pressure—if they are sufficiently organized to recognize inadequate performance by these agencies and to protest effectively. Hence a key function of local residents, especially in neighborhood organizations, is pressuring citywide agencies to deliver services effectively.

To perform this function well, neighborhood organizations need at least some funding sources independent of city government. If all their funds come from city government, they will be reluctant to criticize its agencies strongly. In nonpoor areas, residents can afford to support local organizations through private contributions. But in poor areas, such support must come from elsewhere, probably from foundations or the federal government. In the past, direct federal funding of neighborhood activities has caused political resentment among city government officials and politicians. They were unhappy at being bypassed and fearful of criticism from strong neighborhood organizations. During the height of the antipoverty program, local community action agencies frequently attacked mayors, city councils, and local bureaucrats. The National Commission on Neighborhoods was also critical of local governments, recommending that the federal government fund many neighborhood organizations directly and not necessarily with the approval of mayors or city councils.[1]

This sensitive issue has no easy resolution. Neighborhood organizations

1. National Commission on Neighborhoods, *People, Building Neighborhoods,* Final Report to the President and the Congress of the United States (Government Printing Office, 1979), pp. 7–10.

should be at least partly independent, but the federal government should not systematically undermine the authority of local officials by supporting organizations engaged solely in attacking them. Federal agencies should therefore fund neighborhood organizations only after consulting local governments but should make the final decision themselves.

Neighborhood residents are also normally conservative, opposing changes in their neighborhoods. In fact, most neighborhood organizations were founded to protest some proposed or actual change. Even neighborhood groups seeking change usually want to alter conditions marginally, not introduce new conditions or abolish old ones.

This conservatism is reinforced by the nature of participation in neighborhood affairs. Residents who have made the largest financial or emotional investments in the status quo are normally the most active in neighborhood organizations. People who have been extremely dissatisfied with the status quo probably have moved away. And residents who are indifferent to local conditions or believe they have no prospects of changing them rarely participate in neighborhood organizations. Hence those organizations are dominated by people who want to preserve or marginally improve what is there now.

Certain neighborhood population characteristics probably increase conservatism. One is strong identification with an ethnic group, including location there of cultural institutions associated with that group. Because residents could not easily duplicate their neighborhood's ethnic traits elsewhere, they will resist changes in those traits. Home ownership also increases local conservatism. Owner occupants usually have a large fraction of their assets invested in their homes. They strongly oppose changes they believe would jeopardize those investments.

Neighborhood conservatism has implications for policies concerning the location of certain types of public facilities, as discussed later.

Personal Values and Participation in Local Organizations

As noted in chapter 9, residents' personal values have crucial impacts upon behavior patterns within urban neighborhoods. Many people in concentrated-poverty areas exhibit values adverse to fruitful community life. They might adopt less destructive values if they could gain greater control over their own lives, including better job opportunities and chances to exert more influence over local affairs. These might lead to more positive feelings of self-worth and accomplishment, and create greater local leadership experiences and capabilities.

Such self-development can occur both through the behavior of individuals as individuals and through their participation in local organizations. Therefore, patterns of participation in both organizations within neighborhoods and neighborhood organizations (as defined in chapter 2) affect residents' feelings concerning how much influence they have over their own lives and environments. Such mediating structures include churches, neighborhood organizations, extended families, credit unions, parent-teacher associations, private schools, public schools, clubs, and other nongovernmental structures. All have social locations somewhere between the government and the individual.[2]

Recent studies of Pittsburgh neighborhoods indicate that the attitudes of residents toward their communities are influenced by the degree to which they participate in such mediating structures.[3] The greater their participation, the more satisfied the residents are with their neighborhoods, and the greater their willingness to remain there and help upgrade them. True, not every neighborhood needs additional, or more effective, social structures within its boundaries. Many areas already contain enough to carry out their functions very effectively. But most concentrated-poverty areas do not have numerous enough, or strong enough, mediating structures to provide their residents with many autonomy-encouraging experiences. Hence public policies should try to strengthen such structures in those areas.

Providing more mediating structures there with significant social functions will require at least some local government agencies, and perhaps some at higher levels too, to relinquish certain functions they now perform. These agencies are reluctant to lose any of their existing powers—as are nearly all organizations. Hence two of the key challenges to public leadership concerning neighborhoods are determining which functions should be so shifted and persuading those who now exercise them to yield at least partial control over them to organizations at the neighborhood level. This is discussed later.

2. See Peter L. Berger and Richard John Neuhaus, *To Empower People: The Role of Mediating Structures in Public Policy* (American Enterprise Institute, 1980).

3. Roger S. Ahlbrandt, Jr., and James V. Cunningham, *A New Public Policy for Neighborhood Preservation* (Praeger, 1979).

Raising Neighborhood Consciousness

If organizations within poor urban neighborhoods are to carry out the self-development functions discussed above, the neighborhood consciousness of many key actors must be raised. They need to become more aware of neighborhoods as important social, economic, and political units and to take more account of them in making policies and decisions. Such consciousness raising can begin by the city government's officially defining its neighborhoods, in cooperation with existing neighborhood organizations. Data on these neighborhoods should be continuously collected, analyzed, and published.

City governments can also involve neighborhoods in the processes of government. In New York City, for example, the city administration appoints a local planning council for each major neighborhood or district. This council screens proposals for any actions affecting its area. Its recommendations then go to the citywide planning agency before finally arriving at the city council. In Cincinnati the city administration works with self-generated neighborhood organizations to develop plans for each area. The official boundaries for Cincinnati's forty-four neighborhoods were drawn up in consultation with existing neighborhood organizations, thus officially recognizing their claims to particular "turfs." In Washington, D.C., neighborhood councils have legal functions in the process by which zoning and other land-use decisions are made. Baltimore makes money and technical assistance available to independent neighborhood organizations so they can more effectively cooperate with the city administration in the urban planning process.

The National Commission on Neighborhoods made several hundred recommendations designed to increase the importance of neighborhoods and neighborhood organizations in all aspects of public life.[4] One of its key points is that federal funds should be used to help build neighborhood capacities. For example, federal regulations should require that local government agencies receiving federal funds include neighborhood residents in planning and decisionmaking, and that those agencies develop the residents' capacities to provide their own services and solve their own problems as much as possible. The Department of Housing and Urban Development already funds many neighborhood organizations with small grants. Such direct federal funding of local organizations makes

4. *People, Building Neighborhoods*, pp. 1–16.

sense, partly because local governments in many large cities are so hard-pressed fiscally they cannot afford these innovations. Moreover, the federal government's nationwide jurisdiction empowers it to sponsor experiments and demonstrations in various settings, evaluate the outcomes, and promulgate any resulting lessons to other localities. However, the Reagan administration has recommended eliminating all federal funding of neighborhood activities as part of its budget cutting; so this source of support is in jeopardy.

Transferring Government Authority to Neighborhoods

The ultimate way to raise neighborhood consciousness would be to transfer major elements of government authority to the neighborhood level. Some analysts have called for a two-tier government in urban areas—one tier at the neighborhood or small-community level and the other at the metropolitan-area level.[5] Others argue that certain public powers should be exercised by a new layer of government at the neighborhood level, with officials elected by neighborhood residents.[6] This *devolution* of government powers would presumably transfer the same set of authorities and accompanying resources to the neighborhood level in all parts of the nation, or at least in all parts of any city that carried it out. Such a shift would certainly increase the importance of neighborhood organizations by providing them with tax-raised resources and official powers.

Moreover, placing more government service provision at the neighborhood level would have some definite advantages over present arrangements. Neighborhood organizations would undoubtedly be more responsive to small-area concerns than many citywide bureaucracies are now. Also, this change might allocate more resources to many low-income neighborhoods that now receive unfairly low shares of public services. And it would make citizen participation in neighborhood-level activities far more meaningful.

However, neighborhood government also has serious disadvantages. First, it would be a waste of resources in neighborhoods already well

5. Committee for Economic Development, *Reshaping Government in Metropolitan Areas*, A Statement on National Policy by the Research and Policy Committee (New York: CED, 1970).

6. Milton Kotler, *Neighborhood Government: The Local Foundations of Political Life* (Bobbs-Merrill, 1969).

served by their local governments and other institutions. Most small suburbs do not need separate governments for their neighborhoods. Their elected officials are already highly responsive to local desires. In fact, their small areas, low populations, and population homogeneity often make each resemble a single neighborhood. Similarly, most middle- and high-income neighborhoods in large cities and suburbs already receive high-quality public and private services. Creating another layer of government there is completely unnecessary.

Second, choosing which specific powers should devolve to the neighborhood would be difficult. Just defining what such devolution really means is a complicated task. Would neighborhood officials have the power to decide whether a particular service would or would not be provided there? For services they were required to provide, could they decide what quantity to provide, or what quality, or in what manner those services should be furnished? Who would decide how much money each area received to provide each service? If officials in a neighborhood were allocated funds to provide, say, four services, could they shift the funds from one service to another because of their perception of local needs? Perhaps these questions should be answered differently for each service, but that would make such devolution very complex.

Moreover, those services that activists want controlled at the neighborhood level might be abused there, as powers over the police, schools, and housing regulations have been in the past. Neighborhood organizations are no less virtuous than those at other levels, but they are frequently more parochial because they are often ethnically homogeneous and hostile to outsiders. Sensitive services are more likely to be free of ethnic discrimination and violence if administered at the city level.

Third, neighborhood conditions and capabilities are too diverse even within each city to permit shifting particular powers to that level everywhere. For this and other reasons above, it is both impractical and undesirable to adopt any nationwide, statewide, or even citywide policy of devolving a certain set of powers to neighborhood-level government agencies in all urban areas. Nations like Cuba and China, in which every urban neighborhood has a general government agency, use those agencies partly as instruments of authoritarian control. Their neighborhood-level government agencies perform or influence many social functions: they help decide who goes to college and medical school, provide day-care and health-care services, and allocate housing. But these agencies also promulgate the propaganda of the central government and act as part of its intelligence apparatus to limit dissent. Perhaps the only way to sustain a high degree of citizen participation in neighborhood-level urban organizations is by coupling control over some resources vital to most households' welfare with the coercion of a dictatorship—a high price to pay.[7]

Most proponents of neighborhood government recognize that neighborhood conditions and needs are extremely diverse; so they do not propose nationwide or even citywide devolution. But *any* devolution will meet with difficulty and opposition.

Transferring Delivery of Some Services to the Neighborhood Level

Many neighborhood organizations would be strengthened if they provided their own areas with some of the public services now furnished by citywide government agencies. This could be done selectively, shifting different services to the neighborhood level in each part of a city, commensurate to that part's needs and capabilities. Such an approach would avoid the disadvantages of devolving the same set of governmental authorities to all neighborhoods throughout the city.

Some community development organizations already provide such services as manpower training, housing rehabilitation, land acquisition and development, provision of credit, construction, commercial revitalization, large-scale neighborhood planning, and technical assistance of various types. They usually pay for these services largely with federal funds; sometimes they use state or city funds. Few furnish all these services, but many provide one or a few. Federal agencies should design experiments to demonstrate how other activities can be transferred to neighborhoods. These could include health-care services, garbage and trash removal, day care, housing rehabilitation and insulation, building inspections, feeding and caring for the elderly, property management, anticrime surveillance, personal and employment counseling, and recreation. Some neighborhood organizations might contract with private firms for the actual service delivery; others might perform it themselves.

7. The National Commission on Neighborhoods recommended many specific tactics for shifting power and authority to the neighborhood level, but it stopped well short of prescribing any particular approach to all communities. See its report, *People, Building Neighborhoods*.

Each such experiment or demonstration should last long enough to allow neighborhood organizations to build sufficient capacity to do a good job. Where state legislation prevents local services from being shifted from city to neighborhood agencies, analysis of the legal requirements for such shifts is necessary.

There are major obstacles to transferring service delivery to the neighborhood level. As David J. O'Brien states, "In contrast to [neighborhood] organizers of earlier periods, such as those who formed immigrant groups, the indigenous organizer now must compete with large-scale operations in trying to provide services meaningful enough to induce persons to support collective action."[8] Neighborhood organizations trying to deliver services must receive funding from elsewhere, especially in low-income areas where residents cannot afford to pay full costs. Transfers of these powers and resources will generate conflict with city government agencies that now provide the services. And transfers of power to poor neighborhoods will be opposed by the nonpoor unless the latter also benefit.

These obstacles are most likely to be overcome where the following aspects of shifting service levels are clearly understood and carried out in practice:[9]

1. Different social services require different combinations of centralized and decentralized elements; so each service should be evaluated separately in terms of the costs and benefits of its delivery mechanisms.

2. Per unit costs are more likely to rise than fall when services provided by several small jurisdictions are consolidated into one larger agency, especially where wages were initially unequal and are "equalized upward." However, this does not necessarily mean per unit costs will decline when services are shifted from one large agency to several smaller ones.[10]

3. Different neighborhoods often require different delivery mechanisms and should, perhaps, even have different levels of service provided. Such diversity is likely to result spontaneously if some services are delivered by many different neighborhood organizations across the city. But this kind of inequality may not be legal under existing local or state laws; so those laws may need to be changed.

8. *Neighborhood Organization and Interest-Group Processes* (Princeton University Press, 1975), p. 189.

9. Many of the following observations were taken from David J. O'Brien, ibid., and from National Commission on Neighborhoods, *People, Building Neighborhoods*.

10. See Aaron B. Wildavsky, *Speaking Truth to Power: The Art and Craft of Policy Analysis* (Little, Brown, 1979), p. 332.

4. To avoid abuse, specialized services best performed at the neighborhood level (such as street patrol) and those best performed at a citywide level (such as traffic control and perhaps detective work) need to be spelled out clearly in regulations written by the local government.

5. There should be an easy means for citizens to appeal the actions and judgments of local service deliverers to a higher-level authority.

6. The geographic areas used for service delivery should be separate from those used for taxation; for example, neighborhood service areas versus citywide taxation. Then variations in service levels will not spring from unequal financial resources but from legitimate differences in need.

7. One way to shift power to neighborhood residents is to provide them with vouchers for purchasing services directly. They could buy from public or private suppliers, forcing public service agencies to compete for funds with private suppliers. *Neighborhood corporations* organized on a nonprofit basis could also offer services and compete for voucher funds.[11]

8. Neighborhood organizations cannot deliver services mandated by higher-level governments unless those governments also provide the funds required, since—unlike local governments—those organizations cannot levy taxes.[12]

The purpose of shifting services to the neighborhood level is not just to improve quality but also to encourage self-development of local residents and enhancement of their personal values. Neighborhood self-development usually occurs most effectively through spontaneous, unplanned local efforts—often led by charismatic individuals. In city after city the most effective such efforts have emerged from the dramatic leadership of one or a few unique individuals who took it upon themselves to "do something" about local conditions—and galvanized others into action. Inevitably, their efforts reflect their own unique combinations of talents and are therefore difficult to replicate elsewhere.

Thus, to achieve the most effective self-development efforts in concentrated-poverty neighborhoods, public officials must be willing to

11. Seed money from private foundations or government agencies could get such corporations under way. But they would have to support themselves after that by attracting patronage in competition with other neighborhood corporations in nearby areas or within their own territories, and perhaps with private firms furnishing the same services. Kotler, *Neighborhood Government*.

12. The past practice of federal and state governments of mandating services at the local level without furnishing the required resources will have to be modified if the federal government drastically cuts back financial aids to local governments, as recently proposed.

recognize and encourage an immense variety of approaches to service delivery. Such "letting a thousand flowers bloom" is fundamentally at odds with the bureaucratic tendency to classify and deal with all phenomena in a few standard categories—a practice that stifles creativity. Furthermore, encouraging many diverse projects requires tolerating a very high failure rate. Most projects go nowhere, but it is impossible to know in advance which will work. Hence, to stimulate more effective self-development within concentrated-poverty neighborhoods, public officials at higher levels will have to be more creative themselves, and more willing to allow projects they fund to fail.

These changes of bureaucratic heart are not compatible with current governmental emphases on cutting budgets at all levels and shifting as much activity to the private sector as possible. Neighborhood activities in nonpoor areas can be handled by the private sector, but those in poor neighborhoods cannot, since the local residents cannot pay for adequate services. On the other hand, shifting more power and control down to the lowest geographic level is fully consistent with the conservative philosophy that is becoming more dominant over government politics. Thus, neighborhood-level activities will not achieve their potential unless they are awarded much higher priority in the competition for resources than in the past. Perhaps this can be encouraged by recognizing both its critical importance and its compatibility with the American tradition of placing self-government as close to the people as possible.

Overcoming Neighborhood Resistance to the Location of Key Public Facilities

The natural conservatism of neighborhood residents makes it difficult to select locations for public facilities that provide societywide or citywide benefits but impose undesirable conditions in their immediate vicinities. Facilities such as expressways, power plants, oil refineries, halfway houses, public housing projects, police stations, airports, garbage dumps, incinerators, and sanitary landfills are vital to society; they must be located somewhere. But residents quite rationally do not want them in their neighborhoods, where they would bear all the costs and receive only a tiny fraction of the benefits.

In many cases, the harmful effects of such facilities can be greatly reduced by careful design. For example, expressways can be depressed below grade level to minimize noise. Public housing can be built in small clusters or as single-family homes, rather than in massive projects. The residents themselves should be consulted during the design process to see what features bother them most and what improvements they would consider most acceptable. Their views are at least as important as the ideas of the professional designers. Moreover, the very act of consulting them may mollify some of their resentment.

However, many negative effects cannot be eliminated. Airports always generate loud noise and air pollution, police stations invariably cause flows of "undesirable" persons, and incinerators attract truck traffic. To offset these unavoidable negative impacts, society can compensate those injured with money, or by packaging the unpopular facility with an amenity that neighborhood residents desire, such as a park, a swimming pool, street improvements, or a recreation center.[13] In Japan, the Tohoku Electric Power Company will pay $44 million in compensation to residents of the small city of Onagawa so it can build a nuclear power plant nearby.[14] In Montgomery County, Maryland, residents of an affluent suburb wanted the county government to prevent a large equestrian center near them from being replaced with housing. The county government bought the equestrian center but insisted on placing a few subsidized housing units on the site, too.[15]

Compensation for the adverse effects of a public facility, while fair, is difficult because those effects are hard to measure. What is the value of all the injuries inflicted by a new facility—including intangibles, like disruption of social networks? Also, negative effects are sometimes offset

13. The funds used to pay such compensation should come from taxing citizens benefited by the facility, thus reallocating the facility's net benefits (gross benefits minus the taxes used to pay compensation plus any compensation received). The distribution of benefits then closely corresponds to the distribution of costs. Compensation paid once, in a cash payment, benefits only the current residents. Because the value of local properties would be reduced because of the continuing negative impact of the public facility upon future occupants, the payment should offset that loss. If a permanent amenity is created, existing residents will get only a small immediate compensation, but the value of their properties will not fall, since future occupants will benefit from the amenity. Hence, in theory, if all residents are home owners, it does not matter which form of compensation is used, as long as participants in the housing market are informed about the situation. However, if some residents are renters, they will not gain (or lose) from changes in the capitalized value of properties there, unless such changes also alter rent levels.

14. Atsuko Chiba and Nobuko Hashimoto, "Tokyo Tries to Palliate Plant Pollution by Paying 'Bounties' to Affected Areas," *Asian Wall Street Journal Weekly*, March 24, 1980.

15. Camille Recchia and Paula Tarnapol, "$1.1 Million Voted for Riding Stable by Montgomery," *Washington Post*, June 18, 1980.

by positive effects, such as convenient access to the new facilities. Yet without compensation, local residents will always oppose placing such facilities near them. If each neighborhood has veto power over major changes within its boundaries, building these facilities anywhere may be impossible. This has happened in the cases of airports, oil refineries, power plants, and urban expressways. Therefore, the power to prevent these decisions should be removed from the neighborhood level, though whoever then makes the decisions should be as sensitive to neighborhood impacts as possible.

Conclusion

Activities within urban neighborhoods constitute much of the fundamental stuff of everyday life and establish the foundation for relationships between these areas and larger parts of society. Since neighborhood life in most parts of the United States does not suffer from any major deficiencies, no big changes in public policies concerning it are necessary. But significant policy changes could greatly improve the quality of neighborhood life within many concentrated-poverty areas, especially in big cities. Therefore, policy recommendations in this chapter focus upon strengthening organizations within such neighborhoods as social mediating structures. They can help residents attain greater control over their own lives and develop more positive values concerning community life generally.

But these recommendations must be carried out within the immense diversity of U.S. urban areas; so key officials in each city will have to adapt them to suit the situation in each individual neighborhood. Even so, improvements in neighborhood-level activities have the potential for counteracting some of the most intense and intractable problems in our society—problems for which there seem to be no other possible remedies. Hence trying to improve urban neighborhoods by influencing such activities deserves very large investments of time, money, and effort in most cities, in spite of its inevitable frustrations.

Index

Aaron, Henry J., 105n
Abravanel, Martin D., 77n
Ahlbrandt, Roger S., Jr., 21, 73n, 146n, 175n
Alonso, William, 39
Appleyard, Donald, 169n, 170n
Arbitrage model, 86–89. *See also* Frontier of construction; Transition zones
Austin, Texas, 32, 33

Bailey, Martin J., 87n
Baltimore, 176
Beer, Elizabeth T., 78n, 81n, 148n
Berger, Peter L., 175n
Bernhard, Arlyne S., 63n
Birch, David L., 41n
Black, J. Thomas, 74n
Blacks: housing expenditures, 92; improvement in housing, 93; neighborhood preferences of, 93, 95; neighborhood segregation, 100–02; poverty concentration, 54–55; and property values, 94; spatial neighborhood hierarchy, 47; transition zones, 93, 96–98
Bradbury, Katharine L., 12n, 40n, 103n, 108n, 109n, 110n, 113n, 131n, 137n, 139n
Brashares, Edith N., 55n
Brink, William, 93n
Brophy, Paul C., 73n, 146n
Brown, Richard Maxwell, 54n

Cannon, Donald S., 63n
Castells, Manuel, 111n
Central cities. *See* Inner-city neighborhoods
Chiba, Atsuko, 183n
Chicago, 99
Chicago Urban League, 47n, 92n, 97n

Cincinnati: government-neighborhood organizations joint planning, 176; neighborhood differences, 16
City governments. *See* Local governments
Cleveland: household mobility rate, 32, 33; poverty concentration, 55–56; projections for household growth, 139; resources for renovation, 154n; tax-delinquent housing units, 167
Coleman, Richard P., 13n
Courant, Paul N., 87n, 94n
Crime rate, 54, 79; neighborhood racial change and, 97; revitalization effect on, 82
Cunningham, James V., 21, 175n
Cuyahoga County, Ohio, 55–56

Dayton, 32
de Leeuw, Frank, 105n
Delinquency, 54n
Diamond, Douglas B., Jr., 40n, 105n
Displacement: moving-cost compensation, 146; from neighborhood redevelopment, 114; from neighborhood revitalization, 73, 82–85, 146–49; from urban development, 57
Downs, Anthony, 2n, 12n, 14n, 38n, 40n, 63n, 94n, 99n, 103n, 108n, 109n, 110n, 113n, 115n, 127n, 129n, 131n, 133n, 137n, 139n

Economic Development Administration, 117
Edmonds, Ronald, 131, 132, 133
Education. *See* Schools
Equilibrium: in housing market, 88, 90; in land values, 79

185

Ethnic origin: neighborhood hierarchy based on, 47; and neighborhood transition, 41–42
Ethnic segregation, 51, 84, 86n. *See also* Racial segregation

Federal government: aid to central cities, 126; funding for water and sewer facilities, 135, 151; housing allowance program, 40, 128; housing subsidies, 127, 130; limitations on urban development assistance by, 117–18; policies for neighborhood revitalization, 8–9; proposals for reducing urban poverty, 134–35
Federal Home Loan Bank Board, 129, 130
Federal Housing Administration (FHA) mortgage financing, 144–45
Figlio, Robert M., 54n
Follain, James R., Jr., 91n, 92
Frontier of construction: defined, 87; housing prices in, 88, 89

Gasoline and revitalization, 107–10
Gentrification: defined, 72; housing allowance for, 128; mortgage financing for, 148; prevention of, 149; and revitalization, 73, 74
Goetze, Rolf, 49n, 67n
Graham, Hugh Davis, 54n
Grebler, Leo, 101n
Grier, Eunice, 147n
Grier, George, 147n
Grigsby, William G., 18n
Gurr, Ted Robert, 54n
Guzman, Ralph C., 101n

Hanushek, Eric A., 40n
Harris, Louis, 93n
Hartman, Chester W., 147n
Hashimoto, Nobuko, 183n
Hierarchy of neighborhoods, 43, 44, 47, 87
Hispanics, 86; in-migration to urban areas, 104, 106; in neighborhood change, 100–02
Households, urban, 3; changes in, 105; destructive, 113; effects on surrounding households, 16–17; upgrading, 42–44. *See also* Turnover, household
Housing: arbitrage model, 86–89; capital for financing, 57, 105–07, 129–30, 143; deteriorated, 5–6, 163; as investment, 50–51; link between inner-city and suburban, 3; metropolitan area, 37, 59, 137; neighborhood revitalization effect on cost of, 73; proportion of income for, 40; racial and ethnic discrimination, 91, 144; spatial pattern, 41, 47; substandard, 48; surplus,

59; tax delinquent, 167–68. *See also* Housing construction; Housing standards; Subsidized housing; Trickle down process
Housing Act of *1949*, 147n
Housing allowance program, 40, 128
Housing and Urban Development, Department of (HUD), 31, 126n, 128n, 151n, 161n; efforts to rescue declining cities, 117; encouragement of suburban subsidized housing, 127; funding for neighborhood organizations, 176; neighborhood revitalization program, 129
Housing codes. *See* Housing standards
Housing and Community Development Act of *1974*, 126
Housing construction: inner-city, 3; neighborhood change from, 70–71; for neighborhood redevelopment, 113; population growth and, 137; suburban, 139–41, 142; rate, 4; tax laws, 143; in urban peripheries, 38–39, 59, 112
Housing standards, 38; certificates of inspection, 165; differential enforcement of, 48, 49, 111, 165; effect on neighborhood, 67; purpose, 164, 165
Hughes, James W., 63n
Hu, Joseph C., 78n, 82n, 148n
Humphrey, Nancy, 154n
Hutcheson, John D., Jr., 78n, 81n, 148n

Income: housing location and, 41, 44; neighborhood hierarchy based on, 47; proportion spent on housing, 40; redistribution of metropolitan area, 125–26; slowdown in growth of real, 106, 107
Income-transfer programs: city revenues from, 126; for inner-city revitalization, 9; proposed regional cost-of-living allowance for, 134–35
Incumbent upgrading: defined, 72; financing for, 148; prevention of, 149
Inner-city neighborhoods: housing allowances and subsidies, 128; moving from, 30; population, 137; poverty concentration, 38, 39–40, 56; schools, 112, 131–34; state and federal aid to, 126; and suburban growth, 2, 136–37; taxation, 125–26. *See also* Neighborhoods; Revitalization of inner cities
Integrated neighborhoods: black preference for, 93, 95; racial quotas for, 96, 99–100; stable, 95–96, 98–100

James, Franklin J., 78n, 80n, 141n
Jencks, Christopher, 131n

Keller, Suzanne, 14n, 15
Kern, Clifford R., 41n
Kollias, Karen, 144n
~~Kotler, Milton, 177n, 178n~~

Lachman, M. Leanne, 14n, 49n, 63n, 167n
Land use, 19; neighborhood change and intensified, 61, 67–68; transportation-cost theories of, 41
Land values and neighborhood revitalization, 79
Lane, Roger, 54n
Laurenti, Luigi, 94n
Leven, Charles L., 14n, 63n, 87n, 91, 92n
Levin, Henry M., 133n
Life cycles, neighborhood, 3; explained, 68–69; five stages of, 63–65
Lintell, Mark, 169n
Local governments: action on tax-delinquent properties, 167–68; citizen pressure on, 173; commercial blight, 161, 163; housing deterioration, 163; housing standards enforcement, 164–65; and individual neighborhoods, 159–61; neighborhood revitalization, 9–10; projected spending, 106; real estate assessment, 168–69; resources for city renovation, 153–59; role in neighborhood social functions, 21; slum prevention, 149; support for intensified land use, 68; taxation, 125–26; tax-exempt bonds of, 135, 143; tax gains from revitalization, 81

Malpezzi, Stephen, 91n, 92
Mancini, Paul K., 77n
Mangum, Garth L., 120n
Marciniak, Edward, 19n, 121n
Metropolitan areas, 1n; deterioration, 5–7; housing, 37, 59, 137; income redistribution, 125–26; linking of neighborhoods, 1–2; policies for urban development, 11–12; population, 37, 58, 60, 103–07, 137; poverty concentration, 38, 39–40, 56
Mills, Edwin S., 39, 40, 53n, 77n
Mitchell, James, 63n
Mitchell, Maxine V., 49n
Money flow and neighborhood stability, 26
Moore, Joan W., 101n
Mortgage loans: for new growth areas, 57; for older areas, 129–30; redlining, 129; tax deductibility of interest on, 105, 143; trend in availability of, 105–06, 107
Muth, Richard F., 39, 40, 77n, 87n

National Commission on Neighborhoods, 13, 16n, 173, 176, 179n

Neighborhood deterioration, 3; difficulty of reversing, 66; explained, 61; factors underlying, 18–19, 65–66, 165; from ~~poverty, 149; social contradictions con~~ tributing to, 111–13; from urban development, 5, 7, 111, 117
Neighborhood organizations: allocation of redevelopment funds to, 156–57; defined, 19–20; federal funding for, 173–74, 176–77; to perform public services, 22–23; 179–82; property management by, 166–67; residents' participation in, 174–75, 184; role in urban and neighborhood planning, 176; transfer of government functions to, 177–78
Neighborhoods: agents for changing, 62–63; defined, 13–14; dual nature, 1–2; economic and ethnic transitions, 41–42; functions, 15; hierarchy, 43, 44, 47, 87; as interacting geographic and social units, 15–16; property maintenance, 17, 165; public facilities, 182–84; residents' resistance to change, 172, 174; roles of personal values and social structure in, 119–23. See also Inner-city neighborhoods; Integrated neighborhoods; Neighborhood deterioration; Neighborhood organizations; Neighborhood stability; Redevelopment of neighborhoods; Revitalization of neighborhoods
Neighborhood stability, 1; balancing inflows and outflows, 25–26; defined, 24n; difficulties in maintaining, 49–50; factors influencing, 24–26, 36; social group change and, 3
Neuhaus, Richard John, 175n
New York City, 176

Oak Park, Illinois, 99
O'Brien, David J., 180
Olson, Susan, 167n
Orfield, Gary, 131n
Ozanne, Larry, 105n

Pechman, Joseph A., 105n
Peterson, George E., 154n
Pittsburgh, 21
Polinsky, A. Mitchell, 40n
Population, neighborhood, 16; Cincinnati, 16; stability, 24, 25; turnover rate, 27, 33. See also Turnover, household
Population, urban: age of, 104–05, 106; changes, 37, 58, 60, 137; and housing construction, 137; trend, 103–04; and urban development, 58

Poverty: and neighborhood deterioration, 3, 5–6, 124; and school quality, 131–34
Poverty concentration: and access to public services, 128–29; efforts to deconcentrate, 126–29; ethnic and racial groups, 54–55; housing credit to reduce, 129–30; income redistribution to counteract, 125–26; metropolitan areas, 38, 39–40, 56; and personal values, 120–23; in South, 39; U.S. versus foreign, 53–54
Property owners, 17–18
Property taxes: assessment procedures, 168–69; and neighborhood revitalization, 73
Property values: effect of black occupancy on, 94; and neighborhood revitalization, 73, 81–82
Public policies: failure of, 121–22; inconsistencies in, 119; limitations, 116–18. See also Federal government; Local governments; State governments
Public services: inner-city, 128–29; and neighborhood organizations, 179–82
Pusharev, Boris S., 110n

Quigley, John M., 40n
Quotas, racial, 96, 99–100

Racial change, neighborhood: arbitrage model, 86–89; effects of, 96–98; microdynamics of, 93–96; and racial equilibrium, 90
Racial segregation, 4; in housing, 93, 96; motives for perpetuating, 51; projected trend in, 106; in schools, 39, 51–52; social contradictions in, 112; trickle down process and, 38
Recchia, Camille, 183n
Redevelopment of neighborhoods: allocation of resources, 155–59; availability of public and private resources for, 153–55; commercial blight, 161, 163; explained, 61n; housing strategies, 163–68; potential, 69, 115; rebuilding, 113–14; resistance to relocation, 114; transportation and traffic policies, 169–71; variations, 159–61
Redlining for mortgage financing: defined, 129; responsible versus irresponsible, 145–46
Revitalization of inner cities: balancing displacement and, 146–49; gentrification, 148; mortgage financing, 144–46; prevention of, 149; suburban growth and, 136–41, 150–52; suburban property values and, 83–84; tax policies, 142–44

Revitalization of neighborhoods: benefits, 81–82; city policies, 9–10; costs, 82–84; defined, 61; demand for housing, 75–79; displacement, 73, 82–85; effects on housing costs and property taxes, 73; factors underlying, 65–66; federal and state policies, 8–9; gasoline price and supply, 107–10; gentrification, 72, 73, 74, 128; goals, 147; importance of small households, 77–78; incumbent upgrading, 72; land values, 79–80; neighborhood-level policies, 10–11; potential, 69, 80; private housing renovation, 74; private schools, 134; spontaneous, 73
Rochette, Edward C., 151n
Rutter, Michael, 131n

San Jose, 32
Schelling, Thomas, 94, 95
Schnare, Ann B., 81n, 83n, 161n
Schools: federal and state aid, 132; legal racial segregation, 39; poverty area, 112, 131–32; public support for private, 132–34; socioeconomic segregation, 51–52; young households and, 79
Schur, Edwin M., 54n
Segal, David, 41n
Segregation. See Ethnic segregation; Racial segregation; Socioeconomic segregation
Sellin, Thorsten, 54n
Seninger, Stephen F., 120n
Slum preservation, 149
Small, Kenneth A., 12n, 39n, 103n, 108n, 109n, 110n, 113n, 131n, 137n, 139n, 169n
Smith, Neil, 79n
SMSAs. See Standard metropolitan statistical areas
Social contradictions and neighborhood decline, 111–13
Social costs: destructive households, 113; poor urban neighborhoods, 2–3, 120–21; and suburban growth, 141–44
Socioeconomic segregation: motives for perpetuating, 50–52; projected trend, 106; social contradictions, 112; from spatial hierarchy of neighborhoods, 49; trickle down process and, 38; in urban-periphery new housing, 59
Solomon, Arthur P., 78n, 141n
South Bend, 32, 33
Standard metropolitan statistical areas (SMSAs), 1n, 104, 107. See also Metropolitan areas
State governments: aid to central cities, 118, 126; aid to city schools, 132; authority over local housing codes, 127; housing

subsidies, 127–28; policies for neighborhood revitalization, 8–9; projected spending, 106; tax-exempt bonds, 135; urban growth-control laws, 151

Sternlieb, George, 63n

Stockholm, Sweden: limits on suburban growth, 139n; subsidized housing program, 48

Subsidized housing, 48, 111: for displaced households, 148–49; large units, 130; in revitalized neighborhoods, 73; in suburbs, 127–28

Suburbs: distributing social costs of growth of, 141–44; gasoline price and supply, 109–10; growth effect on inner cities, 2, 136–41; inner-city revitalization effect on, 83–84; proposed limits on growth, 139–41; subsidized housing, 127–28; taxes, 126; trade-off between inner-city revitalization and growth of, 150–52; use of inner-city facilities by residents of, 125

Suttles, Gerald D., 17n

Tarnapol, Paula, 183n

Tax credits: for firms locating in cities, 135; for private school education in cities, 132–33; to replace mortgage interest deductibility, 143

Taxes: biased toward new construction, 143; inner-city versus suburban, 125–26; and redistribution of income, 125–26; on suburban housing construction, 142

Traffic and inner-city neighborhoods, 169–70

Transition zones, 87; housing prices, 88, 89, 91, 93, 96–98; income differentials, 90

Transportation: costs of commuting, 107–10; to improve inner-city neighborhoods, 169–70; housing prices and, 39, 41

Trickle down process: deteriorated housing surplus, 59; ethnic and economic transitions, 41–42; and expanding population, 37–39; household upgrading, 42–44; and poor blacks, 92n, 97; poverty concentration, 38–41; suburban growth and, 136

Tucson, 32

Turnover, household, 24; age differences, 28–29; city differences, 31–33; defined, 22; home owners versus renters, 27, 34–35; housing cost and, 29; income and, 30; neighborhood differences in, 30–31, 33; normal versus neighborhood transition, 26; racial differences in, 29; regional differences in, 27–28

Urban development: displacement from, 57; effect on low-income households, 53–56, 58; effect on high- and middle-income households, 52–53; factors influencing, 4; metropolitan area policies for, 12; and neighborhood changes, 5, 61, 117; and population growth, 58; social problems resulting from, 2–3

Urban Land Institute, 74

Vandell, Kerry D., 97n

Veterans Administration mortgage financing, 144–45

Warren, Donald I., 97n

Washington, D.C., 176

Water and sewer facilities: federal grants to suburbs, 151; proposed federal funds to improve inner-city, 135

Welfare payments, 135

Wiener, Anthony J., 109n

Wienk, Ronald E., 92n, 144n

Wildavsky, Aaron B., 180n

Wilson, James Q., 54n

Wilson, Peter, 154n

Wolfgang, Marvin E., 54n

Yinger, John, 87n, 94n

Zoning regulations, 38, 41; state authority over, 127

Zupan, Jeffrey M., 110n